LOCAL GOVERNMENT FINANCE IN THE THIRD WORLD

LOCAL GOVERNMENT FINANCE IN THE THIRD WORLD

A Case Study of the Philippines

Edited by Roy Bahl
and Barbara D. Miller

PRAEGER

PRAEGER SPECIAL STUDIES • PRAEGER SCIENTIFIC

Library of Congress Cataloging in Publication Data

Main entry under title:
Local government finance in the Third World.

Includes index.
1. Local finance—Philippines—Addresses, essays, lectures. I. Bahl, Roy W. II. Miller, Barbara D., 1948-
HJ9580.L62 1983 336′.014′599 82-18600
ISBN 0-03-063306-0

Published in 1983 by Praeger Publishers
CBS Educational and Professional Publishing
a Division of CBS Inc.

3456789 052 987654321

Printed in the United States of America

PREFACE

Two goals of many developing countries are the mobilization of additional resources through the public sector and the decentralization of government activity. These objectives have led government planners to look toward local governments as a source of administration and fiscal strength that is underrecognized and underutilized. This book is about the possibilities for increased fiscal participation in one developing country, the Philippines. In addition to imparting what we have learned about the Philippines, we hope to contribute to what little is currently known about local public finance in developing countries.

In considering these goals, two questions must be asked: First, what is the spectrum of present performance of local governments in revenue mobilization, capital project activity, and efficient management of local development? Second, given the current structure of the Philippine government, what are the potentials for improving fiscal and administrative roles of local governments?

Within this broad framework for appraisal, several specific issues have been studied. Roy Bahl and Larry Schroeder, in Chapter 1, address the topic of budgeting and financial management of local governments. In Chapter 2, Bahl and Schroeder examine the real property tax in detail, and then provide an analysis of the business license tax in Chapter 3. Chapter 4, by Bahl and Schroeder, provides a critical appraisal of intergovernmental fiscal relations, particularly the grants system. In Chapter 5, David Greytak and Benjamin Diokno present an analysis of the use of local government public enterprises, offering specific details on market enterprises and a case study of Bulacan Province. Credit financing by local governments and the feasibility and form of a specialized local government credit authority are the subjects investigated by Ken Hubbell in Chapter 6. In the final chapter, Bahl reviews the findings and suggests conclusions, alternative policy directions, and future research implications. This chapter is meant to describe a comprehensive rather than a piecemeal program of structural reform; hence, specific conclusions that might otherwise have been placed at the end of individual chapters are provided here.

This book represents an effort that has been collaborative in every sense. The economists who performed several months of fieldwork together—Bahl, Schroeder, Greytak, Diokno, and Hubbell—jointly contributed to the formulation of the research design. The major topics of research were mutually agreed upon by the co-authors and advisers from the government of the Philippines: the Ministry of Finance, the College of Public Administration of the Philippines, and the National Tax Research Center.

The research was conducted under a Cooperative Agreement (PN 936-5303) between Syracuse University's Maxwell School of Citizenship and Public Affairs and the (then) Development Support Bureau of the U.S. Agency for International Development. USAID in Manila originally invited the participation of the Syracuse University team and provided critical support throughout the duration of the research. It requested in return only that the researchers try to be responsive to the needs of the government of the Philippines in pursuing specific research topics and in identifying policy issues.

In undertaking intensive and lengthy fieldwork, the team accrued many personal debts to government officials who generously gave their time and support. In particular, we acknowledge our gratitude to Dean Raul DeGuzman of the University of the Philippines, Director Angel Yoingco of the National Tax Research Center, and Director Lorinda Carlos of the Ministry of Finance. Without their help our work could not have been accomplished, and without their unfailing good humor and patience the whole experience would not have been so pleasant an undertaking.

The present volume is a descendant of the lengthy report, entitled "Strengthening the Fiscal Performance of Philippine Local Governments: Analysis and Recommendations," that the Syracuse team prepared on the basis of their research. Our goal in this book is to provide a substantial amount of the empirical findings because we believe that such will provide a valuable addition to the published literature. We also hope to draw the reader's attention to the more general lessons learned here and to the implications for subsequent work on local government finance in the Third World.

In the process of transforming the earlier report into its present shape, we must thank the secretarial staff of the Metropolitan Studies Program—Esther Gray, Jeanne McGrath, Cheryl Wood, and Debra Sorokin—for their endurance, cheer, and the high level of quality.

The usual disclaimer of responsibility for errors and misinterpretation for anyone except the editors applies here. Furthermore, the opinions expressed throughout the book should not be construed as belonging to any of the governments, organizations, or their representatives involved with the research.

Roy Bahl
Barbara Miller
Syracuse, New York

CONTENTS

PREFACE v
LIST OF TABLES AND FIGURES x
LIST OF ACRONYMS xv

Chapter 1 Local Government Structure, Financial Management, and Fiscal Conditions
by ROY BAHL and LARRY SCHROEDER 1

Chapter 2 The Real Property Tax
by ROY BAHL and LARRY SCHROEDER 46

Chapter 3 The Business License Tax
by ROY BAHL and LARRY SCHROEDER 82

Chapter 4 Intergovernmental Fiscal Relations
by ROY BAHL and LARRY SCHROEDER 100

Chapter 5 Local Government Public Enterprises
by DAVID GREYTAK and BENJAMIN DIOKNO 140

Chapter 6 Local Government Credit Financing
by L. KENNETH HUBBELL 188

Chapter 7 Strengthening the Fiscal Performance of Philippine Local Governments
by ROY BAHL 228

APPENDIX: Research Areas and Sample 257
INDEX 261
ABOUT THE EDITORS 267
ABOUT THE CONTRIBUTORS 269

LIST OF TABLES AND FIGURES

TABLES

1.1	Central and Local Government Expenditure Growth, Selected Years, 1969–78	4
1.2	Per Capita Local Government Expenditure Growth, Selected Years, 1969–78	5
1.3	Means and Coefficients of Variations of Socio-economic Characteristics, Selected Jurisdictions, Metro Manila, and the Nation	13
1.4	Per Capita General Fund Expenditures, Selected Jurisdictions, 1977	17
1.5	Simple Correlations Between Per Capita General Fund Expenditures, Per Capita Income and Urbanized Population, Selected Provinces, 1977	20
1.6	General Fund Revenues Per Capita, Selected Jurisdictions, 1977	23
1.7	Percentage Distribution of General Fund Revenues by Source, Selected Jurisdictions, 1977	25
1.8	Mean Per Capita Revenues and Expenditures by Fund, Selected Jurisdictions, 1977	27
1.9	Tax Effort Ratios for Municipalities by Province and for Cities, 1977	29
1.10	Illustration of Calculation of Components of Tax Effort: Pavia, Iloilo, Tabaco, Albay and Malinao, Albay	32
1.11	Simple Correlations of Municipal and City Property and Business Tax Effort Indexes and Effective Tax Rates with Socioeconomic Variables, 1977	34
1.12	Ordinary Least Squares Regression Results: Effective Tax Rates Related to Local Socioeconomic Characteristics	36
1.13	Cash Balance and Surplus Position, Selected Municipalities and Cities	38
2.1	Growth in Taxable and Exempt Assessed Values, Selected Jurisdictions, 1970–79	56
2.2	Largest Tax Delinquencies in Selected Iloilo Municipalities, 1980	62

2.3	Factors Affecting Property Tax Collection Efficiency	63
2.4	A Comparison of Property Taxation in the Philippines and Other Developing Countries	67
2.5	Per Capita Property Tax Revenues, 1969–79	69
2.6	Indicators of Property Tax Performance	70
2.7	Annual Growth Rates in General Fund Property Tax Revenues, Iloilo and Albay Provinces, 1970–79	71
2.8	Property Tax Collections in Selected Albay Municipalities, 1977–79	72
2.9	Property Tax Collections in Selected Iloilo Municipalities, 1977–79	73
2.10	Property Tax Collections, Iloilo City and Legaspi City, 1977–78	76
2.11	Elasticity of Property Tax Revenues and Property Tax Base	77
3.1	Business Taxes in Iloilo City and Legaspi City, 1977 and 1979	87
3.2	Cross-Sectional Estimates of Income Elasticities of Business License Tax, 1977	91
3.3	Business License Tax Performance in Selected Albay Municipalities, 1977–79	95
3.4	Business License Tax Performance in Selected Iloilo Municipalities, 1977–79	97
4.1	Simple Correlations Between Per Capita Allotments and Selected Independent Variables, for Selected Cities and Municipalities, 1977	104
4.2	Regression Results for Model of Stimulative Impacts of BIR and Specific Tax Allotment Grant System	114
4.3	BIR and Specific Tax Allotment Impacts on Local Government Expenditures	116
4.4	Growth in BIR Allotment	120
4.5	Growth in Specific Tax Allotment	125
4.6	Growth in National Tax Allotment	126
4.7	Barangay Shares and Actual Distribution of BIR and Specific Tax Allotment Programs, 1975–81	128
4.8	Possibilities for Structuring a Grant System	130
4.9	Legal and Actual Classification of Philippine Grant System	132

5.1	Cost Recovery Prospects of Potential Local Government Public Enterprise Activities	144
5.2	Expenditures for Public Enterprise Activities by Type of Public Enterprise and Level of Government, 1977	145
5.3	Population, Local Government Total Revenues, and Gross Revenues from the Operation of Markets, Selected Areas, 1978	148
5.4	Per Capita Market Revenues, Average Stall Fees, Stall Occupancy Rates, and Market Proximity, Selected Local Governments	150
5.5	Market Expenditures, Total and by Type, Selected Local Governments, 1979	153
5.6	Employment and Compensation of Market Workers, Selected Local Governments, 1979	154
5.7	Estimated Book Value of Market Structures, Capital Outlay, and Estimated Capital Costs, Selected Local Governments, 1979	156
5.8	Amortization Payment Required to Reproduce Book Value of Current Market Structure, Selected Local Governments	159
5.9	Profitability of Markets as Reported and as Estimated Under Selected Assumptions About Interest Rate and Asset Life	160
5.10	Estimated Amortization Required to Replace Book Value of Fixed Assets, Excluding Land, Selected Public Enterprises, 1980	166
5.11	Hiyas Cafetorium, Short-Run Performance Indices, 1977–79	170
5.12	Hiyas Cafetorium, Results of Financial Analysis	172
5.13	Hiyas Convention Center, Short-Run Performance Indices, 1977–79	174
5.14	Hiyas Convention Center, Results of Financial Analysis	177
5.15	HACC Slaughterhouse, Short-Run Performance Indices, 1977–79	181
5.16	HACC Slaughterhouse, Results of Financial Analysis	183
6.1	Consolidated Statement of Approved Loans to Local Governments by the Development Bank of the Philippines, the Land Bank, and the GSIS, 1976–80	196

6.2	Approved Loans to Local Governments by the Development Bank of the Philippines (1976–80), the Land Bank (1977–80), and the Government Service Insurance System (1979)	198
6.3	Past Due Local Government Loans with the Development Bank of the Philippines, the Land Bank, and the GSIS, 1980	201
6.4	Debt Limitation of Cities, 1977	207
6.5	Legal Borrowing Capacity and Net Paying Capacity Data for 13 Local Jurisdictions, 1979	210
6.6	Summary Schedule of Local Government Deposits First Quarter, 1978 to Fourth Quarter, 1980	218
6.7	Capitalization of a Credit Authority, 1981–83	221
6.8	Illustrative Lending Terms for a Specialized Local Government Credit Authority	225
7.1	Funding Required from Central Government Sources: A Comprehensive Program for Local Government Financial Reform	251
7.2	Programs to Increase the Efficiency of Local Government Operations	252
7.3	Incentive Programs to Increase Local Government Revenue Mobilization	253
A.1	List of Jurisdictions Included in the Sample	258

FIGURES

1.1	The Structure of Local Government in the Philippines	2
4.1	Model of Expenditure Determination	106
4.2	Components of Allotment Distributed	121

LIST OF ACRONYMS

ARC	Agrarian Reforms Code
ASEAN	Association of South-East Asian Nations
BCLP	Barangay Committee on Land Production
BIR	Bureau of Internal Revenue
BLT	Business License Tax
CIP	Capital Improvement Program
CLT	Certificate of Land Transfer
COA	Commission on Audit
CPI	Consumer Price Index
DBP	Development Bank of the Philippines
DCF	Discounted Cash Flow
EO	Executive Order
FY	Fiscal Year
GAR	Gross Annual Revenue
GF	General Fund
GNP	Gross National Product
GOP	Government of the Philippines
GSIS	Government Service Insurance System
HACC	Hiyas Agro-Commodities Center
HBCC	Hiyas ng Bulakan Convention Center
ICLC	Internal Centre for Local Credit
IF	Infrastructure Fund
IMF	International Monetary Fund
INP	Integrated National Police
IRR	Internal Rate of Return
LBP	Land Bank of the Philippines
LDC	Less Developed Country
LGPE	Local Government Public Enterprise
LOI	Letter of Instruction
LWUA	Local Water Utilities Administration
MAR	Ministry of Agrarian Reform
MLGCD	Ministry of Local Government and Community Development
MOB	Ministry of the Budget
MOF	Ministry of Finance
NAS	National Accounting Service (NEDA)
NCSO	National Census and Statistics Office
NEA	National Electrification Administration
NEDA	National Economic and Development Authority

NPV	Net Present Value
NTRC	National Tax Research Center
PACTAA	Provincial, City and Municipal Treasurers and Assessors Association
PD	Presidential Decree
PIDS	Philippine Institute for Development Studies
PNB	Philippine National Bank
PVB	Philippine Veterans Bank
RA	Republic Act
RDC	Regional Development Council
RDIP	Regional Development Investment Program
RFC	Rehabilitation Finance Corporation
ROP	Republic of the Philippines
RPT	Real Property Tax
RPTA	Real Property Tax Administration
SEF	Special Education Fund
SSS	Social Security System
STA	Specific Tax Allotment
STP	Social Time Preference
USAID	U.S. Agency for International Development
UPCPA	University of the Philippines College of Public Administration

1

Local Government Structure, Financial Management, and Fiscal Conditions

by ROY BAHL and LARRY SCHROEDER

The government structure in the Republic of the Philippines is highly centralized, with the national government selectively delegating powers to its several lower governmental bodies—provinces, cities, municipalities, and barangays (or barrios) (Figure 1.1). The 1959 Republic Act 2264 lifted certain restrictions regarding the taxing power of municipalities, and the new constitution, Article XI, Section 5, allocated power to localities to create their own revenue sources. The centralized orientation, however, has been retained.

The 75 provinces and subprovinces in the Philippines have specific responsibilities and functions. The provincial government collects taxes (some in conjunction with municipalities), constructs highways and bridges, dispenses justice, and supervises the operations of municipal governments. The assessor and treasurer are representatives of the national government rather than the province—a very important feature of the centralized nature of local financial administration in the Philippines.

Each province is fully subdivided into municipalities, which are geographic areas usually containing at least a small semiurbanized market area; there are no unincorporated areas. Currently, there are 1,484 municipalities within the Philippines. The municipality provides some localized services including markets, public works such as local roads, and local justice, and it has some local development responsibilities. The chief financial officers of the municipality, treasurer and assessor, are supervised at the provincial level and therefore implicitly by the central government. A municipal deputy

FIGURE 1.1 The Structure of Local Government in the Philippines

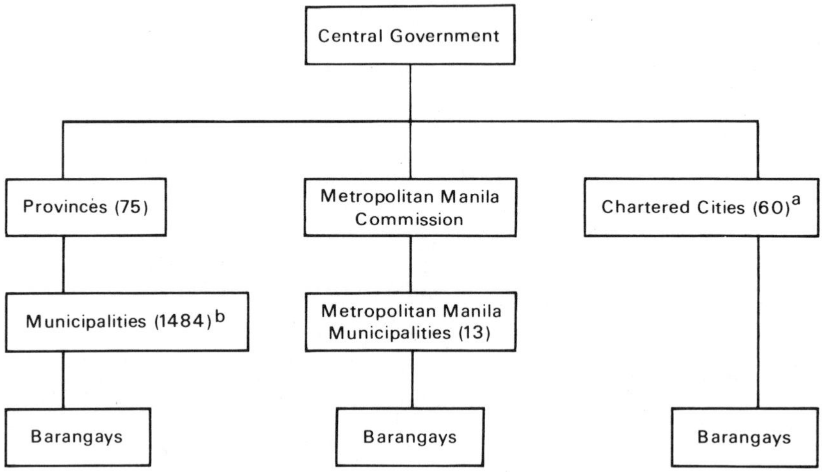

[a]Including cities in Metropolitan Manila.
[b]Including municipalities in Metropolitan Manila.
Source: Philippine Yearbook 1981 (Manila: National Economic and Development Authority, National Census and Statistics Office, 1981).

assessor is appointed by the provincial assessor, but two-thirds of his salary is paid by the municipality.

Juxtaposed against the province and municipality are chartered cities, of which there currently are 60. In general, these cities are more highly urbanized than municipalities, although some contain substantial amounts of agricultural land. Given their administrative independence from provinces, they perform many of the same functions as provinces and municipalities. Their revenue-raising powers are likewise a combination of those prescribed to provinces and municipalities. As in the case of provinces and municipalities, the chief financial officers—treasurer and assessor—are appointed and directed by the central government.

The barangay has existed as a neighborhood unit of local government since the colonial Spanish era. The central government has recently expressed considerable interest in greater participation by the barangays at the local level. They have been given increased grants, increased powers for raising revenues, and increased service provision authority. Most recently the barangay has been used as a means to organize citizens for various civic purposes through a program known as "barangay brigades."

LOCAL GOVERNMENT FINANCES IN THE 1970s

During the 1970s, the Marcos regime enacted strong fiscal reforms that resulted in a dramatic increase in national government revenues. Between FY 1973 and FY 1976, for instance, government revenues increased by more than 30 percent.[1] In 1964, total revenues were between 9 and 10 percent of the GNP, whereas in 1976 they were 14.6 percent of the GNP. But while central government revenues and expenditures grew, there was a continuing decrease in the size of the local government sector relative to that of the central government.

One can approximate that the size of the local government sector relative to that of the central government declined from 20 percent in 1969 to less than 11 percent by the end of the decade (Table 1.1). If the ratio of local expenditures from own sources to central expenditure is charted, the decline is from 9 percent in 1969 to 7 percent in 1979. It is clear that the trend of the 1970s was increased fiscal centralization. Per capita local government spending did increase during the 1970s but mostly because of inflation (see Table 1.2). In fact, if we adjust for increases in population and prices, there has been virtually no growth in Philippine local government spending during the last decade.

Why has the relative and absolute size of the local government sector not been increasing? One possibility is that centralization of government finances is an overt policy of the central government. There is evidence, however, to the contrary. In addition to Republic Act 2264 and Article XI, Section 5, of the new constitution, official statements of the central government point to increased local government revenues as a national priority. For example, in Presidential Decree (PD) 464, Enacting a Real Property Tax Code, President Marcos noted that "this country cannot progress steadily if its local governments are not potent political subdivisions contributing their proportionate shares to national progress" and that it was imperative for local governments to be able to provide "adequate funds with which to underwrite basic and essential public services within their respective areas of responsibility."[2] Then Finance Minister Cesar Virata also emphasized the promotion of local economic development through increased local revenue mobilization as a national goal.[3]

TABLE 1.1

Central and Local Government Expenditure Growth, Selected Years, 1969–78 (millions of current pesos)

	(1) Central Government Expenditures	(2) Total Local Government Expenditures	(3) Local Government Share of Total Central and Local Expenditures (percent)[a]	(4) Central Government Grants to Local Governments	(5) Grants as a Percent of Local Government Expenditures
1969	3,611	817	20.7	490	60.0
1971	4,429	1,033	21.1	558	54.0
1973	7,041	1,465	18.8	700	47.8
1975	20,168	2,202	10.2	863	39.1
1977	22,600	2,914	11.9	1,009	34.6
1978	27,110	3,237	11.0	1,049	32.4
1979[b]	34,380	3,781	10.3	1,474	39.0
Average annual percent change between 1969 and 1978	25.1	16.5	–	8.8	

[a]Grants are excluded from central government expenditures but included in local government expenditures.

[b]Estimates.

Sources: Budget of the national government for fiscal years 1969–75; president's budget message, calendar years 1976–79; Commission on Audit reports on Local Government Expenditures (1969–71); Ministry of Finance, (1972–79) as reported in Daniel Holland, Michael Wasylenko, and Roy Bahl, "An Evaluation of the Real Property Tax Administration Project," Local Revenue Administration Project, Maxwell School, Syracuse University, Oct. 1, 1980, Table 3, p. 16.

TABLE 1.2

Per Capita Local Government Expenditure Growth, Selected Years, 1969–78 (in current and constant 1972 pesos)

	Per Capita Expenditure Current Pesos	Per Capita Expenditure Constant Pesos
1969	44.35	67.20
1971	27.25	29.45
1973	36.43	31.27
1975	52.34	31.36
1977	64.31	32.09
1979	78.57	31.36
Average annual percent increase between 1969 and 1979	5.9	-7.3 (0.8)*

*1971–79.

Sources: Commission on Audit Reports on Local Government Expenditures (1969–71); Ministry of Finance Reports (1972–79); Central Bank Statistical Bulletin, 1978; National Census and Statistics as reported in Daniel Holland, Michael Wasylenko, and Roy Bahl, "An Evaluation of the Real Property Tax Administration Project," Local Revenue Administration Project, Maxwell School, Syracuse University, Oct. 1, 1980, Table 4, p. 18.

In spite of the existence of verbalized government policy regarding the national priority of strengthening local governments, several constraints have temporarily halted progress. The 1970s were years of major social and political changes in the Philippines. Internal economic policy changes altered the nature of investment and there were the outside forces of worldwide recession and the growing energy crisis with which to contend. However, in keeping with the central government's stated view that local governments should become more fiscally independent, this study seeks to provide some insights into how the current system, with some reform, could be made more effective.

LOCAL GOVERNMENT BUDGETING AND FINANCIAL MANAGEMENT

Two important bottlenecks impede increased revenue mobilization and a more efficiently functioning local government sector: the substantial restrictions placed on local government expenditures by the central government, and various shortcomings in the local government budgeting and financial management process. An understanding of the fund structure of the local government accounts and of the extent to which local governments may "control" their budgets is a necessary starting point in evaluating local financial management practices.

Fund Structure

PD 477 (June 3, 1974) established a common fund structure for all local governments in the Philippines. Each jurisdiction has two funds—the General Fund and the Infrastructure Fund. Expenditures from the latter are to be used exclusively for a specified set of purposes, mostly to do with the construction and maintenance of roads, bridges, other public works projects, and public utilities.[4] The General Fund is the source of all other local spending, other than for education. More specifically, the General Fund

> consists of monies and resources not otherwise accruing to any other fund and shall be available for the payment of expenditures, obligations or purposes not specifically declared by law as chargeable to, or payable from, any other fund, though transfers of monies or resources therefrom to other funds of the local government for their augmentation and use may be made by proper appropriation.[5]

The distinction between the General and Infrastructure funds is not synonymous with a separation into current and capital expenditures. Indeed, the General Fund may contain capital construction expenditures, and the Infrastructure Fund obviously contains current spending for maintenance activities on roads, bridges, and so on. Moreover, although expenditures in the Infrastructure Fund are generally developmental in nature, there are also economic development expenditures contained in the General Fund. To complicate matters further, there are substantial interfund transfers.

A third fund (not a focus of this study), administered by the local treasurers, is the Special Education Fund (SEF). It is devoted exclusively to the provision of elementary-level education. The national government directly provides personnel expenditures for education, while nonpersonnel expenditures are supported from the SEF. The primary local revenue source supporting this fund is the real property tax, although in some localities periodic transfers from the General Fund to the SEF are also made.

Budgeting Problems and Issues

A number of issues have arisen in connection with this fund structure and current budgeting practices. These issues concern transfers between the Infrastructure and General funds, the allowing of supplementary budgets, capital budgeting, and the overall supervision of the budgetary process.[6]

Fund Transfers

Although there is a statutory requirement that funds be transferred from the General Fund into the Infrastructure Fund (8 to 12 percent of General Fund net income, depending on the classification of the jurisdiction), additional transfers are permitted if the purpose for the transfer is clearly stated. However, sizable increases in the petroleum excise tax, the principal revenue of the Infrastructure Fund, raise the possibility that local fiscal conditions may now require transfers from the Infrastructure to the General Fund. The Budgeting Regulations (issued in conjunction with PD 477) state that such reverse transfers are possible "only from the unappropriated balance of the (Infrastructure) Fund and to cover exceptionally urgent needs of the local government" and with the approval of the finance minister.[7]

Supplemental Budgets

Budgeting by local governments in the Philippines appears to be less an exercise in fiscal planning or control than a response to particular statutory requirements placed on the financial managers of the locality. Supplemental budgets are used as a general rule rather than as an exception. Under PD 477 there is a "limitation" of one supplemental budget per month unless exceptional circumstances arise, in which case additional supplementals may be prepared. From discussions with local officials, it appears that the one supplemental per month is indeed used and one official bemoaned the fact that only a single monthly supplemental could be used. This practice does not stimulate serious fiscal planning for the full fiscal year, as it is widely recognized that the annual budget need be only a crude first approximation.

Capital Budgeting

Attempts have been made to establish longer term capital planning as a part of the financial management responsibilities of local government. Each local government, even the barangay, is supposed to produce a capital improvements program (CIP), which contains five-year revenue projections, lists proposed capital projects, and is coordinated with the annual budget process. Little evidence exists, however, that such financial planning has been implemented or that it has contributed to improved fiscal planning, perhaps because neither of the motives that typically lead to an effective use of capital budgeting is present in the Philippines. One such motive is the need to understand the relationship between current and capital expenditure requirements, for example, to know the annual maintenance costs associated with the construction of a new road or bridge.[8] The second usual reason for capital budgeting—the planning and scheduling of debt repayment—is not a stimulus in the Philippines because there is little use of credit financing by local governments.

Financial Oversight Problems

Several different central government organizations are involved in the financial oversight of localities. This overlap creates problems in the review process.

The Ministry of Finance (MOF) oversees the principal local fiscal manager—the treasurer—and, until recently, also reviewed the annual as well as all supplemental budgets approved at the local level.[9] After a municipal budget is approved, it is sent to the provincial budget officer, who then sends it with recommendations to the regional Ministry of the Budget (MOB) representative for approval. While this review process considers several aspects of the budget, the only grounds for outright budget veto are conflicts in any way with the several statutory budgetary limitations placed on localities (itemized below).

The budget is also reviewed by the Ministry of Local Government and Community Development (MLGCD). Under PD 144 (March 1973), 20 percent of the Bureau of Internal Revenue (BIR) Allotment to each local government must be spent on "development projects," which, in turn, must be approved by the MLGCD. A memo from the MLGCD (Circular 73-17) indicates that these include agricultural development projects, infrastructure development projects, tourism projects, cottage industries projects, management tools or other devices that would tend to improve financial positions of local governments, and other projects based on local development priorities.

Finally, overall auditing of the financial affairs of local governments is carried out by the Commission on Audit (COA) of the central government. While not directly comparing budgeted amounts with actuals, this commission is charged with at least measuring the financial soundness of local government units.

In essence, then, the local fiscal management function is overseen by at least four different central government bureaucracies, although this by no means is exhaustive of the list of central government agencies that have influence over local authorities. While there may be considerable rationale for this division of labor, such fragmentation imposes costs. Different ministries have different priorities, which leads to possible conflicts in the directives and requirements given to local governments. Because of these conflicts and the time cost of complying with these requirements, local government fiscal management is less efficient than it otherwise would be.

Controllability of the Local Budget

The centralized orientation of local financial management is most evident in the various restrictions placed upon localities in terms of what they can or must budget for certain, specified functions. While this practice, in theory, enhances the direction that the central government can give, it markedly reduces the discretion that local governments have in determining the size and makeup of their budgets. If the bulk of expenditures in a budget cannot be controlled by the public body, ability of the local government to respond to particular circumstances is limited and the local government feels less accountable for its fiscal actions. If revenue bases are narrowly prescribed and tax rate ceilings and the base coverage are fixed, the options for fiscal response are further narrowed.

In fact, the budget options of local governments in the Philippines are substantially narrowed by central government mandates. The restrictions include:

Statutory Reserve: Two percent of estimated revenues from regular sources must be held in reserve to cover unforeseen circumstances.

Election Reserve: Under the Election Code, contributions to election expenses are on the basis of one-third from the national government, one-third from provincial governments, and one-third from the city or municipal government. To ensure that these monies are available for elections, an election reserve based on one-quarter of the local election costs from the previous election must be set aside.

Infrastructure Fund Transfer: Between 8 and 12 percent of annual net income in the General Fund must be transferred to the Infrastructure Fund.

Aid to Hospitals: From 5 to 7 percent of net income is to be set aside as a contribution to the provision of hospital services within provinces.

Integrated National Police (INP): Local police and fire protection is supported by a uniform contribution of 18 percent of total General Fund income from regular sources.

Barangay Development Fund: Each municipality, city, and province is urged to make an allocation from the General Fund to the Barangay Development Fund. The amount transferred is not to exceed ₱500 per year per barangay and, while there is no statutory minimum, our investigation into the accounts of localities suggests that nearly all local governments are making some contribution.

Twenty Percent Development Fund: Twenty percent of the BIR Allotment to the General Fund is to be set aside for "development projects." Two types of eligible projects–training programs for government employees and "other projects based on local priorities"–allow for considerable flexibility within this requirement.

Personnel Expenditures: Several restrictions are placed on personnel expenditures of local governments. One overriding restriction is that total annual appropriations on wages and salaries of all local government employees are not to exceed 45 percent of total annual income from regular sources in first- and second-class jurisdictions (55 percent in jurisdictions lower than second class).[10] This limitation does not include salaries and wages of public school officials and employees, employees of hospitals, health and agricultural services, public utilities, markets and slaughterhouses, or other economic enterprises operated by the jurisdiction.

Emergency cost-of-living allowances are also excluded. The secretary of finance can authorize appropriations that exceed these limits in exceptional cases. Salary ranges for different job titles are set by the central government, although individual jurisdictions can pay the lower bounds in cases of extenuating circumstances.

Likewise, local governments have paid a bonus–for example, some local governments in Iloilo (in 1979) paid "thirteenth month" salaries, thus effectively providing an 8.3 percent increase in pay.

Thus, up to 37 percent of General Fund revenues is earmarked for statutory reserves, Infrastructure Fund transfer, aid to hospitals, and the Integrated National Police (INP). Additional reserves for elections increase this percentage slightly, as does the decision as to how much to transfer to the Barangay Development Fund. Budgetary discretion is further limited by the 20 percent restriction placed on the use of the BIR Allotment. If the allotment accounts for 25 percent of General Fund revenues (a relatively low share), then the use of up to 42 percent of General Fund revenues is in some way restricted.

VARIATIONS IN THE FISCAL PERFORMANCE OF PHILIPPINE LOCAL GOVERNMENTS

The measurement of fiscal performance calls for developing an objective index, but even in countries where data are readily available, this task turns out to be very subjective.[11] On the expenditure side is the problem of not being able to measure public sector output, which in turn prohibits direct measurement of the efficiency of government operations, the productivity of government workers, or the quality of public services provided. On the revenue side, good measures of the potential tax base (the amount of income above subsistence, the full market value of property, and so on) cannot be made; hence, evaluation of revenue effort and collection efficiency is more qualified than one would like. This inability leads most analysts to infer fiscal performance from measurement of actual fiscal outcomes, such as deviations from "normal" revenue and expenditure patterns, fiscal surpluses and deficits, and tax effort.

The measurement of fiscal outcomes is complicated in the Philippines by the absence of comparable, current data. The local government financial statistics used here were taken from audited financial reports from the COA. Unfortunately, the latest available information is for FY 1977; hence, recent important trends and developments are not observable. We have compiled the COA data for selected municipalities–those in the provinces of Albay, Bulacan, Iloilo, and Sorsogon–and for all chartered cities outside Metropolitan Manila.[12] While these data provide considerable insight into variations in the composition of revenues and expenditures, they do not constitute a random sample.[13] (See Appendix A.)

Variations in Socioeconomic Structure

Fiscal performance and potential are related to the socioeconomic and demographic configuration of a jurisdiction. Personal income level and distribution, population size and growth rate, and urbanization are the variables examined here. Due to the lack of more recent detailed data, we rely heavily on the findings of the *1975 Integrated Census of the Population and Its Economic Activities.*[14] Background data on the four provinces and selected comparisons with the rest of the Philippines are presented in Table 1.3.

The upper panel of Table 1.3 shows the province-wide levels for four different indicators of social and economic well-being. Albay stands out as considerably poorer and less urbanized than the other provinces in the sample and in the entire nation; at the other extreme, Bulacan is more urbanized and has a high per capita income. One measure of the industrial development of an area is the proportion of income earned outside the agricultural sector—from wages and salaries, manufacturing, or retail activities.[15] Again Bulacan stands out as being most highly developed. Iloilo and particularly Sorsogon appear to be more dominated by agricultural activity, but with average income levels well above that in Albay.[16] Chartered cities, as might have been expected, are more highly urbanized, less dependent on agriculture, and have higher average income levels. One way to gauge the relative wealth of the four provinces is to compare per capita assessed property values. Again Bulacan and the chartered cities have a much greater level of wealth.

The bottom panel of Table 1.3 addresses the issue of whether there are large variations in these indicators within provinces. An affirmative answer is suggested by the coefficents of variation (the ratio of the standard deviation to the mean of the variable) shown there.

Some interesting conclusions can be drawn from these rather simple calculations. First, there is a great range of urbanization that may affect differential fiscal performance. Second, there is much less uniformity in the per capita property tax base in Iloilo and Bulacan, where the average level of the base is higher. Third, the pattern of coefficients of variation for the pooled sample of all municipalities is

TABLE 1.3

Means and Coefficients of Variations of Socioeconomic Characteristics, Selected Jurisdictions, Metro Manila, and the Nation

Jurisdiction	Per Capita 1975 Income	1975 Urban Population[a]	Percent of Nonagricultural Income, 1975[b]	1977 Assessed Value per Capita	1975 Population[c]
Albay	₱ 797	8.1%	49.5%	₱ 403	657,855
Bulacan	1,035	36.0	70.8	1,407	890,133
Iloilo	935	12.2	43.7	674	998,504
Sorsogon	985	16.6	32.8	460	426,570
Four provinces[d]	941	19.0	52.1	803	2,973,062
Chartered cities[e]	1,258	54.9	63.9	2,244	3,902,508
Metro Manila[f]	2,125	100.0	NA	NA	4,970,000
Philippines[f]	1,111	31.6	NA	NA	42,071,000

(Continued)

TABLE 1.3 (Continued)

Jurisdiction	Per Capita 1975 Income	1975 Urban Population[a]	Percent of Nonagricultural Income, 1975[b]	1977 Assessed Value per Capita	1975 Population[c]
			Coefficients of Variation		
Albay	32.5	97.9	44.8	33.9	46.8
Bulacan	22.2	117.8	20.9	68.8	47.3
Iloilo	31.5	67.6	37.7	98.1	45.1
Sorsogon	27.6	81.0	55.7	33.0	49.7
Four provinces	30.3	123.9	42.4	100.4	53.0
Cities	25.8	80.5	28.5	86.1	78.0

NA = Not available.

[a]Percent 1975 population living in urbanized areas. Based on the 1975 definition of urban by the National Census and Statistics Office.

[b]Income from retail sales, manufacturing, and wages as percent of total 1975 income.

[c]In top panel, entries are totals; in lower panel entries are coefficients of variation across municipalities/cities in sample.

[d]Weighted mean.

[e]Includes only the 42 cities for which complete data were available from 1975 census. See Appendix A.

[f]These are preliminary estimates based on National Economic Development Authority, Regional Development, *Issues and Strategies, Regional Planning Studies Series,* 1 (Manila, 1978), p. 6.

Sources: Data on assessed property value from Commission on Audit; all other data from the National Census and Statistics Office.

not considerably greater than the coefficients within provinces, suggesting that analysis of the pooled sample will provide results not entirely due to differences in the levels of development across provinces. In other words, the inclusion of higher income Bulacan and lower income Albay in the same (pooled) sample will not hamper interpretation of the results. Fourth, chartered cities appear to be much more homogeneous than municipalities with respect to all variables except population size.

Expenditure Structure and Variations: General Fund

For budgeting and financial record-keeping purposes, General Fund expenditures are classified into four major categories: general government, public welfare and safety, economic development, and other. General government includes spending on the offices of governor or mayor, legislative councils, auditor, treasurer, and assessor; public welfare and safety spending includes such items as courts, register of deeds, health, education, and welfare spending, as well as the INP; the economic development category includes expenditures on the offices of the veterinarian and engineer, transfers to the Infrastructure Fund, and spending for enterprises such as markets and slaughterhouses; other spending includes only debt service and the mandated 2 percent budgetary reserve.

Spending by local governments can be considered with respect to level and composition among the three major functional areas of general government, public welfare and safety, and economic development, and in terms of variability across jurisdictions. For the 97 sample municipalities, average per capita spending in 1977 amounted to about ₱17, while the 42 cities spent about ₱56. Obviously, the primary reason for this large difference is that cities are responsible for the combined range of services provided by municipalities and provincial governments.

When the provincial averages are compared, we find an expected pattern of substantially higher spending in Bulacan. On average, municipalities in Bulacan spend twice as much per capita as those in Albay and Sorsogon.[17] This pattern may be due to several factors: Higher income residents demand and are willing to pay for more services; more urbanized areas need to provide more services; provision of services is more expensive in higher income provinces; tax administration is better in higher income provinces and thus there is more money to spend; or there is provincial government assistance in assessment and in planning and implementing projects.

Still, one might ask whether spending in Bulacan in uniformly higher and that in Albay and Sorsogon is uniformly lower, or whether a few municipalities have pulled the average up or down by an inordinate amount. This possibility can be examined by comparing the coefficients of variation within each province. Interestingly, the greatest relative variation is among the 23 municipalities in Bulacan (see bottom row of middle panel of Table 1.4). This finding leads one to conclude that all municipalities in a province do not share equally in the fiscal benefits of a strong economic base.

When attention is turned to the composition of spending by function, other implications can be drawn. The biggest share of municipal expenditures goes for general government. On average, nearly half of total municipal expenditures went to support the general overhead of government (bottom panel of Table 1.4). Economic development spending, the stated motive for mobilizing additional local government resources, claims a much smaller share.

There is variation in the distribution of spending at the municipal level both across and within provinces. The percent allocated to economic development expenditures varies substantially and appears to be a matter of income level (in the case of Bulacan) and, to some extent, the size of the property tax base (in the case of Iloilo). It would be tempting to draw the conclusion that there is a direct and consistent relationship between the economic base of a jurisdiction and the budget share it allocates to economic development, but there are two reasons for hesitation in arguing this point. First, economic development spending tends to be "lumpy," and thus observations in any given year may distort the long-term pattern. Second, because many economic development projects are financed from the Infrastructure Fund, concentration on the General Fund may be misleading. Both qualifications will be dealt with below.

Municipalities in the provinces of Bulacan and Iloilo spend a significantly lower proportion on general government—42 and 44 percent, respectively—whereas in Albay and Sorsogon the shares are 57 and 58 percent. Again a feasible explanation for this pattern is that a local government must spend some minimal amount to support itself no matter how wealthy or poor the underlying economic base. The amount left over for other functions of government—the residual or "surplus" that is usually associated with public service improvements and economic development—is much smaller for poorer jurisdictions. On average, these municipalities appear to spend

TABLE 1.4

Per Capita General Fund Expenditures, Selected Jurisdictions, 1977 (pesos per 1975 population)

	Mean Amounts					
Expenditure Category	Albay	Bulacan	Iloilo	Sorsogon	Pooled Municipal Sample	All Cities[b]
General government	5.71	10.54	7.78	6.28	7.85	17.91
Public welfare and safety	1.98	5.02	5.04	2.07	4.07	20.16
Economic development	2.40	9.56	4.71	2.41	5.12	18.95
Total expenditures[a]	9.95	24.51	17.66	11.52	17.05	56.16
Number of observations in sample	17	23	43	14	97	42

(Continued)

TABLE 1.4 (Continued)

Expenditure Category	Albay	Bulacan	Iloilo	Sorsogon	Pooled Municipal Sample	All Cities[b]
	Coefficients of Variation					
General government	33.77	59.31	35.16	20.95	51.05	41.21
Public welfare and safety	82.40	73.08	66.12	53.23	79.78	70.07
Economic development	58.73	105.25	78.82	68.24	118.88	121.41
Total expenditures	40.53	54.83	39.15	32.47	56.80	63.07
	Percent Distribution					
General government	56.6	42.0	44.4	58.4	46.1	29.8
Public welfare and safety	19.6	20.0	28.8	19.2	23.9	36.9
Economic development	23.8	38.0	26.9	22.4	30.0	33.3

[a]The totals may not equal the sum of the components since all entries in the table are unweighted averages.
[b]Excluding cities in Metropolitan Manila.
Source: Report of the Commission on Audit on Local Governments, 1977.

around 20 percent of their General Fund budgets for public welfare and safety, a consistency that results from the required 18 percent contribution for police services.

Chartered cities exhibit different expenditure patterns. Because they have the combined expenditure responsibility and revenue authority of municipality and province, it is not surprising that they spend significantly more on a per capita basis. They nevertheless allocate a markedly smaller share than municipalities to general government purposes and a larger share to public welfare and safety. These differences, however, are deceptive because of the great variation in financial practices among cities. The coefficients of variation show that there are greater differences in spending patterns among cities than among municipalities in this sample and that the variation is especially pronounced for economic development spending.

These patterns can be explored more systematically through the use of correlation analysis. Table 1.5 contains simple correlations between per capita General Fund expenditures, per capita personal income, population, and the percent of the population living in urban areas. The findings are mixed, but some generalizations are possible.

First, with respect to the 98 municipalities taken together, only the extent of urbanization is strongly correlated with per capita total expenditures and its economic development subcomponent. Neither population size nor personal income is found to be significantly associated with total spending or its component parts.

The correlations at the provincial level are quite mixed. Whereas per capita total spending is strongly related to urbanization and total population in Albay, Bulacan, and Sorsogon, the same relationship does not hold in Iloilo. Per person local government expenditures tend to be higher in more populous and urban places within the highly rural provinces of Albay and Sorsogon but not within Bulacan and Iloilo. The findings with respect to personal income are even more mixed.

When the components of spending are examined, even less consistency in results is obtained. The only general conclusion that can be reached is that in the provinces other than Iloilo, greater urbanization is associated with higher levels of public welfare and safety spending and economic development spending. In the cities, on the other hand, each of these three socioeconomic variables is positively associated with total spending. Where income, urbanization, and population are higher, one may expect to find a higher level of per capita expenditures in general and of per capita economic development expenditures in particular.

TABLE 1.5

Simple Correlations Between Per Capita General Fund Expenditures, Per Capita Income and Urbanized Population, Selected Provinces, 1977

Province	Total General Fund Per Capita Expenditures	General Government	Public Welfare and Safety	Economic Development	Absolute Value Required for Significance at Level[b] .05	.10
Albay						
Per capita income	.480	.311	.093	.543	.53	.46
Urbanized population[a]	.729	.298	.401	.300		
Population	.668	.459	-.030	.711		
Bulacan						
Per capita income	.230	.046	.142	.061	.45	.38
Urbanized population	.399	-.134	.301	.539		
Population	-.101	-.528	-.190	.175		
Iloilo						
Per capita income	-.318	-.288	-.217	-.209	.32	.26
Urbanized population	-.058	.157	-.016	.079		
Population	-.252	-.418	-.383	.238		

Sorsogon						
Per capita income	.082	-.277	-.037	.035	.57	.51
Urbanized population	.617	.289	.455	.362		
Population	.330	-.242	.322	.210		
Four Province Total						
Per capita income	.157	.070	.029	.111	.20	.17
Urbanized population	.421	.116	.239	.541		
Population	-.003	-.227	-.236	.220		
Cities						
Per capita income	.328	.220	.146	.326	.32	.26
Urbanized population	.390	.324	.223	.319		
Population	.346	.097	.291	.297		

[a]Percent of 1975 population classified as urban.

[b]Critical values based on sample sizes and large sample t-test of correlation coefficients.

Sources: Fiscal data from Commission on Audit; per capita income and urbanized population data from National Census and Statistics Office.

Revenue Structure and Variation

Local governments in the Philippines receive grants from the central government and have authority to levy a variety of taxes and fees.[18] Provinces are permitted to levy property taxes, a property transfer tax, and taxes on particular activities including printing, amusement admissions, and specified occupations. Municipalities also derive revenues from the real property tax (RPT), the business license tax, and various fees. Cities, which provide the dual functions of provinces and municipalities, can utilize all of the taxes and fees levied by both provinces and municipalities. In keeping with the centralized orientation of the Philippine finance system, rate ceilings are imposed.

Average per capita revenues of the 98 municipalities and 42 cities included in the sample are shown in Table 1.6.[19] There is substantial variation in the total amounts raised, with municipalities in Bulacan and Iloilo raising substantially more on a per capita basis than municipalities in the other two provinces. The difference is most pronounced for Bulacan, where both business taxes per capita (₱3.95) and total property taxes per capita (₱4.99) greatly exceed the averages in the other three provinces. There is much less difference in the average per capita amounts received from the BIR Allotment. However, municipalities in Iloilo and Bulacan, in spite of their higher than average incomes or assessed valuation, receive a greater per capita allotment, thereby reinforcing their per capita tax revenue advantage.

Variability within provinces, as measured by the coefficients of variation, suggests that greater diversity is to be found where there are higher levels of per capita revenue generation—in Bulacan and Iloilo. Again, this finding is not surprising given that both urbanization and assessed valuation per capita are greatest in Bulacan and Iloilo and also the most varied.

The distribution of General Fund revenues by type of revenue is described in Table 1.7. The business tax, property tax, and BIR Allotment account for 60 percent of revenues to the General Funds of the represented municipalities. Nontax revenues, especially earnings from enterprises, constitute most of the remainder of General Fund income. The minor taxes are minor indeed. When average reliance on various municipal revenues is compared across provinces, some interesting variations emerge. Surprisingly, the business tax is the major source of revenue to municipalities in Albay and Sorsogon, whereas in Iloilo and Bulacan the business tax is of slightly less importance than the property tax. One might attribute this pattern to a kind of

TABLE 1.6

General Fund Revenues per Capita, Selected Jurisdictions, 1977
(pesos per 1975 population)

Revenue Category	Mean Amounts					
	Albay	Bulacan	Iloilo	Sorsogon	Pooled Municipal Sample	All Cities[b]
Revenue from Local Taxation	2.90	10.49	4.32	3.15	5.34	27.40[c]
Business tax	1.50	3.95	1.32	1.55	2.00	8.21[c]
Occupation tax	.03	.08	.02	.01	.03	.27
Residence tax	.19	.56	.20	.17	.28	1.35
RPT–Current	.59	3.66	1.77	.75	1.85	9.00
RPT–Past years	.21	1.11	.43	.30	.53	2.47
RPT–Penalties	.04	.21	.09	.07	.11	.44[d]
(RPT–Total)	(.85)	(4.99)	(2.28)	(1.12)	(2.49)	(11.71)[d]
BIR Allotment	5.24	6.71	6.50	5.90	6.24	13.45
Nontax Revenues	2.31	7.61	7.96	3.25	6.18	18.59
Aids and Contributions	.04	.06	.67	.33	.37	.49
Total Revenue[a]	10.45	24.81	18.77	12.30	17.75	61.41
Number of Observations in Sample	17	23	43	15	98	42

(Continued)

TABLE 1.6 (Continued)

Revenue Category	Coefficients of Variation					
	Albay	Bulacan	Iloilo	Sorsogon	Pooled Municipal Sample	All Cities[b]
Revenue from Local Taxation	49.85	71.14	78.99	48.72	97.09	82.20
Business tax	75.53	98.09	101.86	79.26	120.32	88.24
Occupation tax	64.49	141.04	64.57	97.24	191.83	88.45
Residence tax	55.70	63.33	46.08	45.19	87.39	79.25
RPT–Current	28.98	84.34	147.64	17.88	136.24	139.01
RPT–Past years	50.97	95.80	60.89	47.24	119.62	153.74
RPT–Penalties	38.31	75.02	52.25	42.74	95.75	127.07
(RPT–Total)	(25.60)	(78.55)	(117.20)	(17.54)	(119.47)	(143.90)
BIR Allotment	15.57	34.81	28.66	26.36	29.75	53.12
Nontax Revenues	96.17	107.03	59.34	78.89	92.05	117.95
Aids and Contributions	412.31	260.86	225.03	141.06	287.99	345.64
Total Revenue	34.59	53.65	37.17	30.93	53.95	60.82

[a]Includes sales of assets, borrowing, and so forth.
[b]Excludes cities in Metropolitan Manila.
[c]Number of observations in sample equals 40.
[d]Number of observations in sample equals 41.
Source: Annual Report of the Commission on Audit on Local Governments, 1977.

TABLE 1.7

Percentage Distribution of General Fund Revenues by Source, Selected Jurisdictions, 1977

Revenue Category	Municipality by Province				Pooled Municipal Sample	All Cities[a]
	Albay	Bulacan	Iloilo	Sorsogon		
Revenue from Local Taxation	16.3	42.3	23.0	25.6	30.1	44.6
Business tax	14.3	15.9	7.1	12.6	11.3	13.7
Occupation tax	0.3	0.3	0.1	0.1	0.2	0.4
Residence tax	1.8	2.3	1.1	1.4	1.6	2.3
RPT–Current	5.6	14.9	9.6	6.1	10.4	9.8
RPT–Past years	2.0	4.6	2.3	2.5	3.0	3.8
RPT–Penalties	0.4	0.9	0.5	0.6	0.6	0.7
(RPT–Total)	(8.0)	(20.4)	(12.4)	(9.2)	(14.0)	(14.2)
BIR Allotment	50.1	27.1	35.4	48.2	35.2	24.2
Nontax Revenues	22.2	30.3	44.2	26.2	34.8	29.2
Aids and Contributions	0.4	0.2	3.7	2.7	2.1	0.8

[a]Excluding cities in Metropolitan Manila.

Source: Computed from Table 1.6.

"tax handles" argument. At the earlier stages of development, and with lesser degrees of urbanization, local governments may have little to tax other than the few established businesses, or they may find the administration and collection of a broad-based property tax unwieldy. As the local economy develops, the local government may begin to reach more property owners who have a greater capacity and perhaps willingness to pay property taxes.

The other interesting pattern suggested by Table 1.7 is the heavy dependence on central government assistance, especially in the less urbanized and low property tax base provinces of Albay and Sorsogon. Municipalities in each of these provinces receive about half their total revenues from the BIR Allotment. Nontax revenues—receipts from markets, slaughterhouses, and other enterprises—appear as important and as highly variable, although caution has to be exercised in interpreting importance here because gross revenues rather than profits are reported.

Because of their broader taxing powers, chartered cities show much higher per capita revenues in total and from the several specific sources (Table 1.6). The fact that municipal and provincial governments share the BIR Allotment whereas cities receive a single, but comparable total accounts for the nearly doubled level of per capita shares in cities compared to municipalities. While the mean per capita levels of business and property taxes in cities are considerably higher than in municipalities, the variability among cities is greater. In terms of relative shares, cities rely more heavily on local taxation than do the municipalities (except in Bulacan), whereas municipalities rely considerably more upon the BIR Allotment and on nontax revenues.

Consolidated Budgetary Position

A more complete view of the activity of the local public sector requires aggregating revenues and expenditures in the General Fund, Infrastructure Fund, and Special Education Fund. A truer picture of total economic development spending can be had by including the Infrastructure Fund and a better measure of social service spending by including the Special Education Fund. Interfund transfers have been accounted for in making this consolidation, which shows actual expenditures to be one-fourth to one-third higher when the Infrastructure Fund and SEF are included (Table 1.8).

As noted above, Infrastructure Fund expenditures are used for the building and maintenance of roads, bridges, and other capital

TABLE 1.8

Mean Per Capita Revenues and Expenditures by Fund, Selected Jurisdictions, 1977

	Municipalities					
Fund	Albay	Bulacan	Iloilo	Sorsogon	Pooled	Cities
General Fund						
Total revenues	10.44	24.81	18.77	12.30	17.75	61.41
Total expenditures	9.62	24.93	17.73	11.76	17.16	56.16
Infrastructure Fund						
Total revenues	1.53	2.24	3.29	1.68	2.50	13.04
Total expenditures	1.85	5.17	4.33	2.48	3.83	14.94
Special Education Fund						
Total revenues	0.36	4.29	1.12	0.36	1.63	3.92
Total expenditures	0.30	3.99	1.06	0.55	1.55	3.21
Consolidated Budget						
Total revenues	12.33	31.34	23.18	14.34	21.88	78.37
Total expenditures	11.77	34.09	23.12	14.79	22.54	74.31
Number of Observations	17	23	43	15	98	42

Source: Annual Report of the Commission on Audit, 1977.

projects. For the four provinces, average per capita economic development spending from both the General and Infrastructure funds is ₱4.30 in Albay, ₱14.60 in Bulacan, ₱9.03 in Iloilo, and ₱4.85 in Sorsogon. The results are not different from those reported above: The more developed areas devote a greater share of resources and a greater per capita amount to development spending. If education spending (SEF expenditures) is also classified as economic development, the dispersion is even greater—from a low of ₱4.60 per capita in Albay to a high of ₱18.58 in Bulacan. These findings raise two interesting hypotheses. The first is that the grant system, which is the main support for economic development spending, is not equalizing. The second is that resource availability is the principal determinant of spending variations. Both propositions are investigated below.

Tax Effort

One explanation for the greater levels of taxing and spending in higher income areas is that a greater tax effort is exerted: The higher the average income of the jurisdiction, the more willing are its residents to pay for better services and/or the more able is the jurisdiction to collect a higher level of taxes. The most straightforward measure of tax effort—the ratio of taxes to personal income—oversimplifies because it presumes that communities with the same income have the same capacity to raise taxes. Nevertheless, this measure of tax effort is easily calculated and provides a reasonable idea of the variation in the extent to which taxable capacity is used.

Three different tax effort ratios were computed for the sample of Philippine municipalities and cities: (1) Real property tax (RPT) effort is defined as the ratio of 1977 RPT collections (current year plus past years plus penalties) divided by 1975 census estimates of personal income; (2) business tax effort is an analogous ratio based on 1977 business license tax collections; and (3) the numerator in the total tax effort measure is total 1977 locally collected taxes.[20]

Table 1.9 contains summary data on the jurisdiction-level tax effort ratios. It is clear from these results that local government taxes are quite low. The average effective tax rate for municipalities, even measured against 1975 income, is well below 1 percent.[21] The range (second column), however, suggests much variation. To understand this variation better, a comparison of a municipality's effective tax rate against some norm is needed. We might view the difference between the average tax effort in the province ($\overline{E}_p$) and that in the

TABLE 1.9

Tax Effort Ratios for Municipalities by Province and for Cities, 1977 (in percent)

Province	Range	Simple Average	Aggregate[a]
Albay			
RPT effort	0.05–0.20	0.12	0.11
Business tax effort	0.05–0.52	0.21	0.22
Local tax effort	0.20–0.82	0.42	0.41
Bulacan			
RPT effort	0.22–2.11	0.49	0.42
Business tax effort	0.06–1.40	0.36	0.36
Local tax effort	0.41–3.12	1.00	0.92
Iloilo			
RPT effort	0.05–2.54	0.28	0.24
Business tax effort	0.03–0.88	0.16	0.36
Local tax effort	0.12–2.79	0.53	0.45
Sorsogon			
RPT effort	0.07–0.22	0.13	0.17
Business tax effort	0.05–0.59	0.18	0.19
Local tax effort	0.17–0.88	0.36	0.36
Pooled			
RPT effort	0.05–2.54	0.28	0.26
Business tax effort	0.03–1.40	0.22	0.23
Local tax effort	0.12–3.12	0.60	0.58
Cities			
RPT effort	0.08–9.09	1.04	0.79
Business tax effort	0.00–1.78	0.68	0.85
Local tax effort	0.38–9.99	2.32	2.47

[a]Computed as $\Sigma Tx_i/\Sigma Y_i$, where Tx_i = 1977 taxes in municipality i, Y_i = 1975 income in municipality i, and the summation is across all municipalities in the province. The resulting ratio is essentially a weighted average of the individual ratios.

Source: Computed by authors.

nation ($\bar{\bar{E}}$) as being beyond the control of any particular municipality and, more generally, due to the differences in fiscal capacity and to the goals and leadership provided in the provincial treasurer's and assessor's offices. Hence, the tax effort of the *i*th jurisdiction (E_i) may be compared to the national average from

$$(E_i - \bar{\bar{E}}) = (E_i - \bar{E}_p) + (\bar{E}_p - \bar{\bar{E}}) \tag{1.1}$$

where the first term on the right represents the higher/lower effort of *i*th jurisdiction attributable to its own actions, and the second term is the differential attributable to the generally lower (or higher) level of economic activity and tax administration skill at the provincial level.

This technique has been used to compute tax effort indexes for each of the 98 municipalities in the four sample provinces. An example illustrates the interpretations. The municipality of Pavia in Iloilo collects (municipal) property taxes equivalent to 0.47 percent of personal income. The (unweighted) "national" average collection ($\bar{\bar{E}}$) is 0.28[22] and the provincial mean is also 0.28 (Table 1.9). Thus, Pavia's property tax effort is 0.19 above the national average, that is, $(E_i - \bar{\bar{E}}) = 0.19$. All of this may be attributed to local actions, as the average property tax effort in the province is the same as the national average. To describe this above-average performance, we construct an effort index (I_i) from

$$I_i = \frac{E_i}{\bar{E}_p} \tag{1.2}$$

for each municipality. An index greater than 100 indicates a tax effort performance above the provincial average. In the case of Pavia, in Iloilo, for example, the property tax effort index is 168, which is quite high.

On the other hand, the municipality of Tabaco in Albay makes a property tax effort of 0.07, which is 0.21 below the average national effective rate, that is

$$E_i - \bar{\bar{E}} = -0.21 \tag{1.3}$$

We may attribute 0.16 of this to the generally lower property tax effort in the province, that is

$$\bar{E}_p - \bar{\bar{E}} = -0.16 \tag{1.4}$$

Furthermore, Tabaco exerts a low effort even within the context of its low taxing province, that is

$$E_i - \overline{E}_p = -0.05 \tag{1.5}$$

Thus, Tabaco's effort index is a relatively low 58, and the average Albay index is an even lower 43.

The index and relative effort for business taxes can be interpreted in an analogous way. Computing such indexes for each tax source provides an opportunity to assess the reasons for a high/low effort and to examine tradeoffs in the intensity of use of business and property taxes.[23] Let the total effective rate (E) be equal to the sum of the effective rates for property taxes (E_1), business taxes (E_2), and other taxes (E_3). Hence, for the ith jurisdiction in province p

$$E_i = E_{1i} + E_{2i} + E_{3i} \tag{1.6}$$

Define

$$E_{1i} = \frac{T_{1i}}{Y_i} = r_{1i} \tag{1.7}$$

and

$$\overline{E}_{1p} = \left(\frac{\overline{T}_{ip}}{\overline{Y}_p}\right) = \hat{r}_{1p} \tag{1.8}$$

and define r_{2i}, r_{3i}, r_{2p}, and $\hat{r}_{3p}$ similarly.

Now actual tax yield in the ith municipality (T_i) is

$$T_i = r_{1i}Y_i + r_{2i}Y_i + r_{3i}Y_i \tag{1.9}$$

and potential yield ($\hat{T}_i$) is

$$\hat{T}_i = \hat{r}_{1p}Y_i + \hat{r}_{2p}Y_i + \hat{r}_{3p}Y_i \tag{1.10}$$

The index of tax effort I_i, then, is

$$I_i = [E_i/\overline{E}_p]\,100 = \frac{r_{1i} + r_{2i} + r_{3i}}{\hat{r}_{1p} + \hat{r}_{2p} + \hat{r}_{3p}}\,100 \tag{1.11}$$

and

$$I_i - 100 = \frac{r_{1i} - \hat{r}_{1p}}{S\hat{r}_{1p}} + \frac{r_{2i} - \hat{r}_{2p}}{\Sigma\hat{r}_{2p}} + \frac{r_{3i} - \hat{r}_{3p}}{\Sigma\hat{r}_{3p}}\ 100 \qquad (1.12)$$

The first term in equation (1.12) may be interpreted as the contribution of the property tax to an above- or below-average tax effort index, and the second and third terms to the business and other tax contributions, respectively. Returning to the examples of Pavia in Iloilo and Tabaco in Albay, we may calculate these components of overall tax effort. The results show that Pavia's high effort is due to an above-average performance for all taxes (Table 1.10), which may indicate a generally strong local tax administration. Tabaco offsets a below-average property tax effort with a very high business tax effort. This finding suggests that the commercial/industrial sector is easily taxed, perhaps because of the presence of a few large firms or a generally stronger commercial base; this case might have reduced the pressure to increase property tax effort. Malinao, a poorer municipality in Albay, makes a very low tax effort in total and for each tax, although business tax effort accounts for most of its poor performance.

Do these results provide any clues as to what community characteristics lead to variations in tax effort? To begin exploring this question we have computed the simple correlations between the tax

TABLE 1.10

Illustration of Calculation of Components of Tax Effort: Pavia, Iloilo, Tabaco, Albay and Malinao, Albay

	Pavia	Tabaco	Malinao
Effort index (I_i)	257	126	52
(I_i-100)	157	26	48
Deviation of index from provincial average (I_i - 100) that can be attributed to:			
Property tax	36 (23%)	-12 (-46%)	-7 (-15%)
Business tax	100 (64%)	+41 (158%)	-31 (-65%)
Other tax	21 (13%)	-2 (-7%)	-10 (-21%)

Source: Computed by authors.

effort indexes and per capita income, urbanization, and population for the municipalities in each province as well as for the sample of cities (see upper panel, Table 1.11). For the provinces taken separately there is a consistent negative relationship between per capita income and tax effort. This result suggests that within a province, those jurisdictions with a larger income base tax relatively less of it than do lower income municipalities. On the other hand, total local taxes and especially business taxes are positively related to the relative share of income earned from nonagricultural sources—manufacturing, retail, and wage incomes.

There is a plausible explanation for these seemingly mixed findings. Given that these jurisdictions are predominantly rural in nature, the findings concerning per capita income and nonagricultural shares of income may reflect the fact that farms are exempt from business taxes and that the RPT is not easily collected from the agricultural sector. With respect to the latter, absentee ownership, controlled below-market prices, inadequate assessment and records, land reform, and the physical problems of getting the tax collected are some of the important impediments. If nearly all jurisdictions in a province are predominantly rural in nature (as is especially true in Albay and Sorsogon), the higher incomes in some cannot be "captured" by the tax system—thus the negative correlations.

Most obvious from the charter city analysis is the lack of association between these demographic/economic characteristics and tax effort, although larger cities or cities with stronger nonagricultural economic bases make a greater business tax effort.

The bottom panel of Table 1.11 provides a different perspective regarding tax effort in municipalities in the pooled sample by correlating the effective tax rates (T_i/Y_i) with socioeconomic characteristics. Given the differential average effective tax rates across the four provinces, it is not surprising to find the rather strong positive association between total taxes and both urbanization and nonagricultural incomes. The municipalities of Bulacan are probably a strong influence on this result.

The evidence here suggests that local government taxes in the Philippines are urban taxes. Business tax effort is higher where there are higher levels of per capita nonagricultural income and urbanization. The pattern of property tax effort is less clearly seen from these relationships, perhaps because the pattern is more complicated than can be picked up by simple, zero-order relationships.[24] The major consistent finding is that where per capita income is high—and especially if a large share of this income is earned in the agricultural sector—property tax effort will be low.

TABLE 1.11

Simple Correlations of Municipal and City Property and Business Tax Effort Indexes and Effective Tax Rates with Socioeconomic Variables, 1977

Province	Per Capita Income	Population	Urban Population[b]	Nonagricultural Share of Income[c]
	Simple Correlations with Tax Effort Indexes[a]			
Albay				
RPT index	-.690	-.334	.336	-.412
Business tax index	-.184	.176	.404	.567
Total	-.417	.121	.258	.048
Bulacan				
RPT index	-.174	-.312	-.116	.173
Business tax index	.211	-.173	.263	.540
Total	-.006	-.308	.020	.261
Iloilo				
RPT index	-.266	-.054	-.221	-.304
Business tax index	-.335	-.056	.135	.374
Total	-.358	-.089	-.124	.092
Sorsogon				
RPT index	-.824	-.096	.039	.064
Business tax index	-.282	.460	.664	.439
Total	-.469	.300	.688	.262
Four Provinces				
RPT index	-.258	-.111	-.085	-.018
Business tax index	-.183	.015	.205	.201
Total	-.281	-.065	.069	.109
Cities				
RPT index	-.090	-.094	-.031	-.091
Business tax index	.179	.425	.191	.313
Total	.027	.179	.267	.146
	Simple Correlations with Effective Tax Rates			
Four Provinces				
RPT rate	-.084	-.081	.032	.222
Business tax rate	.016	.112	.354	.456
Total tax rate	-.073	-.010	.224	.387

[a]See Table 2.5 for significance levels.

[b]Urban population in 1975 as a proportion of total population.

[c]Manufacturing, retail, and wage income as a proportion of total income.

Source: Annual Report of the Commission on Audit on Local Governments, 1977.

Measuring Tax Effort: A Digression

The results above treat a high effective tax rate as a high tax effort because of an assumption that all income generates the same level of taxable capacity. Yet we have learned from the above that effective tax rates tend to be larger where urbanization rates and per capita nonagricultural income are higher. We speculated that this is due in part to a generally more advanced stage of development and a greater taxable capacity. Where taxable capacity is high, we may expect a higher effective tax rate, and it is improper to attribute all of an above-average tax performance to "effort," to a greater willingness to pay.

To correct for this we have constructed a tax effort model in the traditional form used in cross-country studies.[25] If taxable capacity varies not only with income level but with per capita nonagricultural income (NY_p), urbanization (U), and population size (P), we may estimate

$$T/_Y = f(NY_p, U, P) \tag{1.13}$$

where T/Y = total local taxes as a percent of personal income.

Under this approach the fitted relationship, if considered adequate, could then be used to measure an "expected tax capacity," $(T/\hat{Y})_i$, based upon the values of the independent variables in the ith municipality. The actual effective rate, $(T/Y)_i$, could then be compared with this expected level to form a new tax effort measure, EE_i, defined as

$$EE_i = \frac{(T/Y)_i}{(T/\hat{Y})_i} \tag{1.14}$$

Rankings of municipalities can then be made on the basis of the EE_i index reflecting whether a jurisdiction is capturing its taxable capacity, where the latter is based upon its own economic characteristics.

Two different forms of the relationship between socioeconomic variables and $(T/Y)_i$ have been estimated, with the results shown in Table 1.12. The first set of regression results shows per capita nonagricultural incomes to be significantly related to effective tax rates (measured as total local taxes per ₱1,000 of personal income), whereas neither urbanization nor population is significant. The second regression suggests that variations in effective tax rates are closely

TABLE 1.12

Ordinary Least Squares Regression Results: Effective Tax Rates Related to Local Socioeconomic Characteristics

Model	Intercept	Percent Urban	Per Capita Non-agricultural Income	Population (1,000s)	Dummy Variables			R^2	F
					Albay	Iloilo	Sorsogon		
1	3.301	1.846	8.782	-.052				.17	6.53*
	(2.60)*	(.62)	(3.62)*	(1.56)					
2	8.711	1.569	4.466	-.061	-3.840	-3.855	-5.077	.24	4.76*
	(3.72)*	(.53)	(1.59)	(1.73)	(2.09)†	(2.44)†	(2.66)*		

Note: Tax rates measured as the ratio of total local taxes to personal income (in ₱1,000).
*Significant at less than the 0.01 level.
†Significant at less than the 0.05 level.
Source: Computed by authors.

related to province-specific factors. Three dummy variables have been introduced to delineate among the four provinces (Bulacan is used as the standard of comparison). Under this formulation none of the three economic variables is significant, while each of the dummy variable coefficients is. This finding suggests an underlying difference in local taxation that depends more on regional levels of development or perhaps provincial government operations than on particular characteristics of the localities.[26]

Several possibilities may explain these results. One grows out of the centralized nature of local tax administration. The role of the provincial treasurer may be so dominant that it swamps the influence of local economic conditions on tax effort and results in no systematic variability in tax effort across jurisdictions within a single province. Another possibility is that the independent variables used here are too crude to pick up subtle differences in stages of development, which account for differences in tax efforts. And a third is that basically random local forces, such as an active municipal mayor, have greater influence on taxing behavior than do the more traditional economically-based variables.

Cash Balances and Surpluses

The question of fiscal health can also be studied by considering trends in the annual surplus/deficit and in the accumulated cash position of local governments. One possibility is a pattern of continuing deficits, exhausted reserves, and general insolvency. Although this scenario is not unknown in developing countries, it fails to describe the situation in the Philippines, at least in the four provinces studied here.

Cash Balances

Municipalities can hold cash either in their own treasuries or in a trust fund administered by the provincial treasurer. Generally, the amounts held locally are minimal—no more than is necessary for the day-to-day operation of the government.[27] To study movements in the cash position of municipalities, COA data are not adequate. Therefore, information was gathered from site visits to a small number of municipalities in the provinces of Iloilo, Bulacan, and Albay.[28] The results of these case studies are summarized in the first two sets of columns in Table 1.13. The first set of columns shows the General Fund balance as a percent of General Fund income for 1977–79. The

TABLE 1.13

Cash Balance and Surplus Position, Selected Municipalities and Cities

	General Fund Cash Balance as a Percent of Revenue			General Plus Infra-structure Fund Cash Balance as a Percent of Total Revenue			General Fund: Unappro-priated Surplus as a Percent of Revenue			General Plus Infra-structure Fund Unappro-priated Surplus as a Percent of Revenue		
	1977	1978	1979	1977	1978	1979	1977	1978	1979	1977	1978	1979
Iloilo												
Dingle	45.5	26.8	9.6	47.5	41.9	26.1	23.7	8.9	14.3	19.5	11.4	14.3
Dumangas	65.0	72.0	66.0	69.0	92.0	80.0	30.0	41.0	34.0	35.0	41.0	34.0
Guimbal	93.5	85.7	85.3	96.3	89.9	113.9	90.3	18.0	18.6	123.1	31.2	18.6
Passi	61.4	133.4	146.0	65.4	126.9	141.1	33.2	9.4	51.4	33.1	19.4	51.4
Pavia	46.8	41.8	42.2	48.1	55.9	44.6	30.9	39.2	9.3	33.9	41.4	9.3
Tigbauan	22.9	21.8	17.0	32.8	30.8	30.3	10.9	13.5	17.7	27.6		17.7
Albay												
Camalig	0.4	0.2	6.4	0.3	0.0	14.5	0.2	7.5	NA	3.2	9.0	NA
Libon	0.5	14.3	4.4	9.7	36.8	22.1	0.2	3.7	NA	8.6	17.9	NA
Malinao	7.8	14.4	2.4	8.9	13.8	7.4	5.4	9.3	6.6	16.2	20.6	7.3
Tabaco	37.3	46.5	51.5	36.0	48.1	47.9	0.1	1.2	NA	0.5	2.4	NA

Bulacan								
Balagtas	0.08	7.14	0.67	5.61	0.12	4.54	1.64	4.31
Baliwag	3.15	21.00	3.94	17.81	1.07	6.32	1.19	5.14
Malolos	38.43	35.91	40.32	36.64	5.81	17.79	6.53	17.16
Obando	34.45	45.89	50.81	66.49	15.94	21.03	17.97	22.09
Sta. Maria	28.12	28.66	26.62	27.95	7.79	7.87	7.71	8.31

	Total General Fund as a Percent of Revenue			General plus Infrastructure as a Percent of Total Revenue*		
	1977	1978	1979	1977	1978	1979
Legaspi City						
Cash						
On hand	6.8	4.9	1.9	6.1	4.3	4.0
Interest-bearing	31.8	49.8	29.7	28.9	46.2	26.2
Unappropriated surplus	41.6	52.6	31.6	36.7	47.2	21.8
Iloilo City						
Cash						
On hand	3.8	27.3	12.2	4.2	25.5	9.6
Interest-bearing	23.9	9.6	8.8	50.6	9.0	6.9
Unappropriated surplus	8.3	12.6	6.9	8.0	12.4	6.2

*Infrastructure Fund "income" in 1979 was ₱4,234,343 in Legaspi but included a loan of ₱2,079,812. The loan is excluded in the computation of these percentages.

Source: Data gathered during field visits to individual municipalities.

next set gives the same information for the combined General and Infrastructure Fund positions. In each case the balances are those held in the provincial treasury.

For most municipalities studied, cash balances are quite large and have been increasing. In Iloilo, even the smallest (1977) balance, relative to revenues, is in excess of 22 percent or equivalent to more than two and one-half months of revenues. The weighted average of the six municipalities in Iloilo (weighted by the amounts of revenue) in 1977 is approximately 57 percent for the General Fund and 61 percent for the two funds combined—an amount equivalent to over half the total year's income. The Bulacan municipalities also have been holding large cash balances, a weighted average for the General Fund of 23.22 percent in 1977.[29] There is, however, considerable variation across the municipalities within this province. The cash position for the Albay municipalities is much less strong, although it did grow during the 1977–79 period.[30]

Substantial levels of cash are also observed for the two chartered cities examined. Especially notable in the cash balances are the large relative holdings in the form of interest-bearing securities. In each of the three years, the stock of interest-bearing balances in Legaspi City was equivalent to nearly 30 percent of its annual flow of income (the percentage was close to 50 percent in 1978). This finding reflects the fact that, as in the case of provinces, cities are allowed to earn interest on cash balances without the approval of a higher level of government. The city of Iloilo relied less heavily on interest-bearing accounts—drawing them down between 1977 and 1978 and then holding them constant through 1979.

The cash position of these local governments is so strong that it causes some questions to be raised—most obviously, the opportunity cost associated with holding these balances. Apparently, only treasuries of provincial and city governments hold assets in the form of interest-bearing time deposits. Municipalities thus incur a real resource loss when these balances become excessive.[31]

Both efficiency and redistributional effects are associated with this policy. For municipalities there is no direct incentive to accumulate excess reserves since it does involve a resource loss. Yet the evidence suggests that, at least in some localities, this disincentive has been overcome through the strong leadership of provincial treasurers. If such is the case, there has been no resource loss associated with the policy, at least when viewed from the perspective of the entire province. However, to the extent that the interest proceeds are not redistributed to the contributing municipalities, there is a resource redistribution. Such redistribution may also affect local tax compliance. If taxpayers in a locality comply with the tax laws but do not observe corresponding increases in public service quantities and qualities, they may become less willing to comply. Beyond possible alterations in the current statutory arrangements, a reasonable administrative policy would be to redistribute some portion of interest proceeds in proportion to the deposits held in the provincial treasury.

Fiscal Surpluses

Cash balances may represent a value of asset holdings by local governments, but they may not be a good measure of the discretionary funds available to local governments because some portion of this liquid wealth may already have been committed to particular purposes. A second approach to the measurement of fiscal well-being, which can take this possibility into account, is to study the trend in the surplus position of a jurisdiction. It should be emphasized that we are not talking here about an annual budgetary "surplus" measure but about the stock of cash available for general purposes. Surplus is measured as the sum of cash in the treasury plus deposits and receivables less payables.

Two different types of "surpluses" are included in the post-closing balance—appropriated and unappropriated. The former includes those funds that, while appropriated for projects, have not yet been spent. Included here are any unspent funds from the 20 percent Development Fund. Unappropriated reserves are, however, essentially free reserves and therefore provide another view of the fiscal reserves of the municipality. These discretionary funds are found in both the General Fund and the Infrastructure Fund. Their size relative to total revenue is reported in the last two sets of columns in Table 1.13 for 1977–79.

One must conclude from the data on the six Iloilo municipalities that substantial financial resources are available and not utilized. By 1979, free reserves averaged (unweighted) 32 percent of total General plus Infrastructure Fund income. While comparable averages in 1978 in Albay (12.4) and Bulacan (11.4) are lower than in Iloilo, the levels in the larger and more urbanized places—Tabaco (Albay) and Obando (Bulacan)—are quite large. The unappropriated surpluses are also very large in Legaspi City—exceeding 50 percent of General Fund income in 1978 and exceeding 20 percent of revenues in all years. The surpluses were not so large in Iloilo City, but nevertheless remained at a substantial level throughout the three-year period.

An obvious question that arises from the finding of these strong cash and reserve positions is, why? Several answers might be suggested. First, it may simply be that these jurisdictions do not "need" these resources and they truly are surplus funds. This explanation, however, does not square with stated needs for public service improvements. Second, the accumulation of balances may be due to a conservative financial management philosophy, espoused at both higher and lower levels of government. At the central government level funds are earmarked for contingency reserves and for capital formation, and, moreover, local government consumption expenditure increases are limited by law. Local treasurers may also contribute to this conservatism in spending by consciously underbudgeting. Local treasurers feel that they have some personal liability in cases of budget deficits and in any case see their performance rating as being based on the fiscal performance of their jurisdictions. It is a truism that in the financial management world, surpluses get good marks. Provincial treasurers have little incentive to revise their conservative practice, for many of these same reasons and because the interest returns on local cash balances accrue fully to the provincial treasury.

A third reason is that it may be these reserves would not accumulate if more imaginative uses of local funds were pursued. That is, there may be "needs" for additional local services, but the system for ascertaining these desires does not work effectively to reflect them in actions. If residents have no effective way of voicing their demands for public services, there is likely to be a tendency to remain with the status quo in terms of services provided rather than undertaking new policy initiatives at the local level. Fourth, and possibly most relevant, is that the kinds of spending necessary to meet the citizens' public service demands require that considerably greater amounts of resources be made available. The balances may be substantial but not by comparison with what is required, for example, to build a market.

CONCLUSION

Three general conclusions may be drawn from the preceding discussion. The first is that not only is local government financing highly centralized in the Philippines in terms of taxing authority and expenditure responsibility but centralization extends to day-to-day influence on fiscal decisions and administrative procedures. The second is that the fiscal importance of the local government sector declined during the 1970s. Third, central government policy may have to share the blame for the failure of local governments to mobilize more resources, for the inefficiencies in local government operations, and perhaps for the wide variation in tax effort.

If increased local government participation in governmental financing is indeed a national objective, the central government may find it necessary to remove certain disincentives to more efficient local government financing and to create incentives for local governments to increase tax effort and development spending. The discussion in this chapter suggests areas where such reforms would seem called for: local budgeting and financial management practices, the central government oversight process, the relaxation of expenditure mandates, and the reduction or management of local government cash balances. We elaborate on these possibilities in Chapter 7.

NOTES

1. Jose Veloso Abueva, "Ideology and Practice in the 'New Society,'" in *Marcos and Martial Law in the Philippines*, ed. David A. Rosenberg (Ithaca, N.Y.: Cornell University Press, 1979), p. 58.

2. PD 464, Preamble, May 20, 1974.

3. This goal was stated by Virata in two recent speeches: "Financing Local Development: Policy Changes, Issues and Problems" (February 4, 1979), and "Local Government Finance: Challenges and Prospects" (no date).

4. *Budget Operations Manual for Local Governments* (Manila: Provincial and City Treasurers and Assessors Association, undated), pp. 8–9.

5. Ibid., p. 8.

6. The fiscal year in the Philippines coincides with the calendar year. Prior to 1976 the fiscal year was July 1–June 30; July 1, 1976–December 31, 1976 constituted the "transition period."

7. *Budget Operations Manual for Local Governments*, p. 82.

8. A review of these issues in the United States is presented in Roy Bahl and Larry Schroeder, "Forecasting Local Government Budgets," Occasional Paper No. 38, Metropolitan Studies Program (Syracuse, N.Y.: Maxwell School, Syracuse University, 1979).

9. This arrangement was altered under PD 1375 (May 1978), when the budget review responsibility was passed to the Ministry of the Budget.

10. Jurisdictions are classified according to the amount of revenue collected.

11. This situation is similar to that facing the U.S. government, which is unable to decide what constitutes a "distressed" city. See James W. Fossett and Richard P. Nathan, "The Prospects for Urban Revival," and Roy Bahl, "The Next Decade in State and Local Government Finance: A Period of Adjustment," both in *Urban Government Finance, Emerging Trends*, ed. Roy Bahl (Beverly Hills, Calif.: Sage Publications, 1981).

12. The municipalities of Jordan, New Valencia, and San Miguel, in Iloilo Province, and Casiguran and Sorsogon, in Sorsogon Province, were excluded

from the sample because the data were not available from COA. Appendix A contains a listing of the jurisdictions included in the sample.

13. The sample was chosen with the advice of the PIDS project directors, using criteria such as accessibility, willingness to cooperate, and variation in income level, economic structure, and quality of financial administration. Some of these criteria may themselves ensure a bias.

14. Obtaining accurate income data from any census is a difficult task. It is even more difficult in rural areas of developing countries, given lower literacy rates of respondents, inadequate record keeping, nonmonetary transactions, and reluctance to divulge financial information. While we recognize the potential weaknesses in the data, they are, nevertheless, the most up-to-date and complete set of economic information available.

15. This term is slightly misleading given the methods used to classify incomes by the census. That is, respondents were asked to indicate from which of several activities (farming/gardening, livestock and poultry, fishing, manufacturing, wages) "the household derived the most income in 1975." Thus, even though only 51 percent of total income of a household may have been earned in a particular pursuit, the entire amount of household income would be classified under that activity.

16. Iloilo has a relatively lower average income level than expected. One possible explanation is the influence of national price controls on sugar and rice production, which are the major crops in Iloilo.

17. It should also be noted that 1975 populations were used to derive these per capita amounts. Hence, differential population growth from 1975 to 1977 could alter these findings slightly by understating the relative per capita amounts for the slower growing municipalities.

18. For a complete listing and discussion of these local taxes and fees, see A. Yoingco and V. Quintos, *Philippine Tax System Under the New Society* (Manila: GIC Enterprises, 1979), especially pp. 238–50 and 262–77.

19. Because of missing financial and socioeconomic data for particular variables, there is some minor variability in the sample of jurisdictions used in the several analyses performed in this and subsequent chapters.

20. While total revenue effort—the ratio of total General Fund revenues less the BIR Allotment to personal income—may be computed, it is less comparable because it includes gross revenues from enterprise activities. It is not reported here.

21. The municipal share of the property tax is only 45 percent.

22. As approximated here by the average across the 98 municipalities, since comparable personal income data were not available for municipalities across the entire nation.

23. The relative effort indexes are shown for all sample municipalities in Bahl et al., *Strengthening the Fiscal Performance of Philippine Local Governments*, Tables II-12a–II-12d, pp. II-47–II-50.

24. This possibility is explored more fully in Chapter 2.

25. See Joergen Lotz and Elliott Morss, "Measuring Tax Effort in Developing Countries," *IMF Staff Papers* 14 (1967): 478–99; Roy Bahl, "A Regression Approach to Tax Effort and Tax Ratio Analysis," *IMF Staff Papers* 18, no. 3 (November 1971): 570–612; Harley Hinrichs, *A General Theory of Tax Structure Change During Economic Development* (Cambridge, Mass.: Harvard Law

School, 1966); Alan Tait, Wilfred Gratz, and Barry Eichengreen, "International Comparisons of Taxation for Selected Developing Countries, 1972–1976," *IMF Staff Papers* 26, no. 1 (March 1979): 123–56; Roy Bahl, "A Representative Tax System Approach to Measuring Tax Effort in Developing Countries," *IMF Staff Papers* 19, no. 1 (March 1972): 87–124; Raja Chelliah, Hessel Baas, and Margaret Kelly, "Tax Ratios and Tax Effort in Developing Countries, 1969–1971," *IMF Staff Papers* 22, no. 1 (March 1975): 187–205.

26. Several other regressions were fit with both intercept and slope dummy variables, under the expectation that both the level of tax effort and its response to economic characteristics differ across provinces. The findings did not, however, bear out this expectation. We also estimated several nonlinear relationships and still could not improve the results.

27. It must be recognized, however, that this measure is of the stock of cash at a point in time (the final day of the fiscal year). This measure can change daily in response to the particular flows of revenues and expenditures in a jurisdiction.

28. The "sampling" scheme was nonrandom; no attempt was made to choose either the "best" or "worst" cases.

29. We were unable to obtain the necessary data for 1979 in Bulacan, so the most recent growth or decline in these stocks cannot be ascertained.

30. This may, however, have to do with the data displayed here—cash held in "other local treasuries." If the municipalities in Albay are not encouraged to hold cash in the provincial treasury, they may well have relatively larger holdings within their own treasuries.

31. Municipalities can earn interest on excess cash balances only with the joint approval of the provincial and municipal councils. Only in the subprovince of Guimaras did we observe this action.

2

The Real Property Tax

by ROY BAHL and LARRY SCHROEDER

As in many countries, the real property tax (RPT) in the Philippines is a principal revenue source for local governments and, as elsewhere, it is laden with administrative and structural problems. In this chapter, we consider the three major problem areas of property taxation: determination of the tax base, tax rate structure, and collection efficiency. Following this description is an analysis of the revenue performance of the property tax: the factors underlying its growth and the variation in its performance within the nation.

In the Philippines, some form of a tax on land or its products can be traced back to the Spanish era. The first property tax similar to today's was implemented in 1901, when Acts 82 and 83 were passed by the Philippine Commission. These acts provided for the organization of municipalities and provinces and allowed municipalities to levy a real property tax of not less than half of 1 percent, with provincial treasurers given the responsibility of supervising assessment and tax collection.[1]

The current system of real property taxation in the Philippines is documented in two major presidential decrees–PD 76, issued on December 6, 1972, and PD 464, issued May 20, 1974.[2] Under PD 76, owners of real property are required to file sworn statements of the current value of their property. Accurate reporting is to be aided by PD 1533, which specifies that the declared values will be used by the government in determining fair value of parcels involved in eminent domain proceedings. In addition, PD 76 stresses uniformity of assessment through requirements that provincial and city assessors prepare schedules of fair market values for different classes of property within their jurisdictions using rules issued by the Ministry of

Finance, and that they revise assessments every five years starting in 1979 (later amended under PD 1621 to every three years).

But it is PD 464, and its more recent admendments and Letters of Instruction (LOI), that constitute the Real Property Tax Code. It defines the base of the property tax, the methods by which assessors are to value property, the timing of reassessments, the rate structure, and how the property tax is to be collected and administered.[3]

DETERMINATION OF THE TAX BASE

A number of steps are required in the determination of the property tax base: legal definition of the base, discovery and verification of property ownership, determination of assessed values, and revisions in property values. Problems in each of these areas have slowed the growth in the taxable property base and constrained it from reaching its potential yield.

Definition of the Real Property Tax Base

Taxable property under the Real Property Tax Code includes all land, buildings, machinery, and other improvements (including such features as productive trees on forest land) except those lands, buildings, machinery, and improvements that are expressly exempt from the tax.[4] These are basically four categories of exemptions: government-owned property, "preferred investments," charitable and religious property, and property of low income persons.[5] Government property is often exempt from local taxation under the principle that government institutions should not tax one another. Nevertheless, local services are rendered to such installations and therefore some payment is justified. A payment in lieu of property taxes that helps to cover thse costs is practiced in other developing countries.[6]

The central government has also exempted a long list of privately owned properties from the local property tax, including dairy farms, pasture and grazing lands acquired from the public domain, machinery of a "new and preferred industry" as certified by the Board of Investments, new investments in tourism-oriented industries (PD 535), and subsidized housing to employees of tax-exempt corporations and partnerships (PD 745). While localities may benefit from additional economic activity resulting from such tax holidays, the nature of the local tax system is such that it is unlikely that the local government will reap revenue benefits from this activity. A payment in lieu of taxes made by the central government would be a reasonable solution to this tax base erosion.

Charitable and religious organization exemptions may be justified on grounds that they are providing certain services that benefit the community—services that would be decreased were taxes levied on their property. Still, care must be taken to ensure that the organizations are truly nonprofit and not competing with similar privately owned facilities.

Real property with a value less than 1,000 pesos belonging to a single owner in any one city or municipality is also exempt from the RPT. Such an exemption may be justifiable both on grounds of equity and administrative efficiency, as the record processing and collection costs associated with extremely low valued parcels may exceed the actual tax yields. On the other hand, one does not want to go too far with such exemptions because of the need to maximize the coverage of the tax roll and hence the involvement of the population in the governmental process.

The taxable base of the real property tax is the capital value of land and improvements with provision for assessment at fractions of current market value. The classes of property to which different assessment ratios are applied are set forth in PD 76. Under this scheme all nonexempt land is classified and assessed according to the following schedule (as amended in PD 1383):

Land Use	Assessed Value as a Percent of Current Market Value
Residential	30
Agricultural	40
Timber and forest	40
Commercial and industrial	50
Mineral	50

Furthermore, all land is to be valued according to its actual use, rather than according to its best use. This classification may initially be based on the use class indicated on the Declaration of Real Property form submitted by the taxpayer. Inspections made by assessors are used as well. When there is a conflict with the use indicated by the owner, the land-use class is usually changed to reflect that determined by the assessor.

Reliance upon actual rather than best use, together with fractional assessments, has potential economic effects that should be recognized in an evaluation of the property tax system. As is the case for nearly all taxes, property taxes can alter choices that individuals would, in the absence of the tax, have made. These distortions of economic choices are not necessarily a disadvantage; for example, some forms of property taxation may be used to discourage land speculation. Unfortunately, the distortions induced by the Philippine system probably do not serve important social goals. Property tax assessments based upon actual rather than best use have the effect of discouraging conversion of the use of property from its current use to an alternative that, at least as judged by the market, is more productive.[7] For example, a parcel of rice land near the edge of an urbanized area may more productively be used as a commercial plot. In this case the potential market price will reflect that fact. Under actual use assessment, however, the land would be assessed the same as a parcel of rice land far from the urban area. If the owner were assessed on the basis of the price the parcel would fetch in the market, there would be an incentive to convert the land to its more productive use.

Fractional assessments also have built-in incentives and disincentives. While the higher fractional assessment of agricultural lands provides an incentive for conversion to residential usage, the higher fractional assessment for commercial or industrial properties discourages conversion to these uses.[8] The fractions noted above were probably applied to promote equity, perhaps under the assumption that ability to pay was greatest for commercial and industrial landowners and least for residential property owners. Nevertheless, the potential inefficiencies similar to the previous example must be recognized.

Buildings, machinery,[9] and other improvements are also assessed at fractional rates. For buildings and other improvements, the fractional values depend both upon use and market value. Once again, there is an apparent attempt to adjust assessments according to the ability of the taxpayer and once again a potential inefficiency results. Here the tax introduces a bias against investing in improvements because the fractional assessment ratio associated with land is less than the ratio applied to nearly all commercial, industrial, and agricultural improvements and less than the ratio applied to a large portion of residential improvements.

Under the current property tax system, total tax liability (T) on a parcel of land and its improvements will be

$$T = r_L a_L V_L + r_I a_I V_I \tag{2.1}$$

where a = fractional assessment ratio; V = market value; r = tax rate; and L and I = land and improvements, respectively.

In any investment decision involving land and improvements, there will be a bias in favor of projects that rely more heavily upon land as long as the value of the improvement is such that the assessment ratio on improvements exceeds that for land. For example, consider a commercial venture where the land is valued at ₱1 million. The investor is trying to determine the type of improvement to place on the land. If he chooses an improvement with a market value of anything more than ₱250,000 (almost a certainty), we can write his tax liability as

$$T = .5 r_L V_L + .8 r_I V_I \tag{2.2}$$

If $r_L = r_I = 0.01$, then

$$T = .005\, V_L + .008\, V_I \tag{2.3}$$

and the improvement will be taxed more heavily than the land. Indeed, in the case of commercial and industrial properties, it is only for the very smallest of improvements, that is, those valued less than ₱30,000, for which the effective tax rate on improvements is not greater than that on land.

A related problem with fractional assessments on improvements is that in order to be placed in a lower assessment bracket, a property owner will attempt to pressure assessors to lower valuations. Pressures could be placed on the assessor or indirectly on politicians. Thus, there is a double incentive to push for a lowered assessment: a lower overall tax base and a lower effective tax rate.

Discovery and Determination of Property Ownership

The base of the RPT is more easily defined than it is measured. A first and difficult step is to discover and document the characteristics and ownership of a property. In the Philippines this problem has recently been exacerbated by the land reform program. The base determination problem has been addressed through tax mapping, required owner declarations of value, and procedures for handling duplicate records.

Tax mapping procedures are the key element in the entire process. Tax maps establish a complete inventory of all real property and assign to each parcel a property identification number (PIN) such that theoretically every parcel in the nation has a unique PIN. The PIN provides a simple means to keep track of all parcels and to link assessment and billing records.

Tax mapping is, however, a lengthy and costly process. Recent estimates of the costs of tax mapping range from ₱10 to ₱20 per parcel.[10] The mapping process itself requires several months, at the least, to carry out; for example, Albay Province planned 267 working days for tax mapping in Tabaco municipality, which comprises approximately 14,500 parcels.[11] Given the per parcel cost, outlays are indeed large for local jurisdictions, especially taking into consideration that one analyst has discovered a pattern of municipal governments contributing 23 percent of the cost of tax mapping and provincial governments 40 percent.[12] Because the results of the mapping will not be reflected in revenues until a year or two after the mapping has been completed, the procedure can be viewed as a long-term investment. Local politicians, who tend to favor investments with highly visible and short-term payoffs, are rarely enthusiastic about increasing local taxes to finance tax mapping projects. One could speculate that relatively progressive local governments with more secure leadership and political support would participate in tax mapping early but that their participation would diminish as the coverage of the project increased. This possibility would point to the need for more loan and/or grant financing and foreign assistance, all of which have been used to some extent to finance tax mapping in the Philippines.

As of August 1980, tax mapping had been completed in 4,820 barangays located in 160 cities and municipalities and had been begun in another 3,710 barangays in 138 localities.[13] Although these achievements are notable, one must keep in mind that there are about 1,600 local governments in the Philippines and that tax mapping has not even begun in 80 percent of the local government areas.

In a different approach to determining property ownership, PD 76 requires self-declaration, while PD 464 (and amendments PD 1383 and PD 1621) requires that such declarations be filed every three years, or within 60 days after any improvement to a property. Included on these declarations are sworn statements regarding the true value of the property and a description of the property "sufficient in detail to enable the assessor or his deputy to identify the same for assessment purposes."[14] While this approach—if performed accurately and promptly by all property owners—would vastly improve the determination of ownership, it has not proven useful.

One of the most frequently cited problems is that of duplicate and missing records. There are several reasons for the existence of duplicate records on the property tax roll.[15] One of these is related to the original filing of tax declarations under PD 76. Apparently, there were cases where different people filed tax declaration statements for the same parcel, which inflates collectibles over that which realistically can be collected and therefore results in an understatement of collection efficiency. In one Albay municipality with 14,000 tax declarations, 2,000 duplicate tax declarations were detected after tax mapping had been completed.[16] A second situation leading to duplicate tax declarations occurs when a property buyer correctly files a tax declaration for a newly purchased property, but the seller's tax declaration form is not removed from the file. Under Section 11 of PD 464, it is the duty of a property owner to inform the assessor of property transfer within 60 days of the transaction, thus placing the responsibility with the previous owner. But there are no penalties for failure of the property owner to inform the assessor and in most cases there are no cross-checks to pick up this problem.

Missing records are also a problem. Although new property buyers must pay the property transfer tax, register the property with the registrar of deeds, pay a registration fee, and fill out a property declaration form, sometimes the final step is omitted. Again, the problem rises from a lack of effective coordination between the registrar of deeds and the assessor.

Another major source of records management problems relates to the land reform program. On the surface, the problem seems relatively simple: Land was transferred (sold) from large landholders to tenants through the Ministry of Agrarian Reform (MAR). Local assessors, however, do not have good records of the particulars of the reformed properties. The previous owners are not willing to pay the tax on behalf of their former tenants nor are the new owners eager to accept their taxpaying responsibilities. The MAR admits that complete mapping of the affected areas is yet another continuing difficulty.[17]

The problem is further complicated because some previous owners were delinquent in payment of property taxes at the time of reform. Large landowners have known since 1972 that it was only a matter of time before some of their lands would be confiscated. Under the statutes, owners could receive payments for their land from the Land Bank upon showing proof of payment of all real property taxes on their holdings through October 1972. Such a system could only lead to delinquency after 1972.

Several aspects of the land reform system make it unlikely to expect a significant amount of compliance from tenants, too. First, there has been a great deal of uncertainty associated with the land reform process. If a tenant is uncertain that the reformed lands will remain in his possession, it is unlikely that he will be willing to pay the taxes. Second, the provision that tenants cannot transfer the land to anyone other than heirs or the government makes ownership of these properties unlike that of other taxed assets, suggesting a different pattern of tax compliance behavior. Third, many tenants were not aware that their rental payments since 1972 would, in fact, be counted as payment toward the purchase of the land. Fourth, there may have been a lack of understanding concerning legal responsibilities associated with property ownership, even in cases where the tenant realized he was the owner of the property. Fifth, there may have been an ability-to-pay problem since these former tenants suddenly found themselves the owners of property, but may still have lacked monetary assets with which to pay taxes.

Finally, local financial officers also must bear some of the blame for their inaction. There was a lack of understanding on the part of local assessors and treasurers of the administrative processes involved in land reform, and there is little evidence of campaigns being carried out in land reform areas to encourage the new landowners to declare their property for tax purposes.

The Assessment Process

The property valuation system is based on a highly systematized set of instructions. Rather than relying upon the subjective judgments of an assessment officer, who unilaterally assigns a value to each parcel, a complete schedule of market values per unit (for example, per hectare of land or per square meter of a building constructed of a particular building material) is compiled before valuation or revaluation occurs. These schedules, constructed for each province and chartered city, are then approved by the Ministry of Finance.

As in most property tax assessment schemes, three different methods are used to estimate market values—comparative sales, income capitalization, and reproduction or replacement cost. The comparable sales approach is the principal technique utilized by assessors in determining the schedule of current market values. Assessors obtain much of this information by asking the opinion of knowledgeable persons, such as bankers and realtors, concerning current prices in certain areas, and many also use their own knowledge of the local realty market.[18] The self-declarations of market value discussed above are seldom relied upon because it is assumed that self-assessment naturally yields downward biased market value estimates. Likewise, property values recorded at the time of sale by the registrar of deeds are felt to understate the actual sales price, and such information is usually discounted by local assessors.

In cases where the income capitalization approach is used, a "normal" rate of return must be determined. In a memo dated July 25, 1977, to all provincial, city, and municipal assessors from the Ministry of Finance, it is noted that the capitalization rate should be "a selected rate prevailing in the locality."[19] No further specification is provided.

The capitalization approach to valuation is not widely used for commercial property due to the difficulties of obtaining adequate financial records from property owners.[20] The approach is, however, utilized in the case of improvements to agricultural lands. The capitalization rate used in Iloilo Province in the latest schedule of values was 14 percent,[21] not an unreasonable rate given rates of inflation in the range of 7 to 10 percent.

The replacement cost method of assessment involves estimating the current cost of replacing a building and requires two steps. The first is to estimate the current cost of constructing the building or purchasing the equipment. To obtain these estimates, assessors usually gather cost information from lumberyards, hardware stores, building contractors, engineers, and so on. The second step estimates the depreciation to be subtracted from the result of the first step and requires information regarding the age of the structure and an assumed depreciation rate. The Ministry of Finance has suggested that assessors use a table of depreciation schedules contained in the 1963 Philippine Assessors Appraisal Manual.[22] These rates range from 2 to 8 percent and are used by many assessors.

Even with these detailed instructions, considerable subjectivity can enter into the determination of assessed valuation. A good example is the case of the classification of agricultural lands. The MOF memorandum of July 25, 1977, establishes productivity classifications for nine different categories of agricultural crops, such as rice land (lowland) with irrigation facilities, rice land (lowland) without irrigation facilities, coconut land, and so on. Within each crop category, several different productivity classes are established. For example, coconut land is classified into first class (more than 70 nuts annually per tree), second class (50 to 70 nuts per tree), and third class (less than 50 per tree).[23] The assessor's discretion can then be used to determine the class of land to which a particular parcel belongs, and one interview revealed that parcels are seldom placed in the first class group.

Equity of the property tax is also closely related to the assessment process. At least two different forms of equity can be considered–interpersonal and interjurisdictional. Within a jurisdiction, interpersonal inequality occurs when two parcels of like value are assessed differently. Although the use of value schedules applied in a similar manner to all properties within a jurisdiction should reduce such inequities, assessor discretion can still introduce inequalities. Likewise, if there are systematic biases built into the schedule of values–for example, if rice land values are understated relative to their actual values while coconut lands are valued accurately–inequities across property types will result.[24] Interjurisdictional inequalities will almost certainly arise in a property tax system that is administered at the local government level. Such tax differentials are less dramatic in the Philippines, where the effective rate of property taxation is not high and centralized assessments minimize the variations.

The final aspect of the assessment process involves reestimating the value of parcels through time. While uniform revaluation cycles every three years are in keeping with the centralized nature of the RPT administration process and produce greater interjurisdictional equality than randomly scheduled reassessments, there are several problems with lump-sum revisions in assessed valuations. The most significant relates to the large jumps in tax liabilities that occur when the new roll takes effect. It was estimated that values increased on the average by about 80 percent between the 1973 and 1977 revaluations[25] and many properties experienced from 80 to 120 percent increases in valuation in 1980.[26]

The revaluation process as currently conducted also creates a problem with the workloads associated with it. The provincial assessor of Albay indicated that of his 29 permanent staff employees, 20 were assigned to the general revision process with an additional 15 casual employees also working on reassessments (out of a total of from 70 to 120 casual employees hired). The number of parcels in Albay in 1979 totaled approximately 180,000. The scheduling of reassessments at particular dates obviously creates fluctuations in workloads that would not arise if the process were spread more

TABLE 2.1

Growth in Taxable and Exempt Assessed Values, Selected Jurisdictions, 1970–79

Year	Iloilo Province Percentage Change		Guimaras Subprovince Percentage Change*		Albay Province Percentage Change		Legaspi City Percentage Change	
	Taxable Assessed Values	Exempt Assessed Values	Taxable Assessed Values	Exempt Assessed Values	Taxable Assessed Values	Exempt Assessed Values	Taxable Assessed Values	Exempt Assessed Values
1970–71	0.2	-0.4	NA	NA	0.1	-2.9	7.2	0.1
1971–72	3.9	0.8	NA	NA	4.9	0.2	11.4	5.8
1972–73	203.7	98.9	NA	NA	55.9	0.9	109.6	38.8
1973–74	11.3	60.9	NA	NA	36.3	4.1	1.8	35.4
1974–75	17.9	1.4	-0.3	6.4	19.4	39.4	4.7	51.2
1975–76	0.1	9.0	3.3	.8	11.8	67.4	3.7	3.5
1976–77	5.8	4.8	11.7	0.1	3.0	0.7	2.9	-0.1
1977–78	2.2	-1.9	0.6	1.2	18.5	43.6	22.3	43.4
1978–79	80.3	96.6	189.5	80.1	6.2	1.7	47.8	6.2

NA: Not available.

*The subprovince of Guimaras became independent of Iloilo Province in November 1979, but prior to that many administrative offices had operated independently of Iloilo Province.

Source: Data supplied by provincial and city assessors.

evenly over time. On the other hand, the scheduling better ensures that all properties will be revalued periodically.

GROWTH IN THE PROPERTY TAX BASE

With revenue yields a primary concern and with property tax rates essentially fixed (or at least limited in range), the principal source of revenue growth is in the tax base, which comes about through property reassessment. Since World War II, general reassessments have taken place in 1949, 1960 (partial), 1974, and 1979. Interim growth in the base can be due to the construction and assessment of new buildings, equipment, and improvements or to discovery of previously untaxed properties as might result from tax mapping.

Examination of the growth in the property tax base for different jurisdictions provides insight into the potential revenue effects of general reassessments. Table 2.1 shows the year-to-year percentage changes in assessed valuations for both taxable and exempt property for the period 1970–79 in the provinces of Iloilo, Albay, and Guimaras (until 1979 a subprovince of Iloilo). The data show a massive increase in assessed valuations between 1972 and 1973 in the wake of PD 76. The less dramatic increases in Albay were apparently due to the longer time period associated with getting the new assessed valuations recorded. The 1979 general reassessment was completed on time in Iloilo and Guimaras, but not in Albay. The increases for the two completed areas suggest that if tax rates were to be held constant and if collection efficiency did not fall, municipalities could anticipate considerable increases in revenues during the 1980 fiscal year. It is doubtful that collection efficiency could remain constant in light of an approximate doubling in tax liabilities.

During the interim periods, there was relatively little growth in the property tax base. For example, in Iloilo, increases in the taxable base were less than 6 percent in each year between 1975 and 1978. This growth is slow in comparison to inflation rates of between 7 and 9.9 percent during the same period. If property tax revenues did not keep up with inflation, but municipal expenditures did, then the pressure on municipal budgets during the late 1970s was in large measure attributable to the low elasticity of the property tax base.

As noted above, the granting of exemptions imposes a substantial opportunity cost on local governments in terms of revenues lost. In 1979 the ratio of exempt assessed values to the total (exempt and taxable) was 7.4 percent in Iloilo and 13.8 percent in Albay. Using the 1 percent tax rate applicable in both of the provinces, these exemptions are equivalent to a ₱1.2 million revenue loss in Iloilo and a ₱0.5 million loss in Albay. To place these costs in some perspective, the provincial government of Iloilo collected only ₱2.4 million in real property taxes in 1979; thus, if all of the exempt property had been taxable and the collection rate had been 100 percent, the province could have increased its property tax collections by nearly 25 percent.[27] An even greater effect would have been observed in Albay, which, in 1979, collected approximately ₱0.697 million at the provincial government level. Using a similar assumption as above, revenues of the province would have increased by 32 percent. The data in Table 2.1 show a generally slower growth in exempt than taxable values, suggesting that the opportunity cost of exemptions has been declining.

PROPERTY TAX RATES AND ADDITIONAL LEVIES

Real property tax rates are limited by statute. Provinces and municipalities can set a basic tax rate of from 0.25 to 0.5 percent while cities are constrained to the range of 0.5 to 2 percent.[28] The statute suggests that provinces and their constituent municipalities can levy differential rates but in fact this is not the case. Item (3) of Section 39 in PD 464 requires that municipal tax rates be approved by the Provincial Board. Moreover, property taxes collected on any parcel are divided among the province, municipality, and barangay (in which the parcel is located) on a 45–45–10 percent basis.

The Special Education Fund rate is a uniform 1 percent, but PD 464 provides that all tax revenues in excess of those collected in 1972 can be placed in the General Fund. This provision aids the revenue elasticity of the property tax for General Fund purposes but, in turn, restricts growth in the SEF. The size of SEF revenues was also limited by PD 1621, which exempted all properties with values less than ₱5,000. PD 464 states that "when the entire total assessed valuation of real property situated in a province or city assessable to any *one person* does not exceed three thousand pesos (altered to five thousand under PD 1621), the additional 1 percent tax herein imposed shall not be collected."[29] The statute thus provides greater revenue capacity to chartered cities.

As of 1975, all provinces[30] and their constituent municipalities were levying the statutorily maximum rates, whereas there was considerable variation in city rates, ranging from 0.7 percent (Tangub) to the legal maximum of 2 percent. There were also three instances of differential rates based either on property usage (Metro Manila), type of property (Palayan), or value (Bais). However, these are not easily explained given the statement in Section 39 of PD 464 that the rate of levy is "a uniform rate of real property tax."

Special Levies

The basic tax and the SEF tax are not the only property-based taxes allowed under PD 464. Sections 42–46 provide the statutory basis for an idle lands tax, and Sections 47–54 provide for special levies to be imposed by local governments. Section 55 allows the central government to impose special assessments on properties affected positively by central government public works projects.

The idle lands tax is an additional levy on land not currently being utilized for productive purposes. PD 464 authorizes a rate of up to 5 percent for this purpose.[31] In the case of agricultural lands, any plot exceeding 5 hectares, where the uncultivated or ungrazed portion of the land constitutes more than three-quarters of the total, is defined as "idle." For urban properties, if more than two-thirds of the parcel is unutilized or unimproved, it can be certified as being idle. There are also provisions for exemptions from this land-use status, for example, if a natural disaster prevents cultivation, if there is lack of peace and order in the area, or if the land, while classified as agricultural, is actually not cultivatable (Section 44).

An idle lands tax has beneficial efficiency effects because it is a penalty against land speculation and encourages a more economic use of land. The taxation of idle lands and the taxation of the gains from land speculations are widely practiced in LDCs.[32] The idle lands tax, however, has never been used in the Philippines, perhaps because of political sensitivity to its use. Land speculators are often very powerful in the community and their influence a substantial deterrent to actions by local treasurers and assessors.

Special levies are a form of benefit taxation where a portion of the costs of particular projects such as street paving or sidewalk construction are recovered from residents in the immediate area. Under PD 464, up to 60 percent of the cost of such projects may be reimbursed through a special levy. The tax is to be applied over a five- to ten-year period, and differential rates can be applied to the different parcels lying within the area affected by the project. While special levies are commonly used in other developing countries, they have not been utilized extensively in the Philippines.[33] Assessors assert that the lack of usage does not stem from the inability of assessors to appraise the differential benefits of spatially defined projects but rather from political pressures and the absence of implementing legislation.

COLLECTION OF THE REAL PROPERTY TAX

The property tax is levied against the owner as of January 1 of each year. Billing must occur by January 31 and payment can be made in four equal installments—on or before March 31, June 30, September 30, and December 31. The taxpayer may choose the installment option without interest or penalty. Furthermore, under LOI 682 (March 20, 1978), a 10 percent discount on taxes due is granted to anyone paying his taxes in full within the prescribed period of time.

The law also provides for penalties against those who are tax delinquent. Yet it is estimated that in 1979, all provinces and cities in the country collected only 57 percent of property tax liabilities. Furthermore, there were provinces with collection rates as low as 5 percent.[34] One could argue that the most pressing problems associated with the property tax in the Philippines have to do with its collectibility rather than with structural weaknesses.

Legal Incentives for Compliance

The major penalty form is that of interest charged on delinquent taxpayers. While the rate is set at 2 percent per month, there is an upper limit of 24 percent charged on the delinquent amount. If a taxpayer is delinquent for more than one year, there is, effectively, no additional cost for subsequent nonpayment. Relatively safe investments in the Philippines yield returns of 12 to 14 percent, so that by comparison the effective penalty is quite low.

In addition to the interest penalty, local governments can use three legal remedies to obtain past due taxes: distraint of personal property, public auction of the delinquent's property, and civil action. Distraint of personal property involves the seizing of personal properties, such as crops, equipment, and personal possessions. PD 464 (Section 69) provides, however, that certain items may not be seized, such as one horse, cow, or carabao (water buffalo) that the delinquent selects, necessary clothing, and necessary household furniture. After proper notice, the confiscated property can be sold at a public auction administered by the provincial or city treasurer, with proceeds of the sale over the delinquent taxes (plus penalties and costs of the sale and seizure) reverting to the delinquent taxpayer.

The public auction remedy involves seizure of the real property on which taxes are due. Once again there must be advance notice of the sale. The proceeds of the sale in excess of what is owed the jurisdiction (including costs) revert to the delinquent taxpayer. Once the property is sold, however, the delinquent taxpayer retains possession for one year and has the right to redeem the property during that time by paying delinquent taxes, penalties, and costs of the sale, plus 20 percent interest on the purchase price. The purchaser of the property is then reimbursed for the purchase price plus the 20 percent interest fee. This final feature makes the purchase of tax-auction property considerably more attractive and helps ensure an adequate number of bidders.

Civil action refers to the fact that the delinquent tax constitutes an indebtedness of the taxpayer to the jurisdiction and therefore, as with any such debt, civil legal proceedings can be initiated. Furthermore, when a parcel on which taxes are delinquent is the subject of court proceedings, the award of ownership will be contingent upon payment of delinquent taxes.

Reasons for Delinquency

Given these strong legal remedies to combat delinquency, the question arises as to why collection efficiency is so low. There are several possible answers to this question.

The most obvious reason is that the legal remedies are seldom used in the Philippines. While a list of the largest tax delinquents is to be prepared annually by the treasurer and submitted to the provincial fiscal officer, the provincial officer often does not carry out any further proceedings against the delinquent taxpayer. This inaction may be due to oversight, an overworked staff, or political pressures against such proceedings. The use of personal property distraint has also been avoided, possibly because of the political ramifications or because the personal property to be seized was removed before the action was taken. Finally, in any rural or sparsely populated area, nearly all residents are known to each other, which makes the successful use of the auction remedy less likely than in a highly populated, more impersonal area.

A second reason for low collection rates has to do with the problems associated with the determination of the legal owner of properties. If duplicate tax declarations exist, with the recorded owner not actually in possession of the property, there will be little chance of collecting the taxes. Likewise, the problems associated with land reform and lack of tax declarations filed by new owners mean that these taxes may go uncollected.

A third reason for delinquency could stem from the management and record-keeping methods used in some localities. Under a properly managed system there would be systematic scanning of the property tax payment records. If the filing system is not adequate or if the workloads due to other day-to-day efforts are too great to check for overdue payment of taxes and to notify the delinquent taxpayer, there is greater likelihood that delinquent taxes will not be paid. In interviews with local officials we found considerable variance in the frequency of checking through the files for delinquents, with stated frequencies ranging from daily to quarterly. Only a few localities actually sent out collectors, usually the person in charge of the property tax or a clerk in the treasurer's office, to meet with the largest delinquents.

TABLE 2.2

Largest Tax Delinquencies in Selected Iloilo Municipalities, 1980

	Total Delinquencies[a]			As Percent of 1979 Current Year RPT Revenues	
Municipalities	Largest Five	Largest Ten	Range Among Largest Ten	Largest Five	Largest Ten
Dingle	44,642	63,765	3,713- 20,759	108.9	155.5
Dumangas	183,083	213,446	3,522-104,551	183.5	214.0
Guimbal	7,542	8,991[b]	247- 2,166	55.1	65.6
Passi	129,792	169,029	4,793- 36,092	115.2	150.0
Pavia	12,050	16,099	342- 4,895	11.8	15.7
Tigbauan	2,463	3,039	108- 795	11.6	14.3

[a]As of May 1980.

[b]Information on only the nine largest delinquents was available from Guimbal.

Source: Data obtained from municipal treasurers.

TABLE 2.3

Factors Affecting Property Tax Collection Efficiency

City/Municipality Province	1979 Collection Efficiency	Characteristics/ Industries of Major Delinquents	Reasons Cited for "Problems"	Reasons Cited for "Success"
Legaspi City	73.4	Agriculture		Tie tax to business license
Libon, Albay	19.0	Rice/grain	Land reform	
Malinao, Albay	29.2	Agriculture	Typhoons and low agricultural prices	Barangay-level campaigns
Oas, Albay	28.8	Rice	Land reform	
Tabaco, Albay	50.1	Agriculture	Low agricultural prices	Send collectors into field
Iloilo City	47.7	Panay Electric (125.3%),* manufacturing, the Church	Estates	
Dingle, Iloilo	52.3	Land reformed estates	Land reform	
Dumangas, Iloilo	57.2	The Church absentee landowners (15.8%)*	Absentee owners, refuse to pay; land reform	Several court cases
Guimbal, Iloilo	63.6	Agriculture	Land reform, poor records	
Passi, Iloilo	42.1	Sugar growers	Land reform, low sugar prices	
Pavia, Iloilo	99.6	Few delinquents		Barangay-level campaign, court case
Tigbauan, Iloilo	97.1	Agriculture		Information program in barangays

*Delinquent taxes of largest delinquent as percent of 1979 current year RPT revenues.
Source: Survey interview data.

A fourth reason relates to the problems of farmlands. Agricultural land is especially prone to periods of low productivity due to unpredictable events such as floods or drought, or low prices can contribute to low incomes from such lands and therefore to an inability of the landowner to pay the due taxes. Because assessments are not altered annually in response to such events, these types of parcels are likely to be delinquent in times of stress.

To understand better the underlying nature of the tax delinquency problem, we have compiled information on the extent (Table 2.2), as well as the causes and means used to stimulate payment (Table 2.3). The example of six Iloilo municipalities (Table 2.2) gives some idea of the concentration of delinquent property taxes among larger taxpayers. The data show that for three jurisdictions, the amount outstanding from the largest delinquents in early 1980 actually exceeded total collections in the previous year. In the case of Dumangas it was more than twice the amount collected. The pattern of concentration of delinquent taxes raises an important policy issue. When one or two delinquents account for the vast proportion of delinquency, legal remedies are likely to be the most effective approach to alleviate the problem. On the other hand, where even the largest of delinquents is quite small, as is true in Guimbal and Tigbauan, extralegal remedies such as campaigns and moral suasion may be more effective.

Table 2.3 provides a different perspective on the problem of property tax delinquencies as observed in several municipalities in Albay and Iloilo provinces and Legaspi City and Iloilo City. Of the two cities represented, Legaspi had a considerably higher collection efficiency in 1979 than did Iloilo. Legaspi carries out a policy that should be especially effective in cities—tying property tax payments to the issuance of mayor's permits. It is interesting to note that Legaspi City's major delinquency problems are related to agricultural properties, which are not subject to business taxes. In Iloilo City the principal delinquent as of 1979 owed considerably more in back taxes than the entire yield of the current portion of the property tax that year.

Of the municipalities represented here, nearly all are agricultural areas, with the result that delinquencies are not nearly as concentrated as in the cities. From the success achieved in Pavia and Tigbauan it seems that campaigns to encourage property owners to pay taxes can be successful, especially when the focus of the campaign is at the barangay level. For the predominantly rural municipalities in these two provinces, however, the two principal cited causes of property tax delinquency are land reform and the uncertainty of agricultural yields and prices.

Another problem associated with tax collection is absentee landlords (cited in Dumangas), where most of the landlords live in a nearby city, refuse to pay taxes, and are difficult to reach. In these cases legal means may be the most appropriate technique to alleviate the problem. The Catholic Church was also noted in both Iloilo City and Dumangas as being one of the largest delinquents. Finding a solution to the Church property problem is not easy because legal means are likely to create political difficulties and campaigns may be ineffective.

Noncourt Methods for Improving Collections

Tax campaigns are an important noncourt method and one especially effective at the local level. The barangay is a natural vehicle for organizing tax campaigns. Because the barangay receives a share of the collection of property taxes, it should be possible to convince taxpayers of the localized benefits to be derived from payment of taxes. Closely related to formal campaigns in the barangays are campaigns eliciting the aid of barangay captains in encouraging their barangay residents to pay property taxes. In Jordan, Guimaras, a ₱2,000 prize is awarded to the barangay with the highest collection rate.

In the same vein, we found that some municipalities (Malinao and Tabaco, Albay) attempted to decrease compliance costs by sending tax collectors to the barangay, thus making it unnecessary for taxpayers to travel to the municipal treasury to pay their taxes.[35] This tactic also may aid in creating a psychological incentive to pay if a taxpayer is among neighbors who are complying with the law.

An innovative program initiated in Pavia, Iloilo, is relatively low in cost and, based upon collection records, productive. Under this program the local treasurer's office sponsors movies in the barangays. During each intermission, of which there are several, the municipal treasurer and barangay captain give short talks on the advantages of paying property taxes. At times public praise or embarrassment is sufficient to prompt tax compliance. For example, in Jordan, a list of the top taxpayers is posted for display in the municipal treasury. We did not encounter any municipality that does the same for the major delinquents; however, this would seem to be a potentially fruitful approach.

REVENUE PERFORMANCE OF THE PROPERTY TAX

The relative burdens of property taxes among different countries can be compared in two ways—on a statutory basis and with respect to actual practices. On a statutory basis the property tax in the Philippines cannot be viewed as imposing an excessively high burden when compared with other developing countries.

Yoingco and Quintos have made a comparison of property taxes in the ASEAN countries.[36] The information provided there suggests that the range of statutory property tax rates (basic tax plus SEF) of from 2 to 3 percent in the Philippines is not out of line. However, the fractional assessment scheme used in the Philippines, together with the several exemptions including the low value exemption, significantly reduces the overall burden of the tax. In a comparison of property taxes in major cities throughout the world the data indicate that statutory rates in Manila are neither excessively high nor very low.[37]

Because the actual burden of property taxes is so closely tied to its administration, an examination of statutory rates often gives misleading impressions about intensity of use. IMF data on property taxes as a percent of gross national product and as a percent of total taxes enable us to compare the Philippines with other developing countries for several years (Table 2.4).[38] These data suggest that since the mid-1950s the role of property taxes within the Philippines has been diminishing both in terms of relative importance in the tax structure and relative to total economic activity. Between the 1953–55 period and the 1972–76 period, property taxes declined from nearly 12 percent to only 3 percent of total tax revenues. Property taxes were also cut relative to GNP during the 1966–68 to 1972–76 period, from 0.8 percent to only 0.3 percent. The Philippines is not alone, however, in these general trends. Table 2.4 indicates that property taxes in other developing countries have declined relative to total taxes and as a percent of GNP.

When compared with other Asian countries, the relative (to GNP) property tax burden in the Philippines for the 1972–76 period was considerably below the regional average. In terms of rank ordering the Philippines is exceeded by only four countries—China, Nepal, Korea, and Sri Lanka.

TABLE 2.4

A Comparison of Property Taxation in the Philippines and Other Developing Countries

	As a Percent of Total Taxes				Ratios to GNP		
	1953-55[a]	1966-68[a]	1969-71[b]	1972-76[c]	1966-68[a]	1969-71[b]	1972-76[c]
Philippines	11.8	8.2	4.4	2.9	0.8	0.4	0.3
Afghanistan	—	—	—	1.7	—	—	0.1
Bangladesh	—	—	—	. . .	—	—	. . .
Burma	—	—	—	. . .	—	—	. . .
China	13.0	11.3	14.5	12.2	1.7	2.6	2.4
India	16.0	9.3	7.8	0.1	1.1	1.0	0.02
Indonesia	0.87	2.1	. . .	0.8	0.2	. . .	0.13
Iraq	—	—	—	0.8	—	—	0.3
Jordan	—	—	—	0.2	—	—	0.03
Korea	5.5	8.3	3.8	4.1	1.0	0.6	0.6
Malaysia	—	12.9	0.5	0.6	2.2	0.1	0.14
Nepal	55.1	26.3	23.8	16.4	0.8	1.1	0.9
Pakistan	7.8	5.7	3.8	2.7	0.5	0.3	0.3
Singapore	—	28.2	27.1	—	3.5	3.6	—
Sri Lanka	3.0	2.9	4.3	2.0	0.5	0.8	0.4
Syrian Arab Republic	—	—	—	1.8	—	—	0.2

(Continued)

TABLE 2.4 (Continued)

	As a Percent of Total Taxes				Ratios to GNP		
	1953–55[a]	1966–68[a]	1969–71[b]	1972–76[c]	1966–68[a]	1969–71[b]	1972–76[c]
Thailand	.09	2.1	3.0	2.1	0.3	0.4	0.3
Turkey	—	—	—	0.5	0.8	—	—
Vietnam	—	5.6	—	—	7.6	—	—
Yemen Arab Republic	—	—	—	. . .	—	—	. . .
Average for:							
Asia	12.6[e]	10.2[e]	8.4[g]	2.7[j]	0.81[e]	1.0[g]	0.3[j]
Other Asian LDCs[d]	12.7	10.4	8.9	2.7	0.80	1.1	0.3
Non-Asian LDCs	6.4	4.8	3.9	1.6	0.75	0.6	0.2
All LDCs	8.3[f]	6.1[f]	5.0[h]	1.9[i]	0.77[f]	0.7[h]	0.2[i]

Key: . . . zero or insignificant amount; — information not available.

[a]Compiled from Chelliah (July 1971).

[b]Compiled from Chelliah et al. (March 1975).

[c]Compiled from Tait et al. (March 1979).

[d]Excludes Philippines.

[e]Includes China, India, Indonesia, Korea, Malaysia, Nepal, Pakistan, Philippines, Singapore, Sri Lanka, Thailand, Vietnam.

[f]Consists of 50 countries.

[g]Same as footnote e, excluding Vietnam.

[h]Consists of 47 countries.

[i]Consists of 63 developing countries.

[j]Includes all the countries as well as the Philippines.

Sources: Raja J. Chelliah, "Trends in Taxation in Developing Countries," *IMF Staff Papers* 18, no. 2 (July 1971): 254–331; Raja J. Chelliah, Baas Hessel, and Margaret Kelly, "Tax Ratios and Tax Effort in Developing Countires, 1969," *IMF Staff Papers* 22, no. 1 (March 1975): 187–205; and Alan Tait et al. "International Comparison of Taxation for Selected Developing Countries," *IMF Staff*

Growth in Tax Yield

Property tax revenues may grow for several reasons: reassessment of existing properties, the addition of new properties to the tax rolls, an increase in nominal property tax rates, and an increase in collection efficiency. But the particular combination of these factors in the Philippines resulted in little growth in per capita real property tax revenues during the early 1970s (Table 2.5). Indeed, there were substantial real declines in some years before the situation was reversed in 1977 and 1978.

In current pesos, the per capita increase was from ₱4.97 in 1970 to ₱16.61 in 1979. To analyze the factors leading to this increase, the 1974-79 period might be used since it includes one full revaluation cycle. There was a general revaluation in 1973 and another in 1979, although the new assessment rolls were not completed in every jurisdiction in either year. Table 2.6 presents data in four components of changing property tax revenues between 1974 and 1979. The number of parcels increased by only about 8 percent over the period,

TABLE 2.5

Per Capita Property Tax Revenues, 1969–79

	In Current Pesos		In Constant Pesos	
Year	Amount	Percent Increase	Amount	Percent Increase
1969	6.07		9.20	
1970	4.97	(19)	6.56	(29)
1971	4.29	(14)	4.65	(30)
1972	5.10	19	5.10	10
1973	6.54	29	5.62	11
1974	7.41	14	4.74	(16)
1975	8.23	11	4.94	5
1976	8.37	2	4.60	(7)
1977	12.94	55	6.46	41
1978	14.44	12	6.72	4
1979	16.61	15	6.63	(2)

Sources: Commission on Audit Reports on Local Governments (1969–71); Ministry of Finance (1972–79); Central Bank of the Philippines, *Statistical Bulletin,* 1978 (CPI, 1972 = 100); National Census and Statistics Office.

TABLE 2.6

Indicators of Property Tax Performance

Year	Number of Parcels	Percent Change	Assessed Value	Percent Change
1974	12,095,287		₱43,911,027,291	
1975	12,588,655	4.08	46,279,928,639	5.39
1976	12,055,681	(4.23)	49,491,049,874	6.94
1977	12,309,845	2.11	55,646,382,125	12.44
1978	13,204,942	7.27	67,302,340,738	20.95
1979	13,073,319	1.00	83,825,748,117	24.55

Year	Property Tax Revenue (million pesos)	Percent Change	Collection Rate*	Revenue/ Assessed Value	Assessed Value per Parcel
1974	307		41.15	.0070	₱3,630.42
1975	346	12.70	43.96	.0075	3,676.32
1976	368	6.36	43.76	.0074	4,105.21
1977	586	59.24	61.95	.0105	4,520.48
1978	674	15.02	58.92	.0100	5,096.75
1979	799	18.55	56.07	.0096	6,402.91

*Collectibles were estimated by using this formula: $[(Av \times .01) + .70(Av \times .01)]$. The assumptions are: (1) Collectibles from the basic property tax equal assessed value multiplied by 1 percent tax rate. (2) Collectibles from the SEF tax equal assessed value multiplied by 1 percent less 30 percent, which is remitted to the national treasurer.

Sources: For assessed values and number of land parcels: "Assessor's Report to the Ministry of Finance." For revenues: Commission on Audit and Ministry of Finance.

TABLE 2.7

Annual Growth Rates in General Fund Property Tax Revenues, Iloilo and Albay Provinces, 1970–1979 (in percent)

	Province	
Fiscal Year	Albay	Iloilo
1970–71	NA	14.5
1971–72	NA	2.1
1972–73	NA	97.9
1973–74	-17.2	12.5
1974–75	-54.8	5.0
1975–76	75.4	30.0
1976–77*	59.6	16.1
1977–78	6.1	0.2
1978–79	13.0	7.2

Note: Includes current year plus previous years plus penalties, but excludes excess SEF collections.

NA: Not available.

*These growth rates are based on FY 1976 (ending June 30, 1976) compared with FY 1977 (ending December 31, 1977). The six-month transition period, July 1–December 31, 1976, has been excluded for comparison purposes.

Source: Computed from data supplied by provincial treasurers.

while assessed value per parcel increased by about 76 percent. The nominal tax rate remained constant over the 1974–79 period, but collection efficiency increased from 41 to 56 percent between 1974 and 1979. Thus, the principal causes of property tax revenue growth over the period would appear to be reassessment of existing properties and improvements in collection efficiency. The pattern, however, has varied from year to year.

Detailed analysis of property tax revenue growth cannot be provided for every jurisdiction, so we performed a case study of two provinces, Iloilo and Albay (Table 2.7). The 10-year history of collections in Iloilo shows considerable variation in the year-to-year increases in property tax revenues—from a low of only 0.2 percent between 1977 and 1978 to the nearly 98 percent increase between 1972 and 1973 in the aftermath of PD 76. The overall growth in property tax revenues during this period, 173 percent, greatly exceeded the population increase of only 12.4 percent. In contrast, Albay experienced declines in property tax revenues

TABLE 2.8

Property Tax Collections in Selected Albay Municipalities, 1977–79 (in pesos)

	Camalig			Libon			Malinao			Tabaco		
General Fund	1977	1978	1979	1977	1978	1979	1977	1978	1979	1977	1978	1979
Current year collection	26,301	37,188	50,140	28,190	27,302	29,509	11,639	21,298	17,488	42,168	45,117	52,172
Previous year collection	9,838	9,275	15,871	19,445	21,414	27,968	4,513	5,099	8,889	11,971	611	4,400
Penalties	1,421	1,948	4,155	3,398	4,746	6,166	898	1,427	1,914	2,304	3,514	2,390
Total from RPT	37,560	48,411	70,166	51,033	53,482	63,643	17,050	27,824	28,291	56,443	49,242	58,962
RPT as percent of total General Fund income	7.9	8.7	11.5	13.8	14.3	15.0	8.7	12.0	11.2	4.1	3.3	3.6
Assessed valuation (in 1,000 pesos)*	12,089	12,280	15,928	33,708	33,968	32,773	12,661	12,766	12,458	23,611	25,102	25,158
Collection efficiency (in percent)	45.8	66.0	70.4	17.8	16.9	19.0	19.3	30.1	29.2	37.4	38.4	50.1

Growth Rates (in percent)

	Camalig		Libon		Malinao		Tabaco	
	1977–78	1978–79	1977–78	1978–79	1977–78	1978–79	1977–78	1978–79
Total from RPT	28.9	44.9	4.8	19.0	63.2	1.7	-12.7	19.7
Total General Fund income	18.3	9.6	1.6	13.1	18.1	8.5	8.3	11.7
Assessed valuation	1.6	29.6	0.1	-3.3	0.1	-2.4	6.3	0.2
Collection efficiency	44.1	6.7	-5.1	12.4	56.0	-3.0	2.7	30.5

*Based on taxable assessed valuation as of December 31 of the previous year.

TABLE 2.9

Property Tax Collections in Selected Iloilo Municipalities, 1977–79 (in pesos)

	Dingle			Dumangas			Guimbal		
General Fund	1977	1978	1979	1977	1978	1979	1977	1978	1979
Current year collection	50,287	45,690	41,002	85,510	101,519	99,755	14,503	13,167	13,697
Previous year collection	14,985	15,890	26,614	39,895	59,945	48,354	4,086	2,287	4,340
Penalties	3,844	3,759	5,802	5,998	11,069	11,432	925	575	1,101
Total from RPT	69,116	65,339	73,418	131,403	172,533	159,541	19,514	16,029	19,138
RPT as percent of total General Fund income	14.9	14.4	13.4	23.2	27.3	22.9	8.3	6.8	7.4
Assessed valuation (in 1,000 pesos)*	16,598	17,262	17,430	27,550	38,544	38,753	4,717	4,726	4,796
Collection efficiency (in percent)	NA	NA	52.3	NA	NA	57.2	NA	NA	63.6

Growth Rates (in percent)

	Dingle		Dumangas		Guimbal	
	1977–78	1978–79	1977–78	1978–79	1977–78	1978–79
Total from RPT	-5.4	12.4	31.3	-7.5	-17.8	19.4
Total General Fund income	-2.4	20.6	11.8	10.3	-0.3	10.1
Assessed valuation	4.0	1.0	39.9	0.5	0.2	1.5

(Continued)

TABLE 2.9 (Continued)

General Fund	Passi 1977	Passi 1978	Passi 1979	Pavia 1977	Pavia 1978	Pavia 1979	Tigbauan 1977	Tigbauan 1978	Tigbauan 1979
Current year collection	121,049	119,229	112,668	56,996	59,829	102,339	23,971	21,492	21,261
Previous year collection	18,477	21,561	31,393	13,296	14,354	21,364	9,189	3,705	9,064
Penalties	2,959	4,017	7,344	3,529	1,608	7,887	1,658	1,007	1,911
Total from RPT	142,485	144,807	151,405	73,821	75,791	131,590	34,818	26,204	32,236
RPT as percent of total General Fund income	12.7	12.0	14.6	14.7	13.5	18.7	10.4	6.4	7.3
Assessed valuation (in 1,000 pesos)*	64,773	65,019	65,318	10,608	10,665	20,042	3,915	3,915	4,009
Collection efficiency (in percent)	NA	NA	49.1	NA	NA	99.6	NA	NA	97.1

Growth Rates (in percent)

	Passi 1977-78	Passi 1978-79	Pavia 1977-78	Pavia 1978-79	Tigbauan 1977-78	Tigbauan 1978-79
Total from RPT	1.6	4.6	2.7	73.6	-24.7	23.0
Total General Fund income	7.3	-14.0	11.4	25.7	20.9	8.8
Assessed valuation	0.4	0.5	0.5	87.9	0.0	2.4

NA: Not available.

*Based on taxable assessed valuation as of December 31 of the previous year.

Source: Compiled from data supplied by provincial treasurers.

between 1973 and 1975. However, since 1975, taxes in Albay have grown more rapidly than in Iloilo.

It is difficult to explain this erratic tax revenue growth behavior when these data are compared with the tax base data (Table 2.1). Some of the differences may be due to the stock nature of the tax base information (measured as of January 1 of each year) and the revenue flow data (since in earlier years the fiscal years did not begin on January 1). More importantly, much of the annual variability can be traced to year-to-year fluctations in collection efficiency. Because collections are made at the municipal level, case studies of individual jurisdictions shed some light on the factors affecting property tax growth and on variations in the pattern among jurisdictions.

For the four selected Albay municipalities (Table 2.8) several generalizations concerning property tax performance are possible. For Camalig, Libon, and Malinao the property tax as a proportion of total General Fund income increased between 1977 and 1979. Moreover, each jurisdiction experienced increases in property tax collection rates. Tabaco, which relies heavily on business taxes as a revenue source (24.2 percent of total 1979 revenues), experienced very little growth in property tax revenues from 1977 to 1979, and this revenue source thus declined in relative importance. Assessed values increased substantially only in Camalig between 1978 and 1979, in the wake of completion of tax mapping in that muncipality. In the other jurisdictions assessed values tended to remain quite constant during this period.

In Iloilo, property taxes play a generally more important role in the overall revenue structure of the municipalities than in Albay, reflecting some combination of differences in their economies and in the way they administer the tax (Table 2.9). There was considerable stability in the base of the property tax, with the exception of large increases in assessed values in Pavia between 1978 and 1979 and in Dumangas between 1977 and 1978. Interestingly, the Pavia collection rate did not suffer in the face of the substantial growth in assessed values, suggesting that much of the increase may have been due to a small number of new properties added to the roll. Indeed, when the largest taxpayers in Pavia are reviewed, one finds that San Miguel Brewery paid ₱128,100 in municipal property taxes in 1979, the first year of operation for the brewery there.[39]

The different performance of the property tax in the two chartered cities compared in Table 2.10 presents an interesting contrast. Iloilo City seems to be deemphasizing the property tax as it moves toward increased reliance on business taxation. Its collection

TABLE 2.10

Property Tax Collections, Iloilo City and Legaspi City, 1977–78 (in pesos)

	Iloilo City			Legaspi City		
General Fund	1977	1978	1979	1977	1978	1979
Current year collection	3,066,983	3,157,772	2,935,949	561,962	752,457	724,216
Previous year collection	792,358	750,949	794,744	152,883	185,110	191,297
Penalties	145,895	152,976	157,717	30,383	36,772	40,380
Total from RPT	4,005,238	4,061,697	3,887,810	745,228	974,339	955,893
RPT as percent of total General Fund income	24.2	21.4	18.7	15.2	17.5	16.5
Assessed valuation* (in 1,000 pesos)	390,432	404,042	410,903	81,232	83,566	102,205
Collection efficiency (in percent)	NA	NA	47.7	NA	NA	73.4

	Growth Rates (in percent)			
	1977–78	1978–79	1977–78	1978–79
Total from RPT	1.4	-4.3	30.7	-1.9
Total General Fund income	14.4	9.6	13.8	4.0
Assessed valuation	3.5	1.7	2.9	22.3

NA: Not available.

*Based on taxable assessed valuation as of December 31 of the previous year.

Source: Compiled from data supplied by provincial treasurers.

TABLE 2.11

Elasticity of Property Tax Revenues and Property Tax Base

Year	Base Elasticity	Rate Elasticity	Total Revenue Elasticity
1975	.38	2.36	.90
1976	.46	.92	.42
1977	.66	4.76	3.14
1978	1.48	.72	1.07
1979	1.01	.76	.77

Note: The rate elasticity is the ratio of the annual percentage change in property tax revenues to the annual percentage change in the assessed value of property. The base elasticity is the ratio of the annual percentage change in the assessed value of property to the annual percentage change in personal income. Total revenue elasticity is the product of the rate and base elasticities.

Sources: Assessed value of property: Reports of Assessors to the Ministry of Finance; personal income: National Economic and Development Authority, NAS Estimates, 1971–79; revenue from the property tax: Ministry of Finance.

rate is relatively low and there have been only minimal increases in assessed valuation. In contrast, Legaspi City has maintained a lower, but approximately constant, property tax share with a much higher collection rate and a general valuation increase in 1978–79.

Another way to consider the revenue yield of a tax is to examine its income elasticity, that is, the percentage response in revenues relative to a percentage increase in personal income in the community. Income elasticities are especially relevant to a discussion of a revenue source since, as incomes increase within a locality, there are likely to be increased demands for public services. It is therefore desirable that yields from a tax source at least keep pace with these service demands—that the income elasticity of the tax be at least equal to the expenditure elasticity of demand. Because we do not know the latter, we might assume that expenditure requirements will grow roughly in proportion to income—hence, an income elasticity of unity would be a reasonable goal for the local tax system.

Table 2.11 reports on property tax base, rate, and total elasticities.[40] The base elasticity, which measures the ratio of the percentage growth of assessed value of property to the percentage growth in personal income, averaged about 0.8 over the 1974–79 period. In other words, the assessed value of property grew only 80 percent as rapidly as personal income. The rate elasticity, which measures the ratio of the percentage growth in property tax revenues to the percentage growth in assessed value, averaged 1.9 over the 1974–79 period. That is, property tax revenues grew almost twice as rapidly as assessed value. If both nominal property tax rates and collection efficiency were constant over the 1974–79 period, the rate elasticity would have an average of unity. Since nominal tax rates were constant, the rate elasticity estimates can be attributed to increased collection efficiency over the period. The total revenue elasticity, which measures the ratio of the percentage increase in revenues to the percentage growth in personal income, averaged about 1.3 over the 1974–79 period. Alternatively stated, property tax revenues—discretionary factors included—grew 30 percent faster than personal income during this period.

Another way to estimate the income elasticity of the property tax is on a cross-sectional basis. The cross-sectional approach has the advantage of holding constant the legal definition of the tax base and the legal tax rate, as data are taken from a single point in time. Cross-sectional relationships, then, must reflect differences among local governments in collection efficiency and in the relationship between assessed value and personal income.

By regressing the natural logarithm of per capita property tax collections against the natural logarithm of per capita municipal incomes in each of the municipalities within a province, it is possible to estimate the cross-sectional income elasticity. The results of this estimation are mixed with the elasticity of current collections significantly different from zero only in Sorsogon.[41] The Bulacan findings show a considerably higher estimate of income elasticity, but there is obviously still a great deal of underlying variability in the collections of property taxes across municipalities. These findings suggest that rather than a consistent relationship with higher income municipalities collecting systematically greater levels of property taxes, other factors play crucial roles in the payment process. It is likely that administrative features are more important in determining relative yields than is simple concern for differences in abilities to pay.

CONCLUSION

The practice of property taxation in the Philippines is far from primitive. In comparison with other developing countries, the structure of the tax is sound and the quality of assessors and assessment practice is impressive. On the other hand, the revenue performance of the property tax has suffered from a poor record of enforcement. This trend can be reversed and the property tax made a more effective means of mobilizing domestic resources if the central government takes a few important and perhaps overdue steps (see Chapter 7). To be sure, there are important administrative and management improvements to be made at the local government level, but in the highly centralized Philippine system the really important reforms and implementing actions must be initiated by the central government.

NOTES

1. Department of Finance, *Manual on Real Property Tax Administration in the Philippines* (Manila, 1975), p. v.

2. A good discussion of the property tax in the Philippines compared to that in other Southeast Asian countries is provided in A. Yoingco and V. Quintos, *Philippine Tax System Under the New Society* (Manila: GIC Enterprises, 1979), pp. 253–61.

3. In studying the operation of the RPT, we have relied heavily upon PD 464, supplementing it with data and observations obtained from interviews and fieldwork.

4. Since there are no unincorporated areas within provinces, the tax rolls of the municipalities and cities include agricultural lands, even though such properties benefit relatively little from municipal services.

5. PD 464, Section 40, as amended by PD 1621, PD 1383, and PD 939. From *The Real Property Tax Code Annotated* (PACTAA), compiled by Conrado G. Sabater and Roberto B. Millena (Manila: Provincial City and Municipal Treasurers and Assessors Association of the Philippines, 1979).

6. For a description of systems in other countries, see Roy Bahl, "The Practice of Urban Property Taxation in Less Developed Countries," in *The Taxation of Urban Property in Less Developed Countries*, ed. Roy Bahl (Madison: University of Wisconsin Press, 1979).

7. See the discussion in Ursula K. Hicks, *Development from Below: Local Government and Finance in Developing Countries of the Commonwealth* (London: Oxford University Press, 1961), pp. 349–59.

8. The strength of these disincentives depends on the rate at which the tax is imposed. The rates in the Philippines, by comparative standards, are not high.

9. For machinery, the fractional system is based only upon usage, with percentages set at agricultural, 60 percent; residential, 70 percent; and commercial and industrial, 80 percent.

10. See Daniel Holland, Michael Wasylenko, and Roy Bahl, "An Evaluation of the Real Property Tax Administration Project," Local Revenue Administration Project (Syracuse, N.Y.: Maxwell School, Syracuse University, 1981), p. 34.

11. *Multi-Year Plan for the Systematic Installation of the RPTA System* (Manila: Ministry of Finance, undated).

12. Eduardo Aguinaldo, "Tax Mapping: Its Significance in Real Property Tax Administration," Master's thesis, National Defense College of the Philippines, 1980.

13. Data supplied by the Ministry of Finance.

14. PD 464, Section 6.

15. The term "duplicate records" is used to refer to instances where the same parcel is listed as belonging to more than one owner.

16. Based on conversations with the provincial assessor of Albay.

17. The Bureau of Lands and the MAR share the responsibility for this mapping. Mapping for land reform purposes involves surveying the tenanted land and determining the boundaries, parcel size, and land use.

18. This is not an unusual practice in developing countries. For a survey see Bahl, "The Practice of Urban Property Taxation in Less Developed Countries."

19. PACTAA, p. 140.

20. One exception occurs in the case of negotiated sales of properties to the government, where the assessor is called upon to determine a fair market value.

21. Data from interviews with the Iloilo provincial assessor.

22. PACTAA, p. 149.

23. Ibid., pp. 145–46.

24. We had neither the time nor resources to study this aspect of property tax administration, even though its implications are extremely important in an overall evaluation.

25. Data supplied by the Ministry of Finance.

26. The problems associated with large increases in assessed values are recognized by the Philippine authorities; LOI 800 (January 30, 1979) provided tax discounts of 5 percent for those experiencing 100 to 200 percent increases in assessed valuation; 10 percent discounts for those with increases in assessments of 200 to 300 percent; 15 percent discounts for those with 300 to 500 percent increases; and 20 percent discounts for those with greater than 500 percent increases in assessed valuation.

27. Assuming a continued provincial government share of 45 percent of collections.

28. In addition, under PD 888, timber and forestlands have a fixed rate of 0.5 percent in both municipalities and provinces (a combined 1 percent rate) and a 1 percent rate in cities.

29. Section 41, PD 464, emphasis added.

30. A complete listing for 1975 is shown in Bahl et al., *Strengthening the Fiscal Performance of Philippine Local Governments*, p. III-38. We were unable to obtain comparable data for a later year.

31. PD 464, Section 42, as amended by PD 1446.

32. For a review, see Roger Smith, "The Effects of Land Taxes on Development Timing and Rates of Change in Land Price," in *The Taxation of Urban Property in Less Developed Countries*, ed. Roy Bahl (Madison: University of Wisconsin Press, 1979), pp. 137–62.

33. William A. Doebele, Orville F. Grimes, Jr., and Johannes F. Linn, "Participation of Beneficiaries in Financing Urban Services: Valorization Charges in Bogota, Colombia," *Land Economics* 55 (February 1979): 73–92. A few instances of special assessments in the Philippines are provided in National Tax Research Center, "The Use of Special Assessment in Metropolitan Manila," *Metro Manila Public Finance Studies* (Manila: NTRC, 1977).

34. From data supplied by the Ministry of Finance. For a complete list of collection efficiency ratios for each province and city in 1979, see Bahl et al., *Strengthening the Performance of Philippine Local Governments*, Table III-7, pp. III-43a–III-43e.

35. The statutes are silent on the use of tax collectors. While this may not be an especially efficient method for collecting taxes in communities where the bulk of the delinquents are small taxpayers, it is a reasonable policy where a few large taxpayers dominate the delinquent list.

36. Yoingco and Quintos, *Philippine Tax System Under the New Society.*

37. Bahl, "The Practice of Urban Property Taxation in Less Developed Countries."

38. Raja J. Chelliah, "Trends in Taxation in Developing Countries," *IMF Staff Papers* 18, no. 2 (July 1971): 254-331; Raja J. Chelliah, Hessel Baas, and Margaret Kelly, "Tax Ratios and Tax Effort in Developing Countries, 1969–71," *IMF Staff Papers* 22, no. 1 (March 1975): 187–205; and Alan Tait et al., "International Comparison of Taxation for Selected Developing Countries," *IMF Staff Papers* 26, no. 1 (March 1979): 123–56. Unfortunately, there are problems using these data to make comparisons across time and countries since the data did not always include local property tax collections.

39. The ₱128,000 includes the basic tax as well as the SEF and therefore exceeds the amount shown in Table 2.9.

40. The usual procedure in public finance is to estimate the revenue income elasticity from a "cleaned" tax series. That is, one would eliminate all discretionary rate and base changes from the revenue series and then estimate the automatic responsiveness to income growth. In this exercise, we have not cleaned the revenue series; hence, we are estimating a combination of the automatic and discretionary response of tax revenues to income increases.

41. The point elasticity estimates together with their absolute t-statistics were

	Income Elasticity	t-Statistics	$\bar{R}^2$
Albay	0.33	1.43	.16
Bulacan	0.83	1.26	.07
Iloilo	-0.17	0.49	.01
Sorsogon	0.32	2.13	.27

Even smaller elasticities and explanatory power are obtained when overdue tax payments are included in the analysis—a reasonable finding given that such payments are probably driven more by random factors.

3

The Business License Tax
by ROY BAHL and LARRY SCHROEDER

The business license tax (BLT) is a major source of city and municipal government revenue in the Philippines. In many jurisdictions it accounts for more General Fund revenues than does the real property tax (see Table 1.6). Despite this importance, and despite the many problems with the tax, little attention has been given to the possibilities for reforming the BLT.[1] In this chapter we consider the problems and reform options in the areas of base determination, rate level and structure, and collection efficiency.

The BLT is an amalgam of three types of business tax or licenses that may be levied by local governments with its statutory basis given in PD 231 (amended). The major form of business tax is a gross receipts tax, with the tax rate varying according to type of business and total sales. The second form is an annual fixed amount levied without regard to the volume of sales, resembling a license paid for the privilege of doing business in the local area. The third is an amusement tax imposed as a flat percentage rate on admissions and so forth but levied only by provinces and cities. Although the overall structure of the BLT is complicated, most revenue is derived from the gross receipts tax.

DETERMINATION AND ASSESSMENT OF THE TAX BASE

Two issues are associated with the determination of the business license tax base: specifying the category into which a particular business falls and determining the amount of taxable gross receipts. The classification of business for tax purposes causes no great difficulty, especially in small localities, where the nature of specific businesses is familiar to nearly everyone.[2] It is considerably more difficult to obtain an accurate estimate of annual gross receipts, and herein lies the major problem with the BLT.

The treasure's office maintains a file of all businesses in the locality and as new businesses are formed, new cards are added to this file. Each card contains the name of the business, its address, the nature of business performed (which serves as the basis for determining which rate schedule is applicable), and space for entering yearly the gross receipts of the business during the previous year, the tax due, and the payment record. This record keeping seems straightforward, but there are many cards and manual manipulation is cumbersome and leaves much room for error.

The measurement of gross receipts is not an easy job nor is it done with great accuracy. For large businesses with verifiable records, the BLT works. The problem comes in the case of small businesses that do not have records that can be easily examined to verify the reported amount of gross receipts. In these cases, the tax becomes almost voluntary. Most treasurers accept on faith the businessman's statement as to the amount of gross receipts and therefore tax liability, which is justified on grounds that the declaration of gross receipts involves a "sworn statement" by the businessman. Moreover, the job of verifying sworn statements would require much more staff than most local treasurers have available. In light of this procedure, it is not surprising that there is a severe underreporting problem.

Some steps have been taken to get a better estimate of gross receipts. One seemingly unsophisticated but effective method used in some jurisdictions is haggling over the amount. Treasurers may not be able to establish the amount of gross receipts, but they may be able to guess that gross receipts have increased. When local treasurers recognize cases where inflation is increasing gross business revenue by large amounts—goods that have price inelastic demands—their haggling powers are strengthened. On the other hand, proper haggling is a time-consuming process and understaffed treasurers' offices cannot engage in it on a large scale. A second method used to increase the accuracy of reporting, at least for large businesses, is to require that the businessman present accounting records to substantiate any self-reported revenue data. This method does, however, require that the treasurer's staff have some ability to analyze an income statement.[3]

Intergovernmental cooperation could help eliminate the reporting problem. The Philippines levies a national sales tax and both personal and corporate income taxes. The submittal of income tax records to the local government could be an efficient and simple method for obtaining evidence regarding past years' gross revenues. This course would require a great deal of cooperation with the central government; and if the BLT could be tied to the central tax structure, perhaps a more effective kind of local sales tax could be developed.

RATE STRUCTURE

The rate structure of the BLT is regressive, that is, firms with higher levels of gross receipts are taxed at lower rates. For example, in the case of retailers and wholesalers operating in cities, firms with gross receipts less than ₱1,000 pay at a 4.5 percent rate (maximum), whereas firms with gross receipts of ₱100,000 pay at a 2.4 percent rate, and firms with gross receipts of ₱1 million pay at a 1.37 percent rate. This general structure of declining effective rates holds across all classes of business activity.

A regressive rate structure makes the revenue elasticity of the BLT lower than it would be under a flat rate or progressive rate structure. As firms increase their gross receipts because of real income growth and inflation, they are "bumped up" into higher gross receipts brackets, where the average tax rate is lower. Under a flat rate structure, real income growth and inflation would generate a greater revenue flow. On the positive side, the current regressive rate structure does not provide the inducement to understate gross receipts that a progressive structure would provide, is less inflationary than a flat rate or progressive structure, and reduces the disincentives to investment and expansion of firm operations.

Notwithstanding these advantages, the present rate structure could be altered to advantage by creating a flat rate at least as great as that currently imposed on the smallest business within each group. This change, itself, would lead to greater revenues from the tax and, more importantly, would increase the elasticity of the revenue source. It would still be possible to retain the current differentials in rates across different types of businesses.[4]

As noted above, not all business activities are taxed on a gross receipts basis. In some cases the rates are specific, for example, per bowling alley lane, or per night in the case of boxing contests. The specific rate structure is clearly inelastic and does not contribute a rapid revenue growth during periods of inflation and income growth. Such a rate structure may also induce undesirable economic incentives.

A greatly oversimplified example may be used to make the point. The BLT on theaters permits a tax of ₱800 per year if the theater contains balcony and orchestra seats for 500 to 999 persons; a similar theater with seating capacity of 1,000 or more persons pays a ₱1,000-per-year tax. Suppose an "optimal size" theater (without regard to the tax) would be built to seat 1,010 persons. Given the tax differential due to the 11 seats, the builder may decide to build a 999-seat theater instead. In this case the differential tax based only upon seats will result in suboptimal investment. Although the BLT rates may not be large enough to have such effects, the possible inefficiencies inherent in such a structure should be recognized.

COLLECTION PROCEDURES AND PROBLEMS

Administration of the BLT is straightforward. Upon determination of the tax base, application of the statutory rate directly yields the total of the tax liability. While the statute declares all business taxes to be due by January 20, it also permits localities to allow for quarterly payments, which is the procedure generally followed. Payment is made directly at the treasurer's office; little use is made of collectors. Collection of the tax is aided greatly by the fact that shortly after the first of the year each business must obtain a mayor's permit, which is a license for doing business within the jurisdiction. Because a prerequisite to obtaining the mayor's permit is payment of the previous year's business taxes, the likelihood that a business will be delinquent on its local tax levy is greatly decreased.

Collection efficiency under the BLT is not easily measured. The usual ratio of collections to collectibles is misleading because it misses the revenue loss due to underreporting. In effect, the traditional measure of BLT collection efficiency refers to the extent to which known taxpayers with a known tax base actually make payment. By this measure, collection efficiency for the business tax appears quite good and is probably due to the fact that businessmen must show proof of past years' payment of the BLT in order to obtain a new mayor's permit.

The major collection difficulty is associated with late payment. As noted above, the tax can be paid quarterly throughout the tax year, but it is not until the subsequent application for the mayor's permit that a major impetus for payment occurs, even though delinquency letters are sent to the businesses after each quarter. Thus, some taxpayers are often late in their tax payment. In such cases late charges are applied to the amount overdue. There are also problems with businesses that do not obtain a mayor's permit and therefore evade the business tax. These, however, do not appear to be major, and some municipalities have tax collectors who enter business establishments to ensure that a mayor's permit has been obtained.

REVENUE PERFORMANCE

Less complete data are available on the business tax base than on the property tax base because gross receipts data are not available in as extensive a form as is property assessment information. We can therefore say less about the base elasticity of the BLT, but we can trace the revenue performance of the BLT over time and across the sample of cities and municipalities.

Sectoral Composition

In order to learn about the base elasticity of the BLT, we extracted data on the revenue composition by industrial sector for the cities of Iloilo and Legaspi for 1977 and 1979 (Table 3.1). These data, although imperfect, tell something about the structure of BLT revenue growth and its potential responsiveness to income and prices. By far the most substantial portion of the business tax in both cities was collected from retailers and wholesalers. Amusement admissions constituted the second most productive source in both cities, with manufacturing of a lower order of importance. The BLT is essentially a tax on traders, placing relatively little burden on producers.

In the three-year period between 1977 and 1979, one can discern patterns in the sectoral composition of revenue growth by comparing the 1977 and 1979 revenue distributions. In total, these taxes grew by over 40 percent in Iloilo City and by nearly 25 percent in Legaspi City. When it is recognized, however, that the consumer price index over this period increased by 25 percent, it becomes clear that real business tax revenues in Legaspi were approximately constant. One cannot infer from these results that the business tax is inherently responsive to inflation even though it is primarily a gross receipts tax on traders.

The faster growth rate in Iloilo City compared to that in Legaspi City could be attributed to several possible causes. First, the economy of Iloilo City could be more broad based than that in Legaspi City so that any cyclical fluctuations that are industry-specific would

TABLE 3.1

Business Taxes in Iloilo City and Legaspi City, 1977 and 1979

	Iloilo City			Legaspi City		
	Percent of Total		Percent Increase,	Percent of Total		Percent Increase,
Tax	1977	1979	1977–79	1977	1979	1977–79
1. Manufacturing	4.2	7.3	147.9	5.9	8.6	81.1
2. Eateries	1.9	1.8	38.0	6.4	5.9	15.0
3. Services	8.4	6.2	4.2	3.9	3.2	3.4
4. Spirits	3.1	2.2	2.6	1.6	1.3	0.2
5. Tobacco	0.7	0.6	12.8	1.5	1.1	-7.5
6. Amusement devices	0.2	0.1	-12.7	0.3	0.2	-23.3
7. Amusement places	3.1	3.6	60.6	1.1	1.0	17.1
8. Amusement admissions	12.8	9.7	7.5	11.9	12.5	29.8
9. Pawnshops/banks	1.7	1.4	15.8	2.2	2.3	32.4
10. Insurance	0.3	0.2	-8.4	—	—	
11. Boarding houses	0.1	0.0	4.1	0.1	0.2	197.7
12. Lodging houses	0.2	0.1	-25.1	—	—	

(Continued)

TABLE 3.1 (Continued)

Tax	Iloilo City			Legaspi City		
	Percent of Total		Percent Increase,	Percent of Total		Percent Increase,
	1977	1979	1977–79	1977	1979	1977–79
13. Hotels	0.3	0.2	-20.4	0.6	0.6	15.6
14. Private detective	0.1	0.1	9.8	0.0	0.0	-24.9
15. Real estate	2.0	2.2	57.3	0.6	0.7	47.0
16. Fish ponds	0.0	0.0	-56.8	–	–	–
17. Cemeteries	0.0	0.0	104.0	–	–	–
18. Billboards	0.3	0.2	-17.6	0.1	0.0	-70.4
19. Printing	0.2	0.2	40.6	–	–	–
20. Mills	0.3	0.2	21.6	0.2	0.0	17.1
21. Delivery trucks	0.3	0.4	95.6	–	0.3	–
22. Peddlers	0.1	0.1	77.5	2.4	0.4	-81.4
23. Retail-wholesale	59.6	63.0	49.8	49.1	51.5	30.2
24. Other	–	–	–	12.0	10.0	3.1
Total amount	P5,461,316	P7,741,495	41.8	P2,010,906	P2,498,921	24.3
Total as percent of total General Fund revenues	33.0	37.3		41.1	43.1	

– = Not available.
Source: Constructed from data supplied by local treasurers.

affect the former city less so than the latter. Second, it may be that in general the local economy in Iloilo City was stronger during this period than in the Bicol region. In this respect, note that the retail-wholesale portion of the tax increased by nearly 50 percent in Iloilo City compared to only 30 percent in Legaspi City. Third, it may be that administrative practices in Iloilo City were more effective than in Legaspi City in capturing the taxable base—despite the fact that we were told there are eight clerks assigned to the BLT in Legaspi City and only six in Iloilo City.

Variations Among Municipalities and Cities

In order to obtain a more systematic view of the relationship between the revenue yields of the BLT and various socioeconomic characteristics of jurisdictions, we carried out a cross-sectional analysis on BLT collections in 98 municipalities in 4 provinces and 42 cities. We studied the variation among municipalities within each province, among all 98 municipalities, and among the 42 cities. Ordinary least squares regression has been used on 1977 data, with the revenue and income variables expressed in natural logarithms, to estimate four models:

1. $BLT_p = a_1 + \beta_1 Y_p$
2. $BLT_p = a_2 + \beta_2 Y_p + \delta_2 U_p$
3. $BLT_p = a_3 + \delta_3 U_p + \gamma_3 NY_p$
4. $BLT_p = a_4 + \delta_4 U_p + \gamma_4 NY_p + \Gamma_4 P$

One measure of the income elasticity of the yield of the BLT can be found by regressing per capita BLT revenues (BLT_p) on per capita personal income (Y_p) as in model 1. However, as suggested in the tax effort discussion of Chapter 1, the BLT appears to be very much an "urban tax"—hence, model 2 includes a variable measuring the percent of population living in urban areas (U_p). The data in Chapter 1 suggested that nonagricultural income was more systematically associated with tax revenues than was total personal income—again an indication of the role of a more developed local economy. Thus, models 3 and 4 use per capita nonagricultural income (NY_p) rather than per capita income and combine it with urbanization in model 3 and both urbanization and population (P) in model 4. Several interesting conclusions can be drawn from the results of this analysis (Table 3.2).

The cross-sectional response to income (income elasticity) varies greatly over the four provinces. The coefficient for Bulacan is more than 2, suggesting that per capita BLT revenues vary among municipalities in the province even more than in proportion to the wide variations in personal income which exist. Since we cannot believe that the income elasticity could be as high as 2.22, we must conclude that high income communities have other characteristics that also stimulate higher BLT revenues per capita. In Albay, the income elasticity is a much lower 0.63, but not statistically significant, whereas in Sorsogon, the statistical relationship is even weaker.

The results for Iloilo are perplexing. They suggest that higher levels of income are associated with lower per capita BLT revenues, which could have a number of interpretations. One is that there are differences in tax rates with higher income communities levying lower rates. Another is that the per capita income measure reflects large amounts of agricultural income, which in turn does not reflect much business taxpaying capacity. The latter appears more likely, because where per capita income is high, there is a high agricultural component and therefore less ability to collect BLT revenues. With respect to all of the estimates of model 1, it is clear that little of the variation can be explained within provinces. Either additional variables must be included to account for different levels of willingness and capacity to collect BLT revenues, or intangible and personal factors that underlie the more effective use of the BLT in some communities than in others must be considered.[5]

The addition of urban population and the nonagricultural measure of per capita income improves the results greatly except in Iloilo, where none of the models is very strong. In Albay the nonagricultural income elasticity of the BLT ranges from 0.50 to 0.66, and approximately half of the variation in per capita BLT revenues can be explained.[6] The Bulacan elasticity is considerably greater, suggesting that municipalities with a 1 percent higher level of per capita nonagricultural income collect nearly 2 percent more in per capita BLT revenues. Again this elasticity is unexpectedly high. One possible explanation is that as development occurs and incomes rise, an associated critical level of population and buying power is reached and the area becomes a marketing center. This growth then creates a business tax base reflecting not only the socioeconomic characteristics of the municipality itself but also its ability to draw economic activity from other areas.

TABLE 3.2

Cross-Sectional Estimates of Income Elasticities of Business License Tax, 1977

		Independent Variables						
Province	Model	Inter-cept	ln (Per Capita Income)	Percent Urban	ln (Per Capita Nonagricultural Income)	Population (in thousands)	R^2	F
Albay	1	-3.98	.63 (1.22)				.09	1.50
	2	-4.04	.60 (1.21)	.03 (1.49)			.22	1.92
	3	-3.88		.03 (1.74)	.66 (2.95)†		.46	6.10
	4	-3.52		.03 (1.98)	.50 (2.15)*	.01 (1.66)	.56	5.51
Bulacan	1	-14.43	2.22 (2.51)*				.23	6.32
	2	-9.64	1.49 (1.58)	.01 (1.73)			.33	4.97
	3	-11.84		.004 (.75)	1.94 (3.46)†		.53	11.27
	4	-10.05		.007 (1.27)	1.72 (2.94)†	-.01 (1.23)	.56	8.21

(Continued)

TABLE 3.2 (Continued)

		Independent Variables						
Province	Model	Inter-cept	ln (Per Capita Income)	Percent Urban	ln (Per Capita Nonagricultural Income)	Population (in thousands)	R^2	F
Iloilo	1	5.02	-.74 (1.99)*				.05	3.97
	2	5.17	-.81 (2.23)*	.02 (1.92)			.16	3.96
	3	-2.16		.02 (1.59)	.32 (1.38)		.10	2.32
	4	-2.51		.02 (1.52)	.44 (1.75)	-.01 (1.24)	.14	2.09
Sorsogon	1	-.12	.05 (.09)				.00	.01
	2	.26	-.09 (.21)	.04 (3.72)†			.53	6.93
	3	-1.02		.03 (3.11)†	.13 (.85)		.56	7.67
	4	-2.04		.02 (2.12)	.25 (1.72)	.02 (2.24)	.70	8.49

Four provinces pooled	1	-2.58	.42				.02	2.27
			(1.51)					
	2	-.35	.04	.02			.24	15.23
			(.17)	(5.25)†				
	3	-3.04		.02	.52		.37	28.27
				(4.06)†	(4.45)†			
	4	-3.04		.01	.51	.002	.37	18.73
				(3.85)†	(4.30)†	(.38)		
Cities	1	-12.13	1.98				.26	12.63
			(3.55)†					
	2	-10.27	1.68	.01			.28	6.89
			(2.70)†	(1.05)				
	3	-4.32		.004	.92		.23	5.19
				(.69)	(2.08)*			
	4	-2.60		.004	.57	.005	.33	5.55
				(.76)	(1.30)	(2.24)*		

Note: Dependent variable: ln (per capita business license tax). Numbers in parentheses are absolute t-values.
*Significant at less than the 0.05 level.
†Significant at less than the 0.01 level.
Source: Computed by authors.

This point may be expanded with the aid of a hypothetical example. Consider two neighboring communities, A and B. Assume that locality A has achieved a higher degree of "development," which is manifest in higher per capita incomes, urbanization, and so on, and has become the marketing center for both communities. It will then earn higher than expected BLT revenues, whereas community B, with its lower per capita income, earns lower than expected BLT revenues. When BLT per capita is regressed on income, a 1 percent difference in income is, not surprisingly, associated with a 2 percent difference in BLT per capita.

In Sorsogon the urbanization variable alone is significantly different from zero and the income elasticity estimate is very low and statistically insignificant. The high *F*-values and nonsignificant coefficients in model 4 for Sorsogon suggest a high degree of multicollinearity, not an unexpected result, as the province contains only a few urbanized areas that serve as regional market centers.

Turning to the municipalities, we find that the pooled data for 98 municipalities show no significant relationship between per capita income and the BLT. Indeed, the simplest model explains only 2 percent of the variability in per capita BLT across all municipalities. On the other hand, both urbanization and per capita nonagricultural income remain significant and positive in each of the models in which they are used and account for between one-fourth and one-third of the variance explained. It is impossible, however, to determine the extent to which the relatively high levels of these variables and BLT per capita in Bulacan are responsible for the results. In any case, the failure to explain more of the variation makes one point clear: The willingness to enforce and collect the tax is an important factor in explaining variations in per capita BLT revenues.

Interestingly, in the case of the cities, per capita income is significant and the implied income elasticity is high (approximately 2). The urbanization variable is not significant (model 2), even when used in conjunction with per capita nonagricultural income (model 3). As may be seen from model 4, population size does seem to matter—larger cities raise more BLT per capita than smaller cities, regardless of their level of income. As in the case of the pooled data, the city models explain one-third or less of the variance.

Increases in Selected Municipalities

Although we lacked a sufficiently complete nationwide time series to study the revenue growth in the BLT, we did observe how

TABLE 3.3

Business License Tax Performance in Selected Albay Municipalities, 1977–79 (in pesos)

	Camalig			Libon			Malinao			Tabaco		
General Fund	1977	1978	1979	1977	1978	1979	1977	1978	1979	1977	1978	1979
Business tax	73,297	88,698	92,087	30,131	32,440	33,469	14,709	34,180	35,229	301,253	361,536	398,451
Business tax as percent of General Fund income	16.5	16.0	15.1	8.2	8.7	7.9	7.5	14.8	14.0	22.1	24.5	24.2

	Growth Rates (percent)							
	1977–78	1978–79	1977–78	1978–79	1977–78	1978–79	1977–78	1978–79
Business tax	21.0	3.0	7.7	3.2	132.4	3.1	20.0	13.2
General Fund income	18.3	9.6	1.6	13.1	18.1	8.5	8.3	11.7

	Socioeconomic Characteristics			
1975 population	41,702	47,890	24,889	65,254
1970–75 population growth (percent)	7.08	9.71	8.32	7.73
Percent urban, 1975	8.64	13.2	0	19.6
Mean 1975 household income (pesos)	6,641	4,523	4,151	7,341
Per capita nonagricultural income (pesos)	767	152	358	835

Sources: Financial data from the provincial treasurer; socioeconomic data from National Census and Statistics Office, "1975 Integrated Census of the Population and Its Economic Activities, Phase II, Albay," no. 289 (Manila, February 8, 1980).

BLT revenues fared in selected Iloilo and Albay municipalities during the 1977–79 period (Tables 3.3 and 3.4). With this extremely small sample it is difficult to reach any definitive conclusions, but the data do not preclude general statements concerning the growth in BLT revenues in particular types of jurisdictions. The most striking feature of this growth pattern is a great deal of year-to-year variation, especially in the case of the Iloilo jurisdictions.

In Albay, Tabaco relies most heavily on the BLT, a reliance that grows out of the fact that Tabaco is the largest of the four Albay municipalities represented here and serves as a market center for several surrounding municipalities. The other three municipalities, more rural in nature and much less important as trading centers, have BLT revenues that are understandably lower relative to total revenue. The extremely large increase between 1977 and 1978 in Malinao is difficult to explain but may be attributable to a new industrial plant that prior to 1978 was exempt from 50 percent of all local taxes under the preferential treatment afforded pioneer industries (Republic Act 5186).

In general, there is much less reliance on the BLT in Iloilo than in Albay. The municipality of Pavia relies more heavily upon this revenue source than the other five jurisdictions represented here. While Pavia's population size and income characteristics are not significantly different from the other jurisdictions, and its location adjacent to Iloilo City may hamper its possibilities as a market center, it has attracted some manufacturing activity that contributes heavily to its BLT base. Interestingly, the highest income community, Passi, has one of the lowest revenue-dependent rates associated with BLT. This may be due partially to its location in a sugar-growing area, implying a relatively high per capita income but a low business tax base. The less urbanized areas in general rely less on the BLT, again suggesting that it is essentially an urban tax.

Annual growth in the BLT is erratic in the six jurisdictions. These fluctuations can usually be traced to two major causes. The first is the location of a new business, which results in a dramatic one-year increase in the tax, particularly if it is a large business, which accounts for a significant share of the total revenue yield. The second reason has to do with enforcement of the tax. If there is a major push to collect the BLT in a particular year, a substantial increase may result; while if enforcement is lax in a particular year, a large decrease occurs. Even a single large, but late, payment of the tax in small communities can greatly influence the annual pattern.

TABLE 3.4

Business License Tax Performance in Selected Iloilo Municipalities, 1977–79 (in pesos)

	Dingle			Dumangas			Guimbal		
	1977	1978	1979	1977	1978	1979	1977	1978	1979
Business tax	48,658	59,856	54,701	37.404	54,711	61,290	45,119	56,435	21,278
Business tax as percent of General Fund income	10.5	13.2	10.0	6.5	8.6	8.8	19.2	24.1	8.2

Growth Rates (percent)

	Dingle 1977–78	Dingle 1978–79	Dumangas 1977–78	Dumangas 1978–79	Guimbal 1977–78	Guimbal 1978–79
Business tax	23.0	-8.6	46.3	12.0	25.1	-62.3
General Fund income	-2.4	20.6	11.8	10.3	-0.3	10.1

Socioeconomic Characteristics

	Dingle	Dumangas	Guimbal
1975 population	25,683	38,457	18,409
1970–75 population growth (percent)	12.80	10.53	10.64
Percent urban, 1975	7.75	4.80	23.66
Mean 1975 household income (pesos)	4,104	4,429	4,389
Per capita nonagricultural income (pesos)	428	335	343

(Continued)

TABLE 3.4 (Continued)

	Passi			Pavia			Tigbauan		
	1977	1978	1979	1977	1978	1979	1977	1978	1979
Business tax	69,666	60,627	54,775	109,100	149,940	153,685	13,950	14,346	14,869
Business tax as percent of General Fund income	6.2	5.0	5.3	21.7	26.8	21.8	4.2	3.5	3.4
Growth Rates (percent)									
	1977–78	1978–79		1977–78	1978–79		1977–78	1978–79	
Business tax	-13.0	-9.6		37.4	2.5		2.8	3.6	
General Fund income	7.0	-14.0		11.4	25.7		21.0	8.8	
Socioeconomic Characteristics									
1975 population		47,017			14,423			27,443	
1970–75 population growth (percent)		23.99			10.44			12.14	
Percent urban, 1975		15.52			18.06			9.57	
Mean 1975 household income (pesos)		9,891			5,961			6,746	
Per capita nonagricultural income (pesos)		443			432			552	

Sources: Financial data from the provincial treasurer; socioeconomic data are preliminary figures furnished by the National Census and Statistics Office.

CONCLUSION

The BLT is a productive revenue source that local governments will continue to rely upon. It is not as good a revenue source as a sales tax shared with the central government could be. Its base assessment problems are substantial and probably insurmountable. Furthermore, it does not automatically grow with income and inflation. On the other hand, it has important advantages: It generates a great deal of revenue, it brings businesses into the local taxpaying community, and it might be used to increase the collection efficiency of the property tax. One might take either of two directions in suggesting a program of reform. First, one can assume that the BLT will remain an important local revenue source and then raise the question as to how it might be adjusted to become more productive. Second, one can consider the alternative of replacing the BLT with a share of central government sales tax. The former is the direction suggested in Chapter 7, which addresses alternative reform possibilities.

NOTES

1. We found only one study of the BLT in Metro Manila done by the NTRC. See *Study on Local Business Taxes in Manila* (Manila: NTRC, 1978).

2. One instance in which classification has caused problems was encountered in Bocaue, Bulacan, where it was stated that since chemical manufacturers and chemical dealers pay different rates, classification decisions can have substantial revenue effects. The Bureau of Internal Revenue was called on for assistance because it also classifies businesses in administering the corporate business tax and several indirect excise taxes imposed at the central government level.

3. In the case of large business operations, the use of an outside expert by the treasurer's office may be well worth the investment.

4. Any further substantial changes in the overall structure of rates should, however, await further in-depth research.

5. See, for instance, the sociocultural insights provided in John T. Omohundro's anthropological study, *Chinese Merchant Families in Iloilo: Commerce and Kin in a Central Philippine City* (Athens: Ohio University press, 1981).

6. That this elasticity is nearly identical to that for the statistically insignificant per capita income variable (and the coefficients on the urban variable in models 2 and 3 are identical) adds credence to the speculation that the systematic income-BLT relationship can be attributed to nonagricultural income, which is more easily capturable by the BLT.

4

Intergovernmental Fiscal Relations
by ROY BAHL and LARRY SCHROEDER

The subject of intergovernmental fiscal relations includes a wide range of considerations: grants and subsidies to local governments; tax sharing among central, provincial, and local governments; approval of tax structure changes and borrowing; monitoring and approving of budgets; and appointment and supervision of local fiscal officers. In this chapter the first two are considered, with the focus on the three grant (allotment) programs used in the Philippines–the BIR Allotment, the Specific Tax Allotment and the National Tax Allotment–and on the role of the barangay unit in local government finances. In each case we ask the same questions: Is the grant program structured so as to encourage the mobilization of additional resources at the local government level? Is it equitable? Does it provide an adequate flow of revenues to local governments? And does it stimulate capital spending?

At the conclusion of this chapter we provide an overall evaluation of the grant system, using the traditional criteria of public finance. Alternative possibilities for restructuring the system, and their impacts, are discussed in Chapter 7.

THE BIR ALLOTMENT

The BIR Allotment system was changed substantially during the 1970s, with the most recent alteration brought about by PD 1741 in January 1981. After a brief review of this history, we turn to an evaluation of the effects of the BIR Allotment on local government budgets.

Before PD 155 (March 3, 1973), 17 percent of national internal revenue collections was distributed to local governments. The basis for the distribution was BIR collections in the preceding year, where 13 percent was allocated to provinces and cities and 4 percent to municipalities. These total amounts were then distributed, 70 percent according to population and 30 percent according to land area. In addition, local governments received an amount equivalent to about 6 percent of the preceding year's national internal revenue tax collections in the form of local shares from the withholding tax and from "excess" income tax collections.[1] This allocation method created an incentive for improved tax collection but biased the distribution of central assistance toward a small number of relatively wealthy provinces. This bias and the desire to make the grant system more equitable prompted reform.

A new system was introduced with PD 144. Its major features were:

1. 20 percent of national internal revenue taxes (not assigned to special funds and accounts) should be transferred to local governments, with the computation based on BIR collections during the third year prior to the current fiscal year.

2. The allocation would be divided among local government levels:
   - 30 percent to provinces
   - 45 percent to municipalities
   - 25 percent to cities

3. These funds would be shared according to a weighted three-factor formula:[2]
   - 70 percent according to population
   - 20 percent according to land area
   - 10 percent according to equal shares

It was also specified that

4. For FY 1974–76, the annual allotment for any local government would not increase by more than 15 percent nor decrease by more than 50 percent of the locality's FY 1971 allotment.

This last feature, then, linked FY 1974–76 allotments to the old system.[3]

Two additional features were included in PD 144. First, economic development expenditures received greater emphasis in that

5. 20 percent of a jurisdiction's allotment was to be earmarked for developmental projects approved by the Ministry of Local Government and Community Development (MLGCD).

Second, the role of the barangay was emphasized in that

6. Each barangay was to receive 10 percent of property taxes collected within the barangay and, in addition, each jurisdiction was to contribute up to ₱500 to each barangay within its boundaries. The provincial treasurer was named custodian of these funds with expenditures requiring MLGCD approval.

The BIR Allotment was amended one year later (September 21, 1974) by PD 559, which specified barangays as co-recipients of the Allotment. Through FY 1976, barangays were to receive ₱56 million that previously had been earmarked for division among provinces, municipalities, and cities. After FY 1976, the split among local governments was to be 25 percent to provinces, 40 percent to municipalities, 25 percent to cities, and 10 percent to barangays.

PD 559 specified that the amount set aside for barangays should be distributed in the form of community development project grants with the distribution administered by the president. Thus, there was an alteration in the BIR grant system away from general grants toward project grants.

The BIR Allotment system was changed again in PD 937 (May 27, 1976). This amendment was made, at least in part, to address the grant distribution during the six-month transition from a July 1–June 30 fiscal year to a January 1–December 31 fiscal year, effective January 1, 1977. In addition, PD 937 specified that in FY 1977 a "hold-harmless" provision (no decreases in the annual allotment) replaced the 50 percent maximum decrease in annual allotments, while allotment increases were restricted to 25 percent of the FY 1976 amount.

PD 144 was further altered by PD 1231 (November 4, 1977), which specifies that allocations for fiscal years 1978 through 1980 would be equal to those determined for 1977 (under PD 937). This temporary measure may be the most important change in the grant system since the enactment of PD 144. In effect, it has held constant the peso level of the grant to be distributed and brought on a drastic decline in the real distribution. By 1980, only about one-third of the actual grant entitlement was being distributed.

In January 1981, PD 1741 was enacted, providing for a grant of additional aid to local governments whose income declined in 1980 due to low crop prices and providing for an allowance of year-to-year increases in allotments beyond the 25 percent ceiling for certain local governments. The second of these provisions is especially important in terms of its effect on the distribution of the allotment. The PD provides that for third-, fourth-, fifth-, and sixth-class local governments, increases of more than 25 percent may be made subject to adequate justification as recommended by the Ministry of Local Government and Community Development and subject to the availability of funds. The PD also notes that if these conditions are met, the allotment may be increased by up to 30 percent (third-class local governments), 35 percent (fourth-class local governments), 40 percent (fifth-class local government) or 45 percent (sixth-class local government). While such additional aid may be justified on equity grounds, it does not provide incentives for increasing tax effort, as governments experiencing revenue declines are more likely to be awarded additional grants than those making greater efforts to maintain revenue flows.

The objectives of the BIR Allotment, as enunciated in presidential decrees 144 and 559, are to create a more equitable distribution of allotments, to stimulate economic development expenditures, and to stimulate the further mobilization of local resources. Additionally, there was much concern at the central government level about whether local governments were accountable for their expenditure of allotment funds. At the local government level, the concern was over the certainty of how much allotment would be received and the elasticity of allotment revenues with respect to income growth and inflation.

Equalization Impacts

Does the BIR Allotment system accomplish an equity objective? The answer in the Philippine case depends, in part, on how one defines equity. The distribution according to land area and population is an attempt to take account of expenditure needs but will be income equalizing only in the unlikely case that the more populous areas are poorer. The recent provision lifting the ceiling on lower class municipalities (see above) may reflect the objective of increasing the flow of resources to poorer municipalities, if lower class

TABLE 4.1

Simple Correlations Between Per Capita Allotments and Selected Independent Variables, for Selected Cities and Municipalities, 1977

Independent Variable	BIR Allotment		Special Tax Allotment	
	Cities[a]	Municipalities[b]	Cities[a]	Municipalities[b]
Per capita personal income	-0.07	0.09	-0.336	-0.138
Per capita assessed value	0.14	0.27	0.038	-0.100
Per capita General Fund expenditures	0.10	0.52	-0.107	-0.191
Per capita General and Infrastructure Fund expenditures	–	–	0.015	-0.142
Population size	-0.02	-0.34	-0.383	-0.263
(Number of observations)	(40)	(96)	(41)	(96)
Correlation required for significance				
At .05 level	.31	.20	.31	.20
At .10 level	.25	.16	.25	.16

[a]Includes the cities listed in Appendix A, less two for which data regarding the BIR Allotment were deemed to be in error.
[b]Includes the municipalities in Albay, Bulacan, Iloilo, and Sorsogon.
Source: Computed by authors.

municipalities tend to have lower incomes. The correlations presented in Chapter 1, however, suggest that this is not the case.

One might turn to the evidence on the actual distribution of the BIR Allotment to understand the equity impact of the system. Working with 1977 cross-sectional data for a sample of 96 municipalities in 4 provinces (Albay, Sorsogon, Iloilo, and Bulacan) and 40 chartered cities throughout the country, we estimated the simple correlation between the per capita allotment received and per capita personal income, per capita assessed value, per capita expenditures, and population size. Statistically significant relationships would indicate that, de facto, allotments were distributed with biases in favor of or against these variables.

The results for chartered cities show no significant relationship with any of the variables, that is, none can explain the variation from a high per capita allotment of ₱36.24 in Bais to a low of ₱4.94 in Baguio (Table 4.1). The absence of a relationship with population is not surprising. Since 70 percent of the city share is distributed on a population basis, the per capita distribution of the allotment should be neutral with respect to population size. But to find no relationship with any of these criteria is a surprise. Either grants to cities—25 percent of the total BIR Allotment—are systematically related to some other variables not included here, or they are distributed in a random manner.

The 40 percent distributed to municipalities shows a more consistent pattern. Significantly greater amounts of per capita allotment were distributed to municipalities that had greater fiscal capacities (as measured by per capita assessed value) and to those that made higher per capita expenditures. Jurisdictions with smaller populations received significantly larger amounts. With respect to municipalities, then, the resulting per capita distribution of allotment does not reflect the intent of the population–land area–equal share formula.

From this evidence on cities and municipalities in the four provinces, three conclusions can be drawn about the equity of the distribution of allotments:[4] (1) the distribution does not appear to equalize, indeed, it may even be counterequalizing; (2) the actual distribution is influenced as much by factors such as mandatory ceilings and maximum increases as it is by formula provisions; and (3) the distribution pattern and equalizing effects differ between cities and municipalities, which implies that the allotment system is not a system at all, but a combination of grant programs.

Fiscal Stimulation

To what extent is the BIR Allotment program stimulative of local government fiscal activities? Does it induce local governments to spend and tax more than they would have otherwise, or is it substitutive in the sense of allowing local governments to tax less than they otherwise would have? Economic theory suggests the latter. A lump-sum grant with no matching requirement or maintenance of effort clause provides no inducement for the local government to increase spending beyond the amount of the grant. Ordinarily one would expect a peso of allotment to be divided between increased expenditures, tax relief, and increased cash balances.

The BIR Allotment, however, may turn out to be less substitutive than suspected. There is a large backlog of unmet public service needs that virtually guarantees that any increased amount of revenue available to the local government will find its way into the local budget. This situation reflects a combination of a high income elasticity of demand for local public goods and the fact that once a government receives grant money, it is more likely to spend the money than return it in tax relief, the so-called "flypaper effect."[5]

Two questions must be considered: the impact of the BIR Allotment on General Fund expenditures and the impact of the BIR Allotment on total economic development expenditures, which may take place in either the General Fund or the Infrastructure Fund. Measurement of these impacts is complicated and requires simultaneous consideration of the BIR and Specific Tax Allotment. The diagram in

FIGURE 4.1 Model of Expenditure Determination

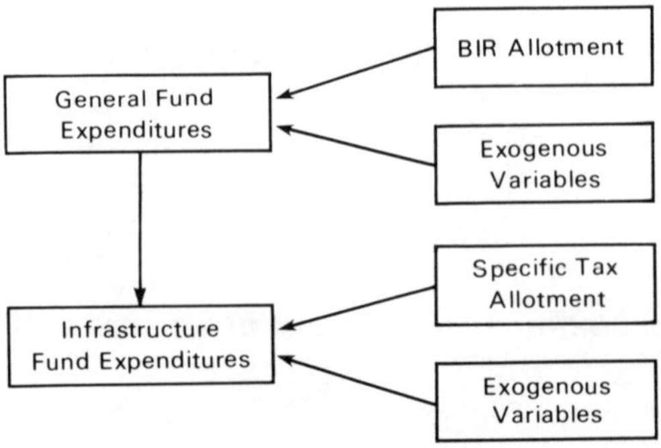

Figure 4.1 is a simplification of this complexity. The BIR Allotment is paid to the General Fund and the Specific Tax Allotment to the Infrastructure Fund, but transfers from the General to the Infrastructure Fund over and above the mandatory proportion of General Fund income may occur. One might suppose that these transfers would be greater (and therefore General Fund expenditures lower and the BIR Allotment much less stimulative) if the Specific Tax Allotment were less.

Expenditure Determinants Model

As described in Chapter 1, the fiscal structure of local governments in the Philippines includes both the General Fund (GF) and Infrastructure Fund (IF). The BIR flows to the former and the Specific Tax Allotment (STA) flows to the latter. There is a statutory minimum transfer of monies from the GF to the IF, but jurisdictions may opt to transfer greater amounts. Furthermore, it is possible for a jurisdiction to transfer funds in the opposite direction (IF to GF). Traditional expenditure determinants approaches, therefore, which consider GF and IF expenditures independently, would be inaccurate. The model developed here recognizes that activity in the two funds is interpendent.

We anticipate that a higher level of Infrastructure Fund spending per capita, IF_p, will be associated with a higher level of General Fund spending per capita, GF_p—that is, $\partial GF_p / \partial IF_p > 0$. We anticipate that the BIR Allotment and the Specific Tax Allotment will directly affect spending in the General and Infrastructure funds, respectively. There are also indirect grant impacts. For example, the provision for inter-fund transfers makes it likely that an increase in Specific Tax Allotment will indirectly generate an increase in General Fund spending—that is, $\partial GF / \partial STA > 0$.

To model this process, we define

$$GF_p = f(AV_p, NAg_p, IF_p, BIR_p) \qquad (4.1)$$

$$IF_p = f(POP, U, GF_p, STA_p) \qquad (4.2)$$

where the endogenous variables are GF_p—per capita General Fund expenditures, and IF_p—per capita Infrastructure Fund expenditures; and predetermined variables are AV_p—assessed value of property per capita, NAg_p—Nonagricultural income per capita; U—percent of population living in urban areas, POP–total population, BIR_p–BIR Allotment per capita, and STA_p–Specific Tax Allotment per capita.[6]

This specification reflects the assumption that spending is jointly determined by demand and fiscal capacity variables, and, as such, the model cannot be interpreted as being built on either a demand-oriented or revenue-determined basis.

As noted above, we hypothesize

$$\partial GF_p / \partial IF_p > 0$$

This implies that the exogenous demand and capacity variables will not fully explain spending in a particular fund and that there are positive cross effects.

We further expect, given the form of the BIR Allotment formula, that

$$\partial GF_p / \partial BIR_p \leq 1$$

In other words, we hypothesize that the grant system does not stimulate local tax effort. The impact of the Specific Tax Allotment may be a different matter, as capital grants may carry some built-in features that stimulate local spending. These are covered below.

Given the interdependent nature of the GF_p and IF_p functions—which we specify for estimation purposes to be linear—a simultaneous equation estimation technique is necessary to yield consistent estimates of the parameters. We have employed a two-stage least squares estimation technique to derive the estimates discussed below.

In estimating the impact of the allotment system on General and Infrastructure fund spending, the direct impact of the BIR on General Fund spending and its indirect effect on Infrastructure Fund spending have been recognized.

The first-stage estimates regress each endogenous variable on all predetermined variables, so that $\hat{GF}_p$ and $\hat{IF}_p$ are generated as follows:

$$\hat{GF}_p = a_1 + b_1 BIR_p + b_2 STA_p + b_3 \bar{\mathbf{X}} \quad (4.3)$$

$$\hat{IF}_p = a_2 + c_1 BIR_p + c_2 STA_p + c_3 \bar{\mathbf{X}} \quad (4.4)$$

where $\bar{\mathbf{X}}$ is the matrix of predetermined variables (specified above); a_1, b_1, b_2, a_2, c_1, and c_2 are estimated coefficients; and b_3 and c_3 are vectors of estimated coefficients. (This notation is used simply to facilitate the discussion here, as we are concerned primarily with the effects of BIR_p and STA_p on GF_p and IF_p.)

The second-stage estimates will be

$$\tilde{GF}_p = a_3 + d_1 AV_p + d_2 NAg_p + d_3 \hat{IF}_p + d_4 BIR_p \quad (4.5)$$

$$\tilde{IF}_p = a_4 + e_1 POP + e_2 U + e_3 \hat{GR}_p + e_4 STA_p \quad (4.6)$$

where $\hat{IF}_p$ and $\hat{GF}_p$ are generated from the first-stage equations (4.3) and (4.4), and all coefficients are estimates.

Substitution of the first-stage results into the second-stage equations and partial differentiation yield

$$\partial GF_p / \partial BIR_p = d_4 + d_3 c_1 \quad (4.7)$$

$$\partial GF_p / \partial STA_p = d_3 c_2 \quad (4.8)$$

$$\partial IF_p / \partial BIR_p = e_3 b_1 \quad (4.9)$$

$$\partial IF_p / \partial STA_p = e_4 + e_3 b_2 \quad (4.10)$$

The estimation of these partial derivatives gives the answer to the grant impact issue.

The second major question to be addressed with this model is the impact of the grant system on total economic development spending. A complication arises because economic development spending may appear in either the General Fund or the Infrastructure Fund. Whereas all Infrastructure Fund spending is development oriented, only a portion of the General Fund can be so considered. To capture these effects, we have specified an expenditure submodel that essentially treats General Fund development spending as residual in nature. That is, general government spending has a large "fixed" component that must be undertaken regardless of the spending capacity of local governments. Likewise, the bulk of public welfare and safety spending is mandated—in this case, linked to revenues.

To capture these features we define total local economic development spending as the sum of IF_p plus the residual of total GF_p from "expected" general government and public welfare and safety spending. The expected levels of general government and public safety expenditures are determined by predicted GF_p and other socioeconomic characteristics of the jurisdiction that could influence community choices about spending for these functions.

More formally, we define

$$\mathrm{DE}_p = (\widehat{\mathrm{GF}}_p - \mathrm{E}^*_p) + \widehat{\mathrm{IF}}_p \tag{4.11}$$

with

$$\mathrm{E}^*_p = \mathrm{GG}^*_p + \mathrm{PSW}^*_p \tag{4.12}$$

where

DE_p	–economic development expenditures per capita
E^*_p	–expected General Fund, nondevelopment expenditures per capita
$\widehat{\mathrm{GF}}_p$	–the predicted value of GF_p from Equation (4.5)
$\widehat{\mathrm{IF}}_p$	–the predicted value of IF_p from equation (4.6)
GG^*_p	–expected general government expenditures per capita
PSW_p	–expected public safety and welfare expenditures per capita

To estimate GG^*_p and PSW^*_p we speciify

$$\mathrm{GG}^*_p = f(\mathrm{POP}, 1/\widehat{\mathrm{GF}}) = a_5 + g_1\mathrm{POP} + g_2\, 1/\widehat{\mathrm{GF}} \tag{4.13}$$

$$\mathrm{PSW}^*_p = .18\widehat{\mathrm{GF}}_p + \mathrm{PSW}^{**}_p \tag{4.14}$$

with

$$\mathrm{PSW}^{**}_p = f(\mathrm{U}, \mathrm{POP}) \tag{4.15}$$

so

$$\mathrm{PSW}^*_p - .18\widehat{\mathrm{GF}}_p = a_6 + h_1\mathrm{U} + h_2\mathrm{POP} \tag{4.16}$$

The GG^*_p equation (4.13) includes population under the assumption that there are certain general government functions that must be expanded above the "threshold level" as the number of residents expands, for example, the number of clerks in service agencies. Yet we also expect that as total spending expands, general government spending will become a smaller proportion of total General Fund expenditures (due to its fixed nature). Equation (4.14) provides specifically for the mandated 18 percent contribution to the INP, whereas

(4.15) suggests that these contributions will be supplemented in response to urbanization and population differences across jurisdictions.[7]

Evaluation of the grant system effect on economic development spending requires an estimation of $\partial DE_p / \partial BIR_p$ and $\partial DE_p / \partial STA_p$. Because the DE_p definitional equation (4.11) implicitly includes both the estimated total expenditure functions ($\tilde{GF}_p$ and $\tilde{IF}_p$) and the expenditure composition functions (GG_p^* and PSW_p^*), evaluation of these partials requires inclusion of the entire model. When fully specified, equation (4.11) can be expressed as

$$\begin{aligned} DE_p = &\{ a_3 + d_1 AV_p + d_2 NAg_p + d_3 [a_2 + c_3 BIR_p + c_2 STA_p \\ &+ c_3 \overline{\mathbf{X}}] + d_4 BIR_p \} - \{ a_5 + g_1 POP + g_2 / [a_3 + d_1 AV_p \\ &+ d_2 NAg_p + d_3 (a_2 + c_1 BIR_p + c_2 STA_p + c_3 \overline{\mathbf{X}}) \\ &+ d_4 BIR_p] \} - \{ .18 [a_3 + d_1 AV_p + d_2 NAg_p \\ &+ d_3 (a_2 + c_1 BIR_p + c_2 STA_p + c_p \overline{\mathbf{X}}) + d_4 BIR_p] \\ &+ a_6 + h_1 U + h_2 POP \} + \{ a_4 + e_1 POP + e_2 U \\ &+ e_3 [a_1 + b_1 BIR_p + b_2 STA_p + b_3 \overline{\mathbf{X}}] + e_4 STA \} \end{aligned} \tag{4.17}$$

When this foreboding expression is differentiated with respect to BIR_p and STA_p, we obtain

$$\begin{aligned} \frac{\partial DE_p}{\partial BIR_p} &= d_3 c_1 + d_4 - \frac{-g_2 (d_3 c_1 + d_4)}{V^2} - .18 (d_3 c_1 - d_4) + e_3 b_1 \\ &= [d_3 c_1 + d_4][.82 + \frac{g_2}{V^2}] + e_3 b_1 \end{aligned} \tag{4.18}$$

and

$$\begin{aligned} \frac{\partial DE_p}{\partial STA_p} &= d_3 c_2 - \frac{-g_2 d_3 c_1}{V^2} - .18 d_3 c_2 + e_3 b_2 + e_4 \\ &= d_3 c_2 [.82 + \frac{g_2}{V^2}] + e_3 b_2 + e_4 \end{aligned} \tag{4.19}$$

where

$$V = [a_3 + d_1\text{AV}_p + d_2\text{NAg}_p + d_3(a_2 + c_1\text{BIR}_p + c_2\text{STA}_p + c_3\bar{\text{X}}) + d_4\text{BIR}_p] \quad (4.20)$$

Thus, again, the overall estimated impact of the grant system depends on a combination of parameters but, given the imposed nonlinearity in the GG_p^* equation (4.13), is expected to depend also on the level of the BIR Allotment.

Statistical Results

Ideally this model should be applied to all local governments in the Philippines or at least to a random, nationwide sample. Data, however, are not available for such an analysis, but we will test for the stimulative effects of the BIR Allotment using our four-province sample of 96 municipalities.

The regression results presented in Table 4.2 confirm the hypothesis that per capita General Fund expenditures are higher where per capita Infrastructure Fund expenditures are higher, even when income level, population size, and other factors are taken into account. This finding leads us to expect that the cross effects of grants (for example, the indirect impact of the Specific Tax Allotment on General Fund spending) are important. As expected, per capita General Fund expenditures are higher where per capita nonagricultural income and per capita assessed valuation are higher.

The evidence makes it difficult to argue that there is a stimulative impact of the BIR Allotment. Our estimation of equation (4.7) does show that a ₱1 higher BIR Allotment is associated with a ₱1.33 higher level of General Fund expenditures (Table 4.3), but the level of statistical significance is low.[8] From equation (4.7), we derived

$$\partial\text{GF}/\partial\text{BIR} = \partial\tilde{\text{G}}\text{F}/\partial\text{BIR} + (\partial\tilde{\text{G}}\text{F}/\partial\hat{\text{I}}\text{F}) \cdot (\partial\hat{\text{I}}\text{F}/\partial\text{BIR}) \quad (4.7')$$

hence

$$\partial\text{GF}/\partial\text{BIR} = 1.33 = 0.72 + (2.69)(0.23) \quad (4.7'')$$

Neither of the estimated coefficients that directly involve BIR_p (0.72 and 0.23) is, however, significantly different from zero. In light of these results, we are hesitant to conclude that the expenditure impact of the BIR Allotment is significantly greater than zero. Such a conclusion suggests a neutral or a substitutive effect. That is, local governments may have either substituted the allotment for what would have been higher taxes or they accumulated it in larger cash balances.

The indirect impact of the BIR Allotment on infrastructure expenditures is negligible (Table 4.3), meaning that larger BIR grants do not free substantially more resources to be transferred to the Infrastructure Fund expenditures. Again, however, the levels of significance are quite low.

The development expenditure submodel gives similar results, providing no evidence of a stimulative impact of BIR Allotments on capital expenditures. The results of the structural equations are sensible and similar to those hypothesized. General government spending has a threshold level and thereafter declines as a percent of total General Fund spending. Public safety and welfare expenditures are quite constant at 18 percent of General Fund expenditures (revenues). A ₱1 higher BIR Allotment tends to be associated with a ₱0.98 higher level of economic development expenditures (Table 4.3) but, as above, the level of significance is too low in the structural equations to provide confidence in this result.

In sum, no strong evidence exists that the BIR Allotment stimulates capital spending, which raises interesting questions about government policy. If there is one clear objective of central government intergovernmental policy, it is to induce local governments to spend more for economic development purposes and less for consumption of goods and services. One approach to achieving this objective has been to require that 20 percent of the BIR Allotment be allocated to development projects. This policy, however, does not ensure that development expenditures will be increased by 20 percent of the allotment, over and above what would have been spent in the absence of the allotment. The evidence, furthermore, shows no such increase.

The problems with our results may be related partially to the sample, which is limited to four provinces, and as always, with the quality of the data used. Broader coverage would reduce the dominance of a "province effect" and would allow for more variability in the dependent and explanatory factors. In addition, the specification of the equations could have improved if more data had been available. Estimation of this model on a nationwide basis should be a high research priority for the future.

Levels of significance aside, the results implied by column 1 of Table 4.3 provide an indication of the capabilities of the model. A ₱1 higher level of BIR Allotment per capita would result in a ₱1.33

TABLE 4.2

Regression Results for Model of Stimulative Impacts of BIR and Specific Tax Allotment Grant System

	First Stage[a]		Second Stage[b]			
Independent Variables	GF_p	IF_p	GF_p	IF_p	GG^{*c}_p	PSW**[d]
Intercept	4.44	.86	-3.65	-.11	14.38	2.20
	(1.18)	(.41)	(1.14)	(.07)	(13.46)	(3.68)
BIR_p	1.40	.23	.72			
	(3.74)	(1.11)	(1.05)			
STA_p	-3.97	.87		1.60		
	(1.76)	(.70)		(1.38)		
AV_p	6.31	1.18	2.84			
	(7.45)	(2.52)	(1.70)			
NAg_p	4.64	.52	8.53			
	(1.47)	(.29)	(2.11)			

U	16.61	3.73		.60		2.05
	(4.64)	(1.88)		(.32)		(1.41)
POP[e]	-.069	-.032		-.020	-.031	-.049
	(1.56)	(1.32)		(.96)	(1.41)	(2.72)
$\hat{IF}_p$			2.69			
			(2.30)			
$\hat{GF}_p$				.177		
				(3.93)		
$1/GF_p$					-80.78	
					(6.08)	
R^2	69	.20	.49[f]	.23[f]	.32	.08
F	33.16	3.76	21.55	6.74	22.24	3.89

Note: Entries in parentheses are absolute values of t-statistics.
[a]Equations (4.3) and (4.4).
[b]Equations (4.5) and (4.6).
[c]Equation (4.13).
[d]Equation (4.16).
[e]Population in thousands.
[f]R^2 statistics are unreliable in the second stage of 2SLS.

TABLE 4.3

BIR and Specific Tax Allotment Impacts on Local Government Expenditures (in pesos)

	Expenditure Response to a ₱1 Higher Amount of	
Per Capita Expenditure Category	Per Capita BIR Allotment	Per Capita Specific Tax Allotment
General Fund	1.33 (4.7)*	2.34 (4.8)
Infrastructure Fund	0.25 (4.9)	0.90 (4.10)
Development expenditures	0.98 (4.18)	2.18 (4.19)

*Numbers in parentheses refer to equation number in text.

higher level of General Fund expenditures per capita and a ₱0.25 higher level of infrastructure spending. Of this net impact of ₱1.58, ₱0.98 is higher economic development spending (₱0.73 in the General Fund), and ₱0.60 is higher general government and public safety expenditure. Of the ₱0.60 in nondevelopment spending, an average of ₱0.24 is automatically siphoned off by virtue of the 18 percent INP requirement. There is clearly much to be learned from further development of this model.

Accountability

Related to the grant impact issue is the question of accountability. Lump-sum grants are criticized on grounds that local governments may spend the money in any way they see fit and with any level of efficiency. The problem of accountability is an old one, and a consequence of separating the pleasure of expenditure benefits from the pain of taxation: If a government must tax its citizens to pay for services, it will be more solicitous in how it spends the money.

How can local governments be made more accountable? First, if matching local funds are required, as in a partial cost reimbursement grant system, local governments must "pay" to receive the grant and thus become accountable to their own citizens with respect to how the grant monies are spent. To institute such a system in the Philippines would call for a complete overhauling of the existing general-purpose grant system. A second approach, more applicable in the case of a general-purpose grant such as the BIR Allotment, is to build in a "maintenance of effort" factor. At present there is nothing explicit in the allocation formula that rewards a higher tax effort. In actual fact, however, the per capita BIR Allotment is positively correlated with the level of tax effort,[9] that is, the simple correlation for 83 municipalities in Albay, Bulacan, and Iloilo is 0.33, suggesting that larger BIR Allotments do flow to jurisdictions making greater efforts.[10] Yet, if the index were to be built directly into the formula, one would anticipate an even stronger relation.

To get some idea of how such a system might work and what its impact would be, consider the following experiment. Assume the formula for distributing the BIR Allotment is changed to 50 percent by population, 20 percent by land area, and 30 percent for tax effort.[11] For our sample, the distribution under the hypothetical formula including tax effort would create substantial gains for municipalities with higher tax efforts.

The differential effect of the inclusion of the tax effort factor may be studied more systematically with a straightforward regression analysis. The current system allocates 90 percent of BIR Allotments according to population (POP) and land area (A). That is

$$\text{BIR} = f(\text{POP}, \text{A}) \qquad (4.21)$$

To explain the variation across municipalities, we may estimate

$$\text{BIR} = a_o + a_1\text{POP} + a_2\text{A} \qquad (4.22)$$

Now, the BIR Allotment per capita, BIR_p, can be inferred from (4.22) as

$$\text{BIR}_p = a_o/\text{POP} + a_1 + a_2(\text{A}/\text{POP}) \qquad (4.23)$$

So we estimate

$$\text{BIR}_p = b_0 + b_1\text{POP}^{-1} + b_2(\text{POP}/\text{A})^{-1} \qquad (4.24)$$

$$b_0 = a_1 = \partial\text{BIR}/\partial\text{POP}, \quad \text{a constant}$$

$$b_1 = a_0 = \text{POP}^2 (\partial\text{BIR}/\partial\text{POP})$$

$$b_2 = a_2 = \partial\text{BIR}/\partial(\text{A}/\text{POP})$$

To equation (4.24), we add tax effort, E_1, and estimate

$$\text{BIR}_p = c_0 + c_1 (\text{POP})^{-1} + c_2 (\text{POP}/\text{A})^{-1} + c_3 E \qquad (4.25)$$

When the BIR Allotment per capita under the current scheme is regressed on the inverse of population (and the inverse of population density–that is, equation (4.24)–we obtain

$$\text{BIR}_p = \underset{}{5.1} + \underset{(3.58)}{32459.6(\text{POP})^{-1}} - \underset{(0.74)}{52.2(\text{POP}/\text{A})^{-1}} \qquad (4.26)$$

$R^2 = .144 \quad F = 6.70$ (t-statistics in parentheses)

The low explanatory power of this seemingly definitional relationship suggests that either certain ad hoc adjustments to the formula are used to allocate the allotment across municipalities or, more likely, the 1977 allotments were based upon population data from 1970 rather than from 1975 as are being used here.

When the tax effort variable (E) is added to explain actual 1977 allocations of the per capita allotments, we obtain

$$\text{BIR}_p = 4.4 + \underset{(3.87)}{32891.3(\text{POP})^{-1}} - \underset{(.75)}{49.5(\text{POP}/\text{A})^{-1}} + \underset{(3.45)}{1.13E} \qquad (4.27)$$

$R^2 = .26 \quad F = 9.05$

The explanatory power of the equation is somewhat increased and the tax effort variable shown to be positive and significant at less than the 0.01 level. This finding suggests that, even without the specific inclusion of tax effort in the allocation formula, the 1977 allotment distribution system did favor areas that were making greater tax effort.

When the alternative scheme suggested here is used, the analogous regression results are

$$\widehat{\text{BIR}}_p = 1.02 + \underset{(14.31)}{44354.0(\text{POP})^{-1}} + \underset{(12.78)}{307.6(\text{POP}/\text{A})^{-1}} + \underset{(32.07)}{3.84E} \qquad (4.28)$$

$R^2 = .95 \quad F = 534.9$

Given that the same population, area, and effort data are used for determining the hypothetical allocation of $\hat{BIR}_p$ and for estimating equation (4.28), it is not surprising that the levels of significance of the explanatory variables are so high. A more interesting result is that after accounting for the other variables in the distribution formula, a 1 percent greater tax effort is associated with a ₱3.84 greater per capita BIR Allotment, or a differential of ₱2.71 compared to the current system.

Such an inducement would be quite substantial; ₱2.71 is equivalent to 43 percent of the average amount received under the present system. For a municipality such as Pavia in Iloilo, tax effort is 1.36 percent, more than twice the average (0.64) of the 83 municipalities studied here. A changeover from the present system to the tax effort formula system, without changing the total amount distributed, would result in an increase of ₱55,603 to Pavia, or 48 percent of the amount it presently receives. An incentive of this kind would undoubtedly result in the mobilization of substantial additional resources.

On the other hand, municipalities with less than average tax effort would receive, under the alternative system, reduced BIR Allotments. For example, Libon in Albay had an estimated local tax effort ratio of 0.28 in 1977 and received ₱244,412 in the form of BIR Allotments during that year. Under the alternative system this allotment would decline to ₱229,922, or a decrease of 5.9 percent. This decrease might be sufficient to encourage the locality to exert greater effort in utilizing its tax capacity.

Elasticity and Certainty

Another criterion for evaluating the BIR Allotment is the elasticity of its revenue yield: Is the BIR yield responsive to income growth and inflation, and in that sense, is it a good substitute for an income elastic, locally raised tax? One might frame the issue as follows: The central government has opted to not give local governments an independent income elastic tax source such as a sales or income tax. It is then reasonable to ask whether the allotment has responded as well to income growth and inflation as an independent tax source would have. Because local expenditure needs respond to these factors, local officials argue that the revenue structure should follow suit.

It is well known among local government officials in the Philippines (and demonstrated in Table 4.4) that the BIR Allotment system is income inelastic–it has responded neither to GNP nor to inflation. There are two distinct components to the allotment elasticity:

TABLE 4.4

Growth in BIR Allotment (in millions of pesos)

Year	Total Allotment Due	Actual Distribution	GNP	BIR Basis	Amount Distributed as a Percent of GNP	Amount Distributed as a Percent of BIR Basis
1981[a]	2,472.6	–	–	12,363.1	–	–
1980	1,853.0	658.9	274,334[b]	9,502.4	0.24	6.93
1979	1,332.6	658.9	220,438[c]	7,593.3	0.30	8.68
1978	1,117.3	658.9	178,543	6,366.3	0.36	10.35
1977	1,140.6	658.9	154,280	6,498.9	0.43	10.14
1976a[d]	422.6	315.1		2,408.2	0.48[e]	13.08
1976	878.2	547.8	131,938[f]	4,391.2	0.42	12.47
1975	599.8	505.4	114,265	2,999.2	0.44	16.85

[a]Budgeted.
[b]Projected.
[c]Preliminary.
[d]Six-month transition.
[e]Based on half of estimated 1976 GNP.
[f]Not final estimate.
Source: Accounting divisions, BIR, MOF, and NEDA.

FIGURE 4.2 Components of Allotment Distributed

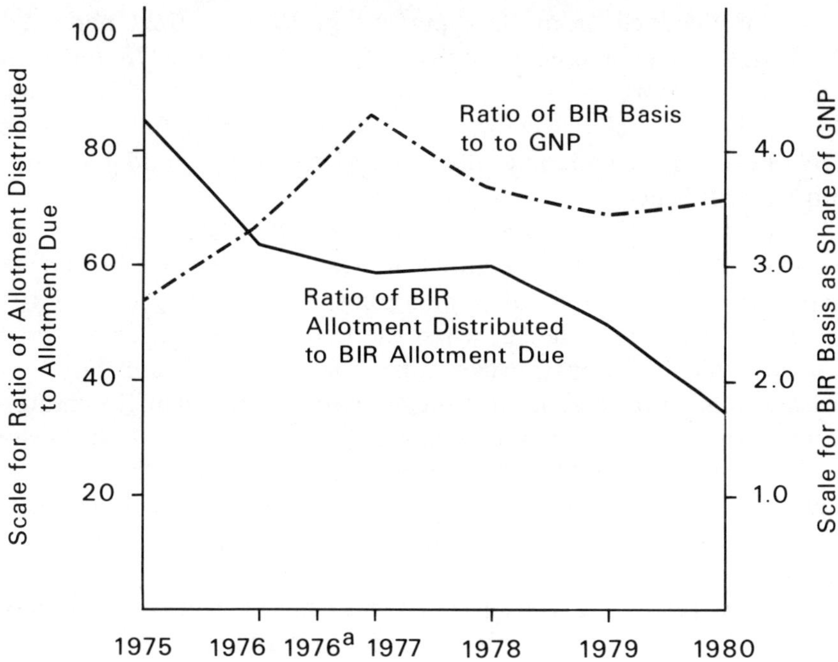

[a]The six-month transition period, July 1–December 31, 1976.

the growth in the amount of allotment actually distributed relative to the amount due and the growth in the BIR basis relative to GNP. The former is the primary explanation of the low BIR Allotment elasticity, which is in turn a result of discretionary government decisions. The government, facing other needs perhaps more pressing than local government finances, has distributed less than the entitled amounts since 1975. The current peso amount distributed was not raised between 1977 and 1980, with the result that in 1980 actual distributions were only about 7 percent of the BIR basis, compared to the 20 percent authorized in PD 144. This decline has been a long-term pattern (Table 4.4 and Figure 4.2). The second component of the elasticity, internal tax revenue collections, has not shown the elastic growth that one might expect. The BIR basis has grown with an erratic pattern relative to GNP, peaking in 1977 and declining somewhat thereafter.

The combined result of these factors has been relatively little growth in the BIR Allotment in recent years. As a share of GNP the allotment declined from 0.44 percent in 1975 to 0.24 percent in 1980, implying an income elasticity of 0.14. Between 1978 and 1980, there was no increase at all in the BIR Allotment; in fact, it declined significantly in real per capita terms. If issued at its full authorized level, however, the income elasticity of the BIR would have been unity over this period.

Even if the BIR Allotment had been fully distributed, the elasticity would not have been unity in every jurisdiction. Indeed, the distribution is on a basis of population (which is changed every fifth year) and land area. Hence, when the nationwide distribution is increased, every recipient receives a proportionate increase. For those jurisdictions with personal incomes growing faster than the national average, the system is income inelastic. For those with relatively slow personal income growth, it is income elastic. Depending on one's view of what causes expenditure needs to rise, the allotment distribution system is a success/failure in getting the pesos to where the needs are.

Closely related to the elasticity maxim for evaluating the BIR Allotment is certainty. Efficient local government budgeting and financial planning require some reasonable estimate of how much can be expected from each revenue source. Capital budgeting requires even longer term revenue projections. Such projections have not been possible with the BIR Allotment in recent years, because distributions have been primarily determined by ad hoc government policy. While this may increase the flexibility of the central government in controlling the total flow of resources, it leaves local governments in a position of being unable to plan effectively their budgets beyond a one-year period.

THE SPECIFIC TAX ALLOTMENT

The second major program of intergovernmental assistance to local governments is based on PD 436 (April 13, 1974), which amended the Internal Revenue Code as it pertained to specific taxes on a variety of petroleum products. More importantly it earmarked a designated portion of these taxes for sharing with local governments. The basis for the Specific Tax Allotment is the designated tax collection in the second preceding year; for example, the basis for the allotment in 1979 is the designated tax collection in 1977.

The sharing scheme is 20 percent to provinces, 30 percent to municipalities, and 50 percent to cities. The allocations are based on the same weighted three-factor formula as used for the BIR Allotment: 70 percent according to population, 20 percent according to land area, and 10 percent according to equal shares. The entire allocation is to the Infrastructure Fund (earlier the Road and Bridge Fund).

As in the case of the BIR Allotment, barangays were included in the allocation scheme in 1974 with the issuance of PD 558 (September 21, 1974). By this PD, one-fourth (25 percent) of the total specific tax was to be retained in a special fund allocated by the president to barangays for road and bridge construction, improvement, and maintenance. These provisions of PDs 436 and 558 have not been altered. The specific tax rates, however, were increased substantially under PD 1122 (April 21, 1977) and again under Executive Order (EO) 550 (August 1, 1979). These changes result in a marked increase in the size of the Specific Tax Allotment Fund.

Equalization Impacts

We can evaluate the Specific Tax Allotment in much the same way as the BIR Allotment. To determine whether the distribution of the Specific Tax Allotment is meeting equity objectives, we shall carry out an experiment similar to that carried out above for the BIR Allotment. At question is how strong is the correlation between the per capita distribution of the Specific Tax Allotment and per capita personal income, per capita expenditures, population, and per capita assessed value.

The simple correlations in Table 4.1 suggest the distributional features of the Specific Tax Allotment system. Among chartered cities there is a pattern to the distribution that is equalizing: Cities with a lower per capita personal income get more and smaller cities get more. The patterns are similar but not as strong in the case of municipalities. The Specific Tax Allotment behaves more like a grant system, that is, the city and municipal components are more alike in their distribution than in the case of the BIR.

Fiscal Stimulation

Clearly, the major goal of the Specific Tax Allotment is to stimulate spending on infrastructure projects. Although the system carries no matching or maintenance of effort clause, it may well achieve this stimulation because the allotment is earmarked to the Infrastructure Fund and because capital projects often require supplementary local government expenditures; for example, road and bridge maintenance or the construction of a new market may require road improvements. On the other hand, three factors might dampen or even negate this stimulation effect: the possibility that higher Specific Tax Allotments will induce local governments to reduce transfers from the General to the Infrastructure Fund; the possibility that the local government would substitute higher Infrastructure Fund expenditures for lower General Fund economic development expenditures, thereby not increasing overall capital expenditures; and the possibility that part of the Specific Tax Allotment will simply be banked in the form of increased cash balances.

To investigate these alternatives, we use the earlier analysis of the stimulative effects of grants, which considered both the Specific Tax and the BIR allotments. As in the BIR Allotment analysis, the problem is the low level of significance of the results. Some interesting conclusions, however, may be drawn from the estimates (Tables 4.2 and 4.3). First, it appears that the Specific Tax Allotment stimulates local government expenditures, certainly more so than the BIR Allotment (Table 4.3). Second, higher Specific Tax Allotments result in higher General Fund expenditures, perhaps because transfers to the Infrastructure Fund are less needed. Finally, Specific Tax Allotments appear to stimulate economic development expenditures, though the process is interesting. A peso more of allotment, on average, means a peso more of Infrastructure Fund spending, but it also means higher spending in the General Fund—₱2.34. About ₱1.28 of this amount shows up in increased economic development expenditures in the General Fund. In sum, a ₱1 higher Special Tax Allotment is associated with a ₱2.18 higher level of economic development expenditures.

Elasticity

The Specific Tax Allotment is not an elastic tax: Since it is not ad valorem it will not respond to income growth or inflation. Revenues will grow only in response to discretionary changes and to increases in the volume of consumption. Volume has been relatively flat. Revenues from the Specific Tax Allotment remained approximately constant for 1976–78, but increased markedly in 1979 because

TABLE 4.5

Growth in Specific Tax Allotment (in millions of pesos)

Year	Total Amount Due	Actual Distribution	GNP	Actual Amount as a Percent of GNP
1981[a]	881.8			
1980	767.0	NA	274,334[b]	
1979	525.1	528.9	220,438[c]	0.24
1978	115.3	94.6	178,543	0.05
1977	115.3	124.8	154,280	0.08
1976a[d]	54.7	144.6	131,938[e]	0.11
1976	118.2			
1975	142.8	NA	114,265	

NA: Not available.
[a]Budgeted.
[b]Projected.
[c]Preliminary.
[d]Six-month transition.
[e]Not final estimate.
Source: Computed by authors.

of specific tax rate increases under PD 1122 in 1977. The rates were increased in 1979 under EO 550, which implies a further revenue increase in 1981 (Table 4.5).

The rationale for tying the Specific Tax Allotment to petroleum taxes is understandable: The intent was to use the funds for road construction and maintenance, and petroleum consumption seemed a reasonable basis for identifying beneficiaries. The program, however, has expanded to a more general infrastructure type of assistance and is an important source of local government revenues. The specific tax does not provide any growth in this important tax base. In any case, changes in petroleum tax rates are more likely to be dictated by energy policy than by the financial needs of local governments. Tying the distribution of grants to energy policy leads to situations such as the current one where increased specific tax rates on petroleum products could bring a revenue windfall to local governments.

TABLE 4.6

Growth in National Tax Allotment (in millions of pesos)

Year	Amount	As a Percent of GNP	As a Percent of Actual BIR Allotment	Amount of Actual Release	Actual Release as a Percent of Total Due
1981[a]	618.2				
1980	475.1	0.17[b]	72.11	20.0	4.2
1979	379.7	0.17[c]	57.63	52.0	13.7
1978	318.3	0.18	48.31	NA	NA
1977	324.9	0.21	49.31		
1976a[e]	120.4				
1976	219.6	0.17[d]	40.10		
1975	150.0	0.13	29.68		

NA: Not available.
[a]Budgeted.
[b]Projected GNP (see Table 4.4).
[c]Preliminary GNP (see Table 4.4).
[d]Not final estimate.
[e]July–December 1976.
Source: Obtained from Bureau of the Treasury, *Final Cash Operations Statements* (annual).

NATIONAL TAX ALLOTMENT

In addition to the establishment of the General and Specific Tax allotments, PD 144 also created an additional Local Government Fund consisting of 5 percent of the BIR revenues, over and above the 20 percent set aside for General Allotment. This fund was to be used for project grants, with projects approved by a committee (specified in LOI 636) consisting of the minister of finance, the minister of the budgets, and the minister of local government and community development.

This fund amounts to earmarking an additional share of BIR collections for local governments, but leaving the distribution—amount and purpose—to the discretion of the office of the president. The National Tax Allotment to the Local Government Fund is not insignificant (Table 4.6), approaching half the size of the BIR General Allotment in some years. But in 1979 and 1980 (the two years for which we have data), only a small proportion of the total amount due was actually released to local governments.

Evaluating the National Tax Allotment is not easy. The primary objective is to increase presidential discretion to finance certain projects in certain regions, perhaps those that are in accord with national goals. On the other hand, this program provides no formal inducement for local governments to mobilize additional resources, nor does it give an incentive to improve financial management. The most important question to be asked here is whether the objectives of this program remain important enough to justify such a large share of total grants to local governments.

The Issue of Barangay Shares

The series of PDs that have redefined intergovernmental relations in the Philippines have made increasing amounts of resources available to the barangay level. PD 144 designated 10 percent of real property tax collections for barangays and provided for a contribution by local governments of up to ₱500 to each barangay within its boundaries; PD 549 required that 10 percent of the BIR General Allotment go to the barangay unit, and PD 558 allocated 25 percent of the Specific Tax Allotment to the Barangay Fund.

The amounts involved are substantial (Table 4.7). However, the actual cash distribution of these amounts and the discretion that barangays have in spending these funds substantially reduce the role

TABLE 4.7

Barangay Shares and Actual Distribution of BIR and Specific Tax Allotment Programs, 1975-81 (in millions of pesos)

Period	BIR General Allotment[a] Amount Due[d]	Specific Tax Allotment[b] Amount Due[d]	Amount of Actual Release[c]	Actual as Percent of Total Due
1981	241.1	293.9	NA	–
1980	185.3	225.7	42.5	10.3
1979	148.1	175.0	25.2[f]	7.8
1978	124.1	38.4	27.0[g]	16.6
1977	126.7	38.4	30.0	18.2
1976	65.0	39.4	80.0	76.6
1976a[e]	46.9	18.3	NA	–
1975	65.0	33.0	NA	–

[a]10 percent Barangay Development Fund (PD 559).

[b]25 percent Barangay Development Fund (PD 558).

[c]These are the combined actual releases for Barangay Development Fund from BIR General and Specific Tax allotments.

[d]Appropriated but not cash supported.

[e]Six-month transition.

[f]₱25.2 (2.6 not yet released plus 22.6 with advice of allotment for actual release).

[g]₱27.0 (26.1 not yet released plus 0.9 with advice of allotment for actual release).

Source: Budget Operation Division, Ministry of the Budget, Tax Statistics Staff, NTRC, January 23, 1981.

of the barangay. The 10 percent property tax share has been distributed for barangay use, with no major restrictions on its use. Use of the ₱500 contribution to the Barangay Development Fund requires approval of the MLGCD. In the case of the barangay share under both the Specific and General allotments, the distribution is administered by the office of the president. The purpose of the BIR General Allotment distribution is community development projects, and the Specific Tax Allotment distribution is for road and bridge (later infrastructure) construction, improvement, and maintenance.

Data have been obtained and tabulated by the National Tax Research Center (NTRC) on the extent to which the barangay shares of the BIR General Allotment and Specific Tax Allotment have been appropriated but not necessarily cash supported, that is, not released. These data (Table 4.7) demonstrate that during the period 1977–80 less than 20 percent of the appropriated amounts was actually transferred to the barangay level in any given year. For the four-year period 1977–80 only 11.7 percent of the total appropriated amount has been cash supported. Thus, while support of barangays as a new and important level of government in the Philippines is a policy initiative, relatively little financial support has been provided.

There are two important advantages to a more active participation of barangays in financing and delivering public services. One is that local government is moved closer to the people and a greater sense of involvement and participation is created, hopefully resulting in improved allocation of resources. Surely barangay officials are better able to determine most local project needs than are provincial and/or national officials. We need to know, however, more about the mechanisms by which barangay-level decisions are made, and how the MLGCD role has been worked out. The other advantage is that this greater local participation and a 10 percent property tax share to the barangay may increase the rate of tax collections, as local officials will see concrete benefits from convincing residents to pay property taxes. Moreover, the support of the barangay captain is more enthusiastically enlisted when it is known that the barangay share of collections will be retained.

Yet increased barangay participation also has its disadvantages. Whether or not equity is a problem (do the poorer barangays get relatively more or less?) is not known because the methods of allocating the General and Specific Tax allotments shares are ad hoc, and data on the actual distributions are not readily available. The property tax share is based on origin of collections and so one would expect a counterequalizing influence, that is, wealthier barangays in general and those in the poblacion (the urbanized area within the municipality) in particular, will benefit most. Perhaps the biggest problem is the capacity of the barangay to absorb revenue increases efficiently. The barangay budget process is not highly developed, and no mechanism or technical expertise to handle large sums of money seems to exist. The lack of technical project planning and financial management might be dealt with by assigning responsibility to a higher level of government, but this defeats the whole purpose of barangay involvement. Finally, there is the question of coordination of barangay project activities with the development plans of the city or municipality.

EVALUATION OF THE PHILIPPINE ALLOTMENT SYSTEM

It is not surprising, or even undesirable, for different grant programs to have different strengths and failings; no single program will accomplish several different objectives at the same time.[12] It is, however, important to examine the workings of the system as a whole: Are allocations being made among grant programs in roughly the desirable proportions? Is the program as a whole equitable? Do the several individual components reinforce each other to increase revenue mobilization by local governments, or are there offsetting effects?

Every grant program has two discretionary dimensions: determination of the total amount to be allocated and determination of the distribution of this amount among local governments.[13] The matrix in Table 4.8 suggests the possible combinations that a country may

TABLE 4.8

Possibilities for Structuring a Grant System

Methods of Distribution Among Local Governments	Methods of Determining the Grant Fund: Shared Tax	Ad Hoc	Cost Reimbursement	Revenue Totals
Origin of collection	*A* (L = 1.5%) (A = 3.2%)	. . .	. . .	L = 1.5 A = 3.2
Ad hoc	*B* (L = 27.0%)	*E* (A = 5.9%)	*H*	L = 27.0 A = 5.9
Formula	*C* (L = 71.4%) (A = 40.5%)	*F* (A = 50.5%)	. . .	L = 71.4 A = 91.0
Cost reimbursement	*D*	*G*	*I*	
(Column totals)	(L = 100.0) (A = 43.7%)	(L = 0) (A = 56.4)		

Key: L = Legal; A = Actual.

Sources: Roy Bahl and Johannes Linn, "Urban Public Finance and Administration in Less Developed Countries" (Washington, D.C.: World Bank), unpublished manuscript.

follow in structuring its grant system. The columns describe the methods of determining the total grant fund, and the rows describe the methods of distribution among local governments. For example, a type C grant is one in which the total grant fund is determined on a shared tax basis, for example, as a percent of BIR collections, and the distribution among local governments is made by formula. Various combinations of these methods are used by developing countries. Programs of the A and C type give local governments more control and autonomy in that the total grant distribution is a fixed share of some national tax, and the share of each local government is determined on some objective basis, that is, according to how much is collected in the local area or according to some predetermined formula. Program E provides maximum central government control because the total grant fund is determined by the central government and subject to change as the need arises, as is the distribution across local units. Programs B, F, and H are also relatively centralized options.

Local Autonomy

In the Philippines, the legal structure of the grant system provides for more local government autonomy than is found in practice. In theory, the system is a mixture of B and C programs, but in practice it is a more centralized combination of C, E, and F. The first column in Table 4.9 shows the typology of Philippine grants according to their legal definition, and the second according to actual practice.[14] Columns 3 to 6 compare amounts due with actual distribution and show that only about half of these funds were distributed in 1979. With these data we may compare the legal grant system with the grant system in practice, by entering legal and actual distributions in Table 4.8.

By law, all grant funds are to be determined as shared taxes (column 1) and 71 percent of this amount is to be distributed among local governments on a formula basis (row 3). In fact, only 43.7 percent of the total grant amount is determined on a shared tax basis, and 91 percent is distributed among local governments on a formula basis. The government has chosen to distribute only about half of total entitlements, and to do so primarily on a formula basis. Even here, however, the formulas frequently have been adjusted or constrained by PD.

One important concession to the formula distribution intent of the Philippine grant system came about with the increased allocation

TABLE 4.9

Legal and Actual Classification of Philippine Grant System (amounts in millions of current pesos)

Program	Legal Definition	Actual Practice	1979 Amounts Due	Percent of Total	Amounts Distributed	Percent of Total Distribution
Barangay share of local property tax collections	A	A	40.0[a]	1.5	40.0[b]	3.2
Barangay share of BIR General Allotment[c]	B	E	148.1	5.7	25.2[d]	1.9
Barangay share of Specific Tax Allotment[c]	B	E	175.0	6.7	25.2[d]	4.0
National Tax Allotment	B	E	379.7	14.6	52.0	4.0
Province, city, and municipal shares of BIR General Allotment	C	F	1,332.6	51.2	658.9	50.5
Province, city, and municipal shares of Specific Tax Allotment	C	C	525.1	20.2	528.9	40.5
Total			2,600.5	100.0	1,305.0	100.0

Note: Excludes local government contributions to barangay.

[a]1977 amount is latest available.

[b]Actual amounts distributed are not known.

[c]Amounts due.

[d]₱25.2 (2.6 not yet released plus 22.6 with advice of allotment for actual release).

Source: Computed by authors.

to the barangays. Paradoxically, this program, which was designed to move government closer to the people, resulted in a greater degree of centralization of the grant system, because it places a substantially greater amount of grant distribution under central government discretion. If these amounts are increasingly distributed, they will reduce the share of grants distributed on a formula basis, that is, they will be E-type grants.

Elasticity

Grants are not an income elastic revenue source for local governments. They have declined as a share of GNP in recent years, and this decline is in part responsible for the declining share of local governments in total government finances in the Philippines. In theory, however, the grant system has a much greater responsiveness to GNP than it has in practice, a problem that has come about because of central government policies.

Legally, all grants are tied in some way to tax collections. In the case where the basis is lagged BIR collections, this would have the decided advantage of a steady growth in the overall grant amount and a responsiveness of grants to real income growth and inflation. Much of this potential advantage has been lost—perhaps because of higher priority national economic objectives—by central government limits on the actual distribution. As a result, the BIR Allotment share of GNP has fallen from 0.44 percent in 1975 to 0.24 percent in 1980. The sharing of the tax on petroleum products does not result in an automatic growth in the grant fund because the tax rates are specific and the volume of petroleum consumption has not been increasing. Discretionary increases in the tax rates have been necessary to stimulate growth in the Specific Tax Allotment amount. The barangay shares of both allotments, and the National Tax Allotment, are shares of BIR collections and thus are responsive to inflation and real income growth, but again, only a small proportion has been distributed. Finally, there is a barangay share of the local property tax that is actually distributed but that is tied to a basically income inelastic tax. The most elastic component of the grant system—the BIR Allotment—has a statutory elasticity of about unity. From this, we guess that the statutory elasticity of the total grant system is less than unity.

The income elasticity of grant receipts to individual jurisdictions will vary depending on the rate of personal income growth in the community relative to the growth in lagged BIR collections. Because the system allocates increments more or less in proportion to the existing distribution, communities with more rapid income growth would face a lower grant income elasticity. For those grants allocated on an ad hoc basis, the income elasticity for individual jurisdictions depends heavily on the equalization objectives of the government. The more equalizing the distribution, the less elastic the system for jurisdictions with more rapid income growth.

Data are not available to allow an aggregate estimate of the income elasticity of the grant system. It is clear, however, that the grant share of total local government financing has been declining and that grants have been declining as a share of GNP. The grant system is not providing an adequately growing source of revenue for Philippine local governments. This finding raises an important problem. In a highly centralized system such as the Philippines, grants are given to local governments as a substitute for local government taxes in order to enable local governments to finance more than simply housekeeping functions. The income elasticity and responsiveness to inflation are important elements of the grant system in that they help the local government to keep up with growing expenditure needs. If the central government is not prepared to maintain at least the higher legal elasticity of the grant system, then it must consider the options of relinquishing a more elastic tax base to the local government, taking back some of the expenditure responsibility it has assigned them, or initiating a major program to improve local tax administration. An income inelastic grant system is simply not compatible with the decentralization objectives that are part of national government policy.

Equity

Again, the absence of data on actual grant distribution makes it difficult to determine whether grants are distributed, in aggregate, on an equalizing basis. The analysis above suggests that the BIR General Allotment is counterequalizing with respect to its distribution among municipalities, but neutral in its distribution among chartered cities. The Specific Tax Allotment, on the other hand, appears to be distributed on a mildly equalizing basis for both cities and municipalities. These two programs, which account for roughly 60 percent of all grants in the system and about 90 percent of all grants distributed, then, have offsetting effects. There are no data on the distribution of the barangay shares or the National Tax Allotment.

On a conceptual level, there is no reason to expect that the grant system in total will be equalizing. Measures of fiscal capacity or personal income do not enter into any of the distribution formulas. Indeed, that the Philippine grant system has not done a good job of distributing grant funds on an equalizing basis may not be a flaw in government policy. One could argue that the objective of equalization may only be accomplished by sacrificing the use of the grant system as a tool to mobilize more local government revenues. It is the local governments with greater fiscal capacity that have the leverage to use grant funds to increase local resource mobilization. Some smaller and poorer local governments may actually not be able to absorb increased grant flows. If one believes that the fiscal stimulation objective is paramount, then one could argue that equalization issues ought to be left to the national tax system and to the distribution of central government expenditures.

Stimulation of Tax Effort

We found no convincing evidence that the grant system is stimulative of local tax effort. Although the statistical analysis provides only tentative conclusions, it appears that the Specific Tax Allotment is more stimulative than the BIR Allotment, perhaps because capital expenditures require local matching in the form of supplementary expenditures or maintenance costs. In theory, the system is not designed to be stimulative of tax effort. No tax effort provision enters the formulas, and the grants are not conditional upon the local government providing a matching share of costs. For these reasons, if the barangay shares and the National Tax Allotment were fully distributed, the overall system would be even more substitutive. More data and testing are needed, but the evidence currently available points to a grant system that in practice is not stimulative, and if fully distributed could be substitutive.

Again, individual local jurisdictions might respond to the grant stimulus in different ways, and the estimates we have made are of the average behavior. We can speculate, however, about how different types of communities might respond. Where income is higher and the local budget is larger, the stimulative effect may be greater. Such communities have many potential advantages in leveraging grant funds: They can more easily raise additional taxes for maintenance and supplementary expenditures, they have a greater capacity to borrow, and they have better technical and financial management ability to absorb increased grants.

Economic Development Expenditures

Our results suggest that the Specific Tax Allotment does lead to more economic development expenditures than otherwise may have occurred. This change happens in two ways. First, the Specific Tax Allotment paid to the Infrastructure Fund is spent. Second, a higher level of grants to the Infrastructure Fund dampens the transfer from the General Fund to the Infrastructure Fund and results in more economic development expenditures in the General Fund. A single grant program of the same amount, such as a consolidated BIR, would not have accomplished as much stimulation of economic development expenditures.

Inasmuch as very little of the barangay aid or the National Tax Allotment has been distributed, we can say little about their effects on economic development expenditures. Potential effects will depend largely on whether steps are taken to ensure that these funds are not used as substitutes for other sources of funding.

Financial Management

The Philippine grant system could provide better incentives for effective financial management. A grant system that does not require a locai contribution is not as likely to induce local governments to be as accountable for how they spend the funds as is a system that requires some payment on the part of local governments. Furthermore, the grant system does not presently encourage effective financial planning. In its legal form, where the basis for grants is lagged three years (BIR) and two years (Specific Allotment), and where formula distributions are easily calculated, the system could be effectively integrated into the local government budgeting process. As practiced, however, the total grant amount is decided on an ad hoc basis, with much less certainty about the amounts to be distributed. This situation does not provide an incentive for effective financial planning and will be a deterrrent to any reform designed to make better use of local budgets as financial plans.

Central Government Flexibility

A final criterion in evaluating the grant system is the flexibility that the national government has in adjusting the system to meet the exigencies of national economic and social objectives. Particularly important here is the question of how easily the national government can shift the regional distribution of funds or slow the total flow to the local sector to accommodate more pressing national needs. The law suggests that the government has a great deal of control over the former via the ad hoc distributions of the National Tax Allotment and the barangay shares, but relatively little control over the latter because of the shared tax bases of determining the grant funds. In practice, just the opposite has resulted. Presidential decrees to limit the increase in grants and suspensions of full distribution have provided substantial flexibility to the central government. However, because the barangay shares and National Tax Allotment have been held back, the distributions actually made are formula-based, thus reducing the government's flexibility to affect the regional flow of funds.

NOTES

1. Under RA 2343, local units received 30 percent of the income taxes collected (in a jurisdiction) above the 1959 level.

2. Apparently the 1970 census results were to be used in computing the allocation, thus no jurisdiction-level changes would be made in the allocation formula until the 1975 census results were processed.

3. Whether this constraint is binding depends, oddly enough, on the rate of growth in BIR collections. PD 144, as amended, provides that the total grant fund (F) be related to BIR collections as

$$F_t = .2\,BIR_{t-3}$$

The municipal share is 40 percent, or

$$F_t^m = .08\,BIR_{t-3}$$

Any given municipality would receive an allotment (A_i) from

$$A_i = .7F_t^m P_i \Sigma P + .2F_t^m L/\Sigma L + (.1)(.00067)F_t^m$$

where the .00067 equals 1/1,500 (there are approximately 1,500 municipalities in the country). Substituting and eliminating the last term as inconsequential, we derive

$$A_{it} = (.056\;P_i/\Sigma P + .016\;L_i/\Sigma L)BIR_{t-3}$$

where A_i is the amount received, provided that it is not more than 15 percent above the 1971 allotment. The 1971 total grant fund (F) was

$$\hat{F}_t = .2\,BIR_{t-1}$$

and

$$\hat{F}^m_t = .08\,BIR_{t-1}$$

For any given municipality

$$\hat{A}_{it} = .7P/\Sigma P\hat{F}^m_t + .3\ L/\Sigma L\hat{F}^m_t$$

substituting

$$\hat{A}_{it} = (.056\ P/\Sigma P + .024\ L/\Sigma L)BIR_{t-1}$$

Now we may write, for example, that the entitlement for a municipality in 1977 is

$$A_{i,77} = (.056\ P_i/\Sigma P + .016\ L_i/\Sigma L)BIR_{74},\ \text{or,}$$

$$A_{i,77} = 1.15(.056\ P_i/\Sigma P + .016\ L_i/\Sigma L)BIR_{70}$$

whichever is less.

In this case, if the growth in BIR collections between 1971 and 1974 was greater than 15 percent, the constraint is not binding.

4. The city and municipal shares constitute only 65 percent of the total BIR Allotment in any single year. Barangays share in 10 percent of the total, and provincial governments account for the remaining 25 percent. Unfortunately, we were unable to gather the necessary data to analyze the equity implications of the provincial government distribution. Because there are no good data on the socioeconomic characteristics of barangays, analysis of this lowest level of government was also impossible.

5. Edward Gramlich, "Intergovernmental Grants: A Review of the Empirical Literature," in *The Political Economy of Fiscal Federalism,* ed. Wallace Oates (Lexington, Mass.: Lexington Books, 1977), Chapter 12.

6. Originally, we estimated the fiscal impact of BIR_p and STA_p using indirect least squares. Using various combinations of income, population, and urbanization variables, we were unable to explain much variability.

7. Equation (4.14) implicitly assumes that General Fund spending equals General Fund revenue, as the INP mandate refers to revenue, not spending. In light of the discussion of cash balances and surpluses in Chapter 1, this is obviously unrealistic; yet to encompass these features would greatly complicate the model and there are not adequate data on cash balances in any case. We would like to be able to fall back on the justification that our sample is large enough for these cash balances to wash out, but we do not have enough information to know if that is a reasonable assumption.

8. We realize that the t-statistics are only approximations in the second-stage equations and that, strictly speaking, we should not base our conclusions on the level of significance. Still, in the first stage results, the explanatory significance of the IF_p equation is quite low, which suggests that the predicted values

of IF_p will not vary a great deal around the mean. Moreover, the STA_p and BIR_p are not significant in three of four cases. Finally, the BIR_p variable shows a low level of significance in the second-stage equation.

9. Tax effort is measured here as the ratio of own source tax revenues (T) to personal income (Y).

10. Throughout this section Sorsogon is omitted from the analysis because of data problems.

11. The tax effort component, S_i, in the formula would simply be based on the size of a jurisdiction's tax effort relative to that of all other jurisdictions, that is,

$$S_i = \frac{T_i/Y_i}{\sum_i (T_i/Y_i)}$$

where T is total own source tax revenues in jurisdiction i and Y_i is personal income for the same jurisdiction.

12. Two good reviews of grant systems in developing countries are Lady Ursula Hicks, "Intergovernmental Relations with Special Reference to the Developed Countries," Occasional Paper no. 29, Metropolitan Studies Program, Maxwell School (Syracuse, N.Y.: Syracuse University, 1976); and Richard M. Bird, "Intergovernmental Fiscal Relations in Developing Countries," *World Bank Staff Working Paper No. 304* (Washington, D.C.: World Bank, 1978).

13. This approach is fully developed in Roy Bahl and Johannes Linn, "Urban Public Finance and Administration in Less Developed Countries" (Washington, D.C.: World Bank), unpublished manuscript.

14. We include as grants all intergovernmental transfers: the three allotment programs, the barangay share of the local property tax, and the local government grant to the barangay.

5

Local Government Public Enterprises

by DAVID GREYTAK and BENJAMIN DIOKNO

A more widespread and intensive use of local government public enterprises (LGPEs) is consistent with decentralization objectives of central governments. The advantages and disadvantages of using LGPEs for this purpose, however, vary for different kinds of enterprises and depend on the intended purpose of the enterprise.[1] An analysis of the relative merits and demerits is the purpose of this chapter. We first describe the general practice of LGPEs in the Philippines and then move to analysis of the success with market and commercial enterprises. Chapter 7 provides options for improved use of the LGPE form.

APPROPRIATE USE OF LOCAL GOVERNMENT PUBLIC ENTERPRISES

The undertaking by governments of what are termed enterprises has a long history in the developing countries. The operations have been of two general types. The most common variety relates to goods and services whose provision is characterized by high fixed costs—public utilities, for example. The second relates to the provision of a good or service that cannot or should not be trusted to the private sector. This latter category includes production activities whose provision is often undertaken by the private sector in developed countries but whose capital requirements, importance to development or stabilization, or social importance dictate the need for a government monopoly in developing countries—steel, airlines, mining, grain marketing, and liquor, for example.

One important question that arises is which public sector activities are proper candidates for provision through LGPEs. We offer three considerations that would aid in selection: management and accounting, marketability, and cost recovery through pricing.

A first criterion is that the efficient operation of a local government enterprise requires separate management. Consider the advantages. If the undertaking can be set off from the other public financing activities of the local government, then its pricing policies, production management, personnel management, and so forth, should also be separable. The public enterprise form frequently requires specialized, relatively expensive employees and services, which necessitates separation from the general public administration and its often limiting salary schedules. There are also accountability issues. Without some degree of administrative independence, it will not be possible to hold management of the entireprise accountable for the efficiency of its operations and for its financial performance. Additionally, the management of the enterprise can be effectively monitored only if there are separate accounts.

In theory, all local government activities other than general administration could fit this criterion of separate management and accounting, but for some it would be much less efficient to separate their operations than others. For example, a water supply system and a hospital might lend themselves to separate management more easily than the courts or public parks. The latter are too highly complementary with other local government activities (for example, police and fire, public works and maintenance) to make it efficient to separate their operations. Moreover, for some functions, input costs are so entangled with other local government purchases that separate accounts are impossible.

The second criterion involves marketability and pricing. The activity or operation should be involved in the production, distribution, or provision of marketable goods or services. This criterion excludes general government activities, such as tax collection and budgeting, as well as services that are not easily divisible into units of consumption.

The third criterion, cost recovery, requires that it be possible and feasible to price the output and to measure costs of production, and that there be some relationship between cost levels and price determination. If cost recovery is to be an objective, then some pricing rules must be followed.[2] The basic rule of efficient pricing is that price should be set equal to the current economic cost of the last unit produced, that is, price should be set equal to marginal cost. With this policy, resources would be allocated among productive activities in a manner consistent with the preferences of and benefits received by all consumers. Moreover, in the normal case, where unit costs are increasing, a marginal cost price would not only cover all costs but would generate a profit or surplus.

In the case of LGPEs, this basic pricing rule has two problems. The first is the sheer difficulty in identifying marginal cost, especially when the LGPE is selling a service such as access to a public market. The second problem arises when LGPEs are capital intensive and face decreasing unit costs of production.[3] In this case, an efficient (marginal cost) price will not lead to cost recovery and will require a general subsidy.

Regardless of the pricing rule followed, other impediments to cost recovery will arise. Some problems are related to income distribution considerations, such as regulating market fees to help maintain low prices for foodstuffs. In these cases the extent of cost recovery may not be realized under any pricing rules. Cost recovery requirements should be developed by the government with a view to determining what cutoff would make the enterprise form unacceptable. Again, it is most important that cost recovery be considered in light of the objectives of the specific enterprise form, particularly whether those objectives justify a public subsidy to guarantee continued operation or whether revenue generation itself is sought for the local government.

IDENTIFYING LOCAL GOVERNMENT PUBLIC ENTERPRISE POSSIBILITIES IN THE PHILIPPINES

The basic responsibilities and activities of local governments in the Philippines are set out in the Local Tax Code, PD 231, and in subsequent amendments. The types of enterprise activities that local governments may undertake to finance services are implied in Article 5, which states that local governments may levy fees, tolls, tuitions and charges for public markets and slaughterhouses, public utilities, cemeteries, schools, roads, bridges, canals, ferries and fisheries, and similar bases. Thus, local governments have broad authorization—explicit or de facto—to impose fees and charges.[4]

Legal Restrictions on Enterprise Profitability

Although it appears that income generation as a goal for LGPEs is being encouraged, it is not clear that the government has decided to permit local governments to substitute enterprise profits for general taxes. The possibility of enterprise surpluses has been recognized and there exists a general directive concerning the disposition of any surplus that may result from local government undertakings: They "shall be spent solely for the improvement of the public utility or the economic enterprise concerned" (PD 477, Section 13) or should revert to the General Fund.

However, the general legal intent appears to call for restricted use of any such surpluses. That is, profits available for general use are limited to 10 percent on net investment in the case of utility services and the use of profits from tolls for public works. Whether restrictions of this type would be applicable to any type of enterprise activity undertaken by local governments is uncertain, for there has been no clear specification of what constitutes a utility service. This concept needs to be clarified by the government if confusion about the use of many types of activities as alternatives to taxes as revenue sources is to be avoided.

Local Government Public Enterprise Options

We derived a comprehensive list of over 30 potential LGPEs from the COA account categories for local government. Many of these do not satisfy any of the three criteria discussed above and so are not considered here. There remain a number of more plausible candidates for LGPEs.

We grouped potential LGPE activities according to degrees of potential cost recovery (Table 5.1), based on the following considerations: Is the venture purely commercial, or are there social goals to be accomplished (and costs subsidized)? Does high fixed investment preclude a price that is both efficient and cost recovering? Is the size of the market adequate?

Full cost recovery is desirable for several reasons. First, where the social benefits from the enterprise are limited, subsidies are not justified. Second, full cost recovery requirements may act as a disciplinary measure, leading public enterprises to seek the most efficient and least costly means of serving their clientele. An additional consideration in classifying activities according to potential for cost

TABLE 5.1

Cost Recovery Prospects of Potential Local Government Public Enterprise Activities

All Areas	
Low	High
Schools (secondary)	Public markets
Zoos and other cultural institutions	Slaughterhouses
Airport landing fields and terminals	Farms and cattle ranches
Docks and wharves	Rock quarries
Tool roads, bridges, and ferries	Ice plants
Canals	Other private sector-type activities (stores, restaurants, manufacturing, processing, and so on)
Small Areas Only	Large Areas Only
Telephones	Telephones
Waterworks	Waterworks
Electric power	Electric power

recovery has to do with the relation between benefits and pricing, or more precisely with the degree to which the activity is beneficial to persons and groups other than those who directly pay for the use of the product or service. With efficient prices, individual purchases will be determined in relation to individual benefits; however, when there are externalities—the activities are also beneficial to society in general—too little of the good or service will be produced.[5] Common examples are immunization against contagious diseases and family or community improvement due to better education and/or cultural awareness. Thus, full cost recovery would be undesirable for hospitals, schools, and cultural activities such as zoos and museums.

For certain activities, an efficient (marginal cost) price may result in a loss. This is often the case with activities that require large initial investment outlays and for which, once the facility is in operation, the cost of providing additional units of service is relatively low. The appropriate pricing policy under these conditions is one that encourages consumption or use of the facility and thus reduces the average or per unit cost of providing output (or utilization of the facility). However, the efficient or marginal cost price will, in this

TABLE 5.2

Expenditures for Public Enterprise Activities by Type of Public Enterprise and Level of Government, 1977 (in thousands of pesos)

	Markets and Slaughterhouses	Waterworks	Cemeteries	Electric Plants	Other Public Utilities*	Total
Provinces	259	2,784	551	2,268	17	5,879
Cities	27,212	5,175	813	1,918	29,275	64,393
Municipalities	39,475	8,189	1,138	6,490	72	55,361
All local units	66,946	16,148	2,502	10,677	29,364	
			Percent Distribution by Level of Government			
Provinces	0.4	17.2	22.0	21.2	0.1	4.7
Cities	40.6	32.0	32.5	18.0	99.7	51.3
Municipalities	59.0	50.7	45.5	60.8	0.2	44.1
All local units	100.0	100.0	100.0	100.0	100.0	

*Primarily telephones and ice plants.

Source: Commission on Audit, *Report on Local Governments*, 1977.

case, result in something less than full cost recovery and will require a subsidy. Traditional examples of this type are toll roads, bridges, airports, and public utilities.

An important, although frequently overlooked, factor is the dependence of cost recovery on market size. When the initial investment costs are spread over large volume, the price that must be charged to achieve cost recovery can be lower. These considerations suggest that some activities like public utilities, bridges, and docks are quite expensive and will likely be able to recover costs only in more densely populated areas. Others, markets and slaughterhouses, are not so expensive and thus hold prospects for cost recovery in smaller or less densely populated areas.

Use of Local Government Public Enterprises in the Philippines

Available data on enterprise activities indicate that municipal governments account for the major share of traditional types of public enterprise—markets and slaughterhouses, waterworks, cemeteries, and electric plants (Table 5.2).[6] Cities are generally more active than provincial governments in using the public enterprise form and account for virtually all of the activity. Local government involvement with less traditional enterprise activities and business-type ventures is rare.[7] Revenue data in the COA accounts are not adequate to permit judgments about which enterprises and levels of government were most successful at cost recovery. Available data would suggest, however, that the provinces have done relatively well and that all three levels have experienced some success with markets and slaughterhouses.

PROBLEMS AND POTENTIALS OF MARKET ENTERPRISES

Public markets are the most common form of public enterprise activity in the Philippines. Markets also come close to fitting most of the criteria suggested above: Management and accounts can be separated, the "product" can be marketed to individuals, prices can be related to costs, and there are good possibilities for cost recovery. Even so, the financial success record of market operations has been questionable. To understand more clearly the financial success of market enterprises and the barriers to improved financial performance, we have undertaken a set of comparative case studies.

A cross section of 11 local government market operations was chosen for study. Although not drawn on a random basis, the sample is diverse. One city and one municipality are in Albay Province, one city and six municipalities are in Iloilo Province, and two municipalities are in Sorsogon.[8] Thus, one of the cities and three of the municipalities are located in the slow-growing Bicol region, and one city and six municipalities are located in the more prosperous Eastern Visayas region.

Fiscal Importance of Market Undertakings

Markets account for a significant share of the fiscal activity of local governments in the Philippines. In one sense, the gross revenue from markets may be compared to total local government taxes because it is claimed from the same underlying tax base, local area personal income.[9] When viewed this way, the fiscal importance of markets, particularly in smaller areas, comes to the fore. In most of the municipalities, the contribution of markets to total revenues ranges upward from about 15 percent. In two areas, Tabaco and Gubat, market activities account for roughly one-third of total revenues (Table 5.3).

Comparisons of gross market revenues with local government revenues raised from other sources again exhibit much variation. Yet even in those areas where the contributions of markets to locally raised revenues are smallest—Iloilo City, Oton, and Legaspi—they constitute more than one of every ten pesos. More commonly, markets account for upward of 20 percent of locally raised revenues; and in two areas, Tabaco and Gubat, the percentage is closer to 50 percent. An equally revealing comparison is that of market revenues to taxation. In Passi and Tabaco, gross revenues obtained from markets are about the same as those from taxation, whereas in Gubat, gross revenues obtained from the market exceed those from taxation by a rather substantial margin. Clearly, markets are important revenue sources to local governments.

Determinants of Revenues from Market Activities

All market undertakings are not equally successful in terms of cost recovery. The problem could lie either with inadequate revenues

TABLE 5.3

Population, Local Government Total Revenues, and Gross Revenues from the Operation of Markets, Selected Areas, 1978 (in thousands of pesos)

Local Jurisdiction	Population	Gross Revenue from Operation of Public Markets	Market Revenues as a Percent of Total Local Revenues	Market Revenues as a Percent of Locally Raised Revenues[a]	Market Revenues as a Percent of Local Taxes[b]
Barotac Nuevo (1979,[d] NA[e])	32,926	187	21.18	31.27	52.67
Dumangas (1974, 1964)	38,457	96	15.19	21.72	40.68
Iloilo City (1975, NA)	210,423	1,670	9.60	11.71	16.06
Miagao (1979, NA)	40,501	102	14.72	21.42	53.40
Oton (1976, NA)	36,120	51	8.99	13.21	36.43
Passi (1975, NA)	47,017	191	15.86	31.36	87.21
Tigbauan (1979, 1974)	27,443	77	18.97	29.84	45.29
Legaspi City[c] (1976, 1974)	89,613	544	9.59	11.38	18.29
Tabaco[c] (1979, 1974)	67,814	426	31.42	44.51	100.47
Gubat[c] (1979, 1976)	37,724	234	36.00	55.19	178.62
Sorsogon[c] (1978, NA)	52,075	153	14.93	19.82	38.44

[a]Locally raised revenue is revenue from taxation plus nontax revenue net of allotments and aids and contributions.
[b]Local taxes refers to revenue from taxation net of BIR allotments.
[c]Computed using 1977 figures.
[d]Date of present market fee ordinance.
[e]Date of previous market fee ordinance.

Sources: Population for 1975 is from several special releases of the Office of Executive Director, National Census and Statistics Office. Fiscal data are from selected local government financial reports to the Commission on Audit.

or with excessive costs. If the problem is on the revenue side, it may be with an inadequate pricing or market fee policy, or it may lie with an inadequate volume of business in the market. If the problem is on the cost side, it may stem from high operating cost, such as higher than necessary employment levels or from excessive capital cost. The revenue shortfall possibilities are explored here for the sample of 11 jurisdictions.

The Local Tax Code specifies that market stall fees must be set per meter of space per month/day and that higher rates be set for more favorable locations. Occupancy and entrance fees are no more clearly defined in the Local Tax Code except for a provision that entrance fees may be imposed on any convenient unit of measure, for example, weight or bundle, and they may not exceed the occupancy fee. The code also specifies that the schedule of market fees is established after public hearing by the local council, and the ordinance setting the fees is subject to review by the provincial treasurer in the case of municipalities and the Ministry of Finance in the case of cities.

In general, the sample markets conform to the specifications of the Local Tax Code. There is, however, substantial variation. Two markets prescribed a limited range of stall rental fees (Sorsogon and Passi), one relied heavily on entrance fees (Oton), and others opted for a combination of rental, entrance, and occupancy fees, which in one case (Tigbauan) involved a large number of different rates.

Revisions of market fees and rental schedules do not appear to be frequent (see Table 5.3). In five of the eleven areas, the ordinance governing market fees and rentals in 1980 was four or more years old. The other six had revised their ordinance in 1978 or 1979. This small sample suggests that the market rental and fee ordinance is revised every four or five years. The one factor said to hasten revisions is growth in the volume of market activities.

Recommendations for fee increases are generally made by the treasurer and mayor, in light of discussions with vendors or vendor associations. However, in a variety of instances, the levels finally passed by the Sangguniang Bayan (the local council) were reported to be below those recommended by the treasurer and/or the mayor. The reason given for the lower rates was the fear that higher fees would be passed on to consumers and thus be inequitable. The belief that market fees should be higher seems stronger among those whose concern is with fiscal position–mayors, treasurers, the Ministry of Finance, and the Ministry of Local Government and Community Development.[10] Alternatively, those most directly responsible to local constituencies, the members of local councils and committees,

TABLE 5.4

Per Capita Market Revenues, Average Stall Fees, Stall Occupancy Rates, and Market Proximity, Selected Local Governments

Local Jurisdiction	Per Capita Market Revenue (in pesos)	Average Stall Fees[a] (in pesos)	Stall Occupancy Rates[b]	Number of Smaller Markets Within 20 Kilometers	Number of Larger Markets Within 20 Kilometers
Barotac Nuevo	5.68	₱1.00	99.2	NA	NA
Dumangas	2.50	0.78	100.0	0	2
Iloilo City	7.94	NA	100.0	5	0
Miagao	2.52	0.31	100.0	2	1
Oton	1.41	1.50	84.8	NA	NA
Passi	4.06	1.77	98.5	3	0
Tigbauan	2.81	1.45	100.0	1	1
Legaspi City	6.07	0.37	100.0	1	0
Tabaco	6.28	0.34	100.0	2	0
Gubat	6.20	1.36	NA	2	1
Sorsogon	2.92	1.49	NA	NA	NA

NA = Not available.

[a]Average stall fee (ASF) for i^{th} jurisdiction is computed as follows: $ASF_i = (\sum_{j=1}^{m} r_{ij}) / n_{ij}$, where n_{ij} = number of commodity classification rates considered (see Table 5.11) and r_{ij} = the market rental rate for j^{th} commodity in the ith local jurisdiction.

[b]Stall occupancy rate is defined as the number of fixed stalls occupied as a percent of the total number of fixed stalls.

Source: Case study survey data.

favor lower market rentals and fees. In our sample, the price stability and equity concerns have been dominant.

The structure of market fees also reflects equity considerations. Rental rates for meat, fish, and dry goods stalls are consistently among the highest; those for fruits and vegetables are generally the lowest. In the absence of data on the consumption of the various classes of goods sold in the markets, it seems reasonable to assume that expenditures for meats, fish, and dry goods are likely to be larger on the part of higher income groups. Alternatively, the more plentiful and less luxurious foodstuffs such as fruits and vegetables probably constitute a larger part of the diets of low income households and are of less importance in the budgets of higher income families. The general structure of market fees and rental rates then appears to have been influenced by equity considerations.

A reasonable argument can be made, however, that increases in fees charged vendors would have no appreciable effect on very low income families. Whether the burden of market fees and fee increases is shifted to consumers is a matter of conjecture, but, given the relatively low market rates, it is unlikely that an increase would have a significant effect on the prices charged in the market. For example, if the stall fee for a meat vendor were ₱2.00 per square meter per day for a stall of four square meters, a 10 percent increase in the rental fee would increase the cost by only ₱.80 per day.[11] This would seem to be a small amount; indeed, it would be less than half of 1 percent of revenues if the vendor had sales of no more than ₱160 per day. For lower fee rates, such as ₱1 per meter per day and smaller stalls of three square meters, for example, the corresponding amount is 30 centavos per day, which would be half of 1 percent of revenues if sales were as low as ₱60 per day. This implies that even if the entire increase were passed on to consumers, a 10 percent increase in fees would have a very small effect on prices (less than 0.5 percent) and indeed not all such increases would fall on low income consumers.

Another constraint to increasing market fees is the fear that occupancy rates would fall because some vendors might take their business elsewhere. For this to be a valid concern, profit margins would have to be quite small or a competitive private sector market would have to exist. While we have no estimates of the income earned by market occupants, it would seem that existing market fees are not so high as to discourage market occupancy. Of the markets considered here, all or most fixed stalls are occupied (Table 5.4).

The volume of sales is an important determinant of total revenues. If the minimum volume is not there, the market will not be a financially viable proposition, no matter what the pricing policies. Volume, not pricing, is the key to the success of municipal markets. However, growth in volume is determined largely by external factors.

The municipal officials surveyed on this issue responded that the volume of market activities depends greatly on whether the local market is able to draw consumers from other municipalities. We have no direct information on the commuting range for market activities, but indirect evidence suggests that larger and more accessible markets are more successful. If vendors come to the more popular markets in greater numbers, then larger revenues from increased entrance and occupancy fees will result.

It does appear that markets in adjacent jurisdictions compete with each other. Those markets that produce large amounts of revenues relative to the population of the municipality in which they are located are within 20 kilometers of smaller markets. The clear implication is that the influence of larger markets is spread over broad areas, creating a degree of competition among markets. Whether the competition is such that some smaller markets are rendered unprofitable cannot be determined from available data. But this gives rise to the possibility that the smaller ones may have difficulty in making the market a profitable undertaking.

Expenditure Levels

There is a substantial variation in the level of expenditures among the markets included in this survey (Table 5.5). Clearly, expenditures for the larger markets are larger, but size alone cannot account for all of the variation.

The search for a more efficient market operation inevitably leads to consideration of whether market employees are overpaid relative to the work they perform. In our sample this problem does not appear to be major, as the standards for rates of public employee compensation are set nationally. In fact, it has been suggested that higher wages and salaries for market personnel could lead to improved market efficiency.[12] A more general concern, and one that has been expressed in a number of market studies, is that employment levels may be too high and that market employees are not put to effective use.[13]

An examination of the average employee compensation (Table 5.6) reveals a consistent pattern. Compensation rates are higher in the cities and larger municipalities and lower in smaller municipalities.

TABLE 5.5

Market Expenditures, Total and by Type, Selected Local Governments, 1979 (in thousands of pesos)

Local Jurisdiction	Total Expenditures (1)	Expenditures on Current Operations: Total (2)	Personal Services (3)	Maintenance and Repairs (4)	Capital Outlays (5)
Barotac Nuevo	222.7	143.1	87.2	55.9	79.6
Dumangas	212.8	206.1	35.9	170.2	6.7
Iloilo City	2,237.1	1,215.7	702.7	513.0	1,021.4
Miagao	36.5	35.6	22.4	13.2	0.9
Oton	71.8	71.8	57.8	14.0	0.0
Passi	374.4	238.5	165.3	73.2	135.9
Tigbauan	105.3	52.2	40.8	11.4	53.1
Legaspi City	405.6	355.0	164.5	190.5	50.6
Tabaco	232.3	230.7	177.4	53.3	1.6
Gubat	98.7	95.7	84.2	11.5	3.0
Sorsogon	1,705.4	173.6	119.5	54.1	1,531.8

Notes: Column (1) is the sum of columns (3), (4), and (5). Column (2) is the sum of columns (3) and (4).

Includes expenditures for travel and transportation, supplies and materials, printing and binding, freight and delivery service, repair of equipment, rental of building and grounds, maintenance and repair of fixed property, illumination and power service, communications, adjudications, contracts, losses, discretionary, and other services.

Source: Case study survey data.

In part, these differences reflect the fact that compensation rates are set in relation to the type and class of the governmental unit. A more important reason for the variation in compensation rates is the composition of employment. In the cities and larger municipalities, markets are supervised by a separate administration that, although located within the treasurer's office, is basically self-contained. In these cases, the market plantilla (work force) includes administrative positions of higher salary grades, such as market master; higher level staff positions, such as senior level collectors; and a number of skilled clerical positions, including bookkeepers and accountants. In the

TABLE 5.6

Employment and Compensation of Market Workers, Selected Local Governments, 1979

	Number of Workers	Personal Service Expenditure per Worker	Market Revenue per Worker	Productivity Index*
Barotac Nuevo	16	P2,325	P17,275	172.75
Dumangas	10	3,590	9,170	117.56
Iloilo City	99	7,091	18,896	NA
Miagao	8	2,800	14,012	452.00
Oton	NA	NA	NA	NA
Passi	29	5,700	10,769	60.84
Tigbauan	NA	NA	NA	NA
Legaspi City	23	7,152	26,400	713.52
Tabaco	28	6,336	20,475	602.23
Gubat	11	4,927	23,682	174.13
Sorsogon	18	6,639	14,244	95.60

NA = Not available.
*Market revenues per employee (in 100 pesos) divided by average stall fees.
Source: Case study survey data.

smaller areas, market administration is a function of the treasurer, who, along with his staff, discharges the supervision and clerical duties of the market operation. As a result, in smaller markets, staff listed on the plantilla of the treasurer's office perform many of the administrative and support tasks necessary for the operation of a market, while the market plantilla consists primarily of staff positions (collectors, cleaners) of the lower salary grades. Thus, the composition of market plantillas explains a large part of the variation in average compensation levels.

A frequent practice is to gauge the effectiveness of the market plantilla in terms of market revenues per employee. This measure is rough, as the ratio may vary because some jurisdictions charge higher market fees, because of more efficient utilization of the work force, or because of scale economies—that is, a work force is inherently more productive in larger markets. In our sample, revenues per employee are lower in the smaller markets and higher in the larger markets (Table 5.6). On a weekly basis, market revenues per employee range between a rough average of ₱544 in Legaspi to about ₱200 in Passi and Dumangas. On average, the amounts are surprisingly low. However, when compared with the rates of employee compensation, the revenue ratios do not appear so low. In fact, revenues per employee in most cases are two to four times larger than per employee personal service costs. These differences imply that expenditures on market personnel are well spent.

The possibility still remains that some markets operate more efficient than others, that is, that fewer employees are required to perform a given amount of work. This proposition is particularly difficult to evaluate because there is no flawless way of separating the effects of market charges from the effects of employee efficiency on revenue productivity. By dividing market revenues per employee by average stall fees, however, it is possible to construct a productivity index that identifies employee productivity (Table 5.6).[14] The index gives a rough approximation of the number of employees required to earn a fixed amount of revenues in a standardized market size. A low index indicates low productivity and a high index indicates high productivity.

Limitations notwithstanding, the distribution of this index suggests a separation of these case study areas into two groups, one characterized by higher productivity and the other by lower productivity. In the former group are areas with relatively large market plantillas: Iloilo City, Legaspi City, and Tabaco. The areas in which the productivity indexes are low are those with the smaller market plantillas: Barotac Nuevo, Dumangas, Gubat, and Sorsogon. Between these two groups the difference in the indexes is quite large, suggesting the possibility that the number of employees required to operate markets increases less than in proportion to the volume of market activities. That is to say, there may be scale economies to be realized in the operation of public markets. Areas with a population of less than 40,000 (Barotac Nuevo, Dumangas, and Gubat) all score low on the productivity indexes, and higher productivity indexes are associated with the larger areas (Legaspi City, Tabaco, Miagao, and Passi). The one exception to this pattern is Sorsogon's low productivity, which can be traced to the interruption of its market activities by the major renovation of its facilities.

The second major component of market expenditures is capital outlays. The problem with comparing capital expenditures across jurisdictions is that they are "lumpy." That is, they are large in years of construction and small at other times. Some of the areas

TABLE 5.7

Estimated Book Value of Market Structures, Capital Outlay, and Estimated Capital Costs, Selected Local Governments, 1979 (in thousands of pesos)

Local Jurisdiction	Estimated Book Value of Market Structures	Capital Outlay	Annual Capital Cost	Ratio of Capital to Total Expenditures	
				Budget	Our Estimate
Barotac Nuevo	469	79.5	70.8	25.1	33.1
Dumangas	124	6.7	18.7	3.1	8.3
Iloilo City	2,899	1,021.4	588.7	45.7	32.6
Miagao	294[a]	0.9	44.4	.3	55.5
Oton	162	0.0	24.4	0	25.3
Passi	243	135.9	36.7	36.3	13.3
Tigbauan	475	53.1	71.7	50.4	57.8
Legaspi City	NA	50.6	—	12.5	—
Tabaco	1,255[b]	1.6	189.5	.7	45.1
Gubat	800[c]	3.0	120.8	.3	55.9
Sorsogon	1,580[d]	1,531.8	238.6	89.8	57.9

NA = Not available.

[a]Computed from the Commission on Audit Financial Report, 1978, unadjusted and undepreciated.

[b]Based on the Government Service Insurance System loan in 1965.

[c]Based on the Development Bank of the Philippines loan of ₱800,000 for market construction and improvement.

[d]Major reconstruction valued at ₱1,004 million was done in 1979.

Sources: Columns (1) and (2), unless otherwise noted, are from the case study survey data. Capital outlays are those capital expenditures reported in the market accounts. Estimated capital costs are calculated as the annual amortization payment required to pay off a 14 percent, 20-year loan in the amount of the book value of the market structure.

surveyed in 1979 were involved in the construction or major renovation of market facilities (Table 5.7) and thus their reported capital expenditures are higher than might normally be the case, which, of course, gives a distorted picture of annual capital costs and profitability. From an analytic point of view, we are interested in measuring capital costs as the use or depletion of resources that result from market operations during a given year. Such values are not generally reported, and moreover, annual capital outlays as reported in market accounts do not provide a measure of the opportunity cost of capital. These values are related to the annual costs of "using up" the market facilities. This problem led us to develop a method of estimating annual capital costs.

To determine annual capital costs, we used estimates of the book values of market structures and a set of assumptions about depreciation rates. The data in Table 5.7 contrast reported capital expenditures with estimates of the annual amounts by which the book value of the market structure depreciates, assuming a 20-year useful life and an interest rate of 14 percent. That is, we have estimated capital cost as the annual amount of money that would be required to repay a loan in the amount of the book value of the market structure at the indicated terms. These are probably low estimates of capital cost for two reasons: First, our assumed borrowing rate of 14 percent is low, and, second, the loan amounts required are based on the book value of existing structures and therefore represent the original cost of construction rather than current replacement costs.

Given the concern with the extent to which public markets recover costs, accurate estimation of capital costs is essential. Our calculations, conservative as they are, might be used to indicate the importance of capital costs in market operations. To obtain such a measure we divide our estimate of capital costs by the sum of the operating costs and estimated capital costs. This yields a measure of the capital share of the total costs of market operations, which may be compared with the ratio of capital to operating expenditures actually reported in the government accounts (see Table 5.7). Note first that the share of capital expenditures as reported in local government budgets is, with only three exceptions (Iloilo City, Passi, and Sorsogon), lower than our estimate of capital share of market costs. The implication is that local government accounts generally understate the importance of capital as a determinant of the costs of local markets. Note, too, that when measured in terms of local government budget data, markets in most areas (seven) do not appear to be capital intensive, as their capital outlays account for less than 25 percent of total expenditures. However, when measured in terms of estimated annual capital costs, the capital share appears to exceed 40 percent.

One consequence of underestimating capital costs and therefore overestimating profitability warrants special mention. Central government regulations limit the profits of "utility" services to an amount equal to 10 percent of net investment. Surplus in excess of that amount is to be plowed back into the service either for price reductions or for the improvement of the facility. If markets were governed by this regulation, an interesting situation could arise. The "excess" profits—resulting from improper cost measurement—could put pressure on local officials to maintain market charges and fees at levels that are already too low. Instead of stimulating cost recovery by permitting rate increases, this regulation may well add to the deficit.

It might also be noted that as the cost of constructing or improving markets tends to be paid during the relatively short period in which construction actually takes place, costs reported in a market account will be high and profits low during the construction period. It appears that this is the reason for the high capital outlay and apparent low profitability in the four areas (Barotac Nuevo, Iloilo City, Passi, and Sorsogon) where major market investments were underway. Once construction is completed and construction costs are paid, capital outlays will fall and reported profits will rise. Thus, they too eventually may be subject to pressures to maintain market fees and rates at low levels.

These considerations shed some light on the shortcomings of current procedures for measuring capital costs. As noted, a more appropriate measure of the cost of using capital is some estimate of the value of resources that are used up by the operation of the market. We have suggested that one approach is to measure the cost of replacing the market structure, an approach similar to the general accounting convention of establishing depreciation and investment reserve accounts.

This approach, though it may require some crude assumptions, clearly identifies the determinants of what investing in a market may cost a local government. The initial cost is, of course, the outlay required to build a facility. Certainly the larger and more elaborate the building or the improvements attached to it, the greater the capital costs. Construction expenditures, however, do not give a full measure of capital costs, for the very act of tying up resources in a structure means that the local government must forego the opportunities to use those resources for other purposes. That is to say, by tying up resources in a market, the local government's ability to spend on other activities or to reduce tax loads is reduced, not just during the period of construction but in the future. One way to see this drain is to consider the implications of funding the construction by means of credit financing. In this case, the recurrent amortization payments reduce the amounts of revenues available for other uses.

The extent to which amortization payments are a drain on local tax resources depends on the length of the amortization period and the rate of interest charged, as well as on the amount borrowed. We

TABLE 5.8

Amortization Payment Required to Reproduce Book Value of Current Market Structure, Selected Local Governments (in thousands of pesos)

Local Jurisdiction	Rate of Interest = 14%			Rate of Interest = 18%		
	$n = 10$	$n = 15$	$n = 20$	$n = 10$	$n = 15$	$n = 20$
Barotac Nuevo	89.9	76.4	70.8	104.4	92.1	87.6
Dumangas	23.7	20.2	18.7	27.6	24.4	23.2
Iloilo City	747.5	634.8	588.7	867.6	765.8	728.4
Miagao	56.4	47.9	44.4	65.4	57.7	54.9
Oton	31.0	26.4	24.4	36.0	31.8	30.3
Passi	46.6	39.6	36.7	54.1	47.7	45.4
Tigbauan	91.1	77.3	71.7	105.7	93.3	88.7
Legaspi City	—	—	—	—	—	—
Tabaco	240.6	204.3	189.5	279.2	246.5	234.4
Gubat	153.4	130.2	120.8	178.0	157.1	149.4
Sorsogon	302.9	257.2	238.6	351.6	310.3	295.2

Note: n is the number of annuity periods (years). The values of market structures considered in the computation are from column (2) of Table 5.7.

Source: Computed by authors.

TABLE 5.9

Profitability of Markets as Reported and as Estimated Under Selected Assumptions About Interest Rate and Asset Life (in thousands of pesos)

			Estimated Profitability			
	Reported Profitability		Overall Surplus (in thousands)		Percent Return on Book Value of Asset	
Local Jurisdiction	Surplus[a]	Surplus on Current Account[b]	Low Capital Cost[c]	High Capital Cost[d]	Low Capital Cost	High Capital Cost
Barotac Nuevo	53.7	133.3	62.5	41.2	13.3	8.8
Dumangas	-121.1	-114.4	-133.1	-138.8	-107.3	-111.1
Iloilo City	-204.4	817.0	228.3	51.2	7.9	1.8
Miagao	75.6	76.5	32.1	18.8	10.9	6.4
Oton	-22.6	-22.6	-47.0	-54.4	-29.0	-33.6
Passi	-62.1	73.8	37.1	26.1	15.2	10.7
Tigbauan	-19.6	33.5	-38.2	-59.8	-8.0	-12.6
Legaspi City	245.1	295.7	NA	NA	NA	NA
Tabaco	340.7	342.3	152.8	95.8	12.2	7.6
Gubat	169.3	172.3	51.5	15.2	6.4	1.9
Sorsogon	-1,395.7	136.1	-102.5	-174.2	-6.5	-11.0

NA = Not available.

[a]Revenues from market operations less total (current and capital) expenditures.

[b]Revenues from market operations less operating expenditures.

[c]Interest rate of 14 percent and loan maturity of 20 years.

[d]Interest rate of 18 percent and loan maturity of 15 years.

Source: Revenues from market operations are from case study data. Total expenditures and total expenditures on current operations are from Tables 5.7 and 5.8.

have constructed different estimates of capital costs based on different loan assumptions. In one set we have assumed an interest rate of 14 percent and three repayment periods—10, 15, and 20 years. In the second set we have assumed an interest rate of 18 percent and the same repayment periods (Table 5.8). Thus, there are six different estimates of capital cost.

One interesting result of these calculations is the sensitivity of annual payments to the maturity period and to the interest rate. Lower interest rates and longer repayment periods reduce the annual repayment costs. In the case of Sorsogon, for example, at an 18 percent interest rate for a 15-year period, annual capital costs are estimated at ₱310,300. Alternatively, at a lower interest rate, 14 percent, for a period that more closely approximates the 20-year life span of a market building, the capital cost is ₱238,600. The difference, ₱71,700, is a substantial amount and shows the potential impact on local treasuries of alternative capital costs. Even at relatively favorable terms (14 percent and 20 years), amortization payments can amount to as much as 50 percent of market expenditures. Given this finding one might be tempted to question the advisability of policies that are designed to stimulate local government investments in public markets unless pricing policies are to be adjusted or further subsidies provided.

Profitability of Markets

At first blush it would appear that as a general proposition the operation of markets by local governments as profit-generating or even as cost-recovering activities is doubtful (Table 5.9). When profits are calculated from the revenues and cost data reported in the local budgets, only five of the areas surveyed report current revenues in excess of current operating expenditures and capital outlays, while the remaining six show a deficit. Although these data imply that the operations of markets are as likely to require a subsidy as to produce a surplus, such a conclusion may be misleading because of the problems in defining "profitability" and measuring capital costs.

Considering the question of profitability first, an analysis of the current account position shows that nine of the eleven markets studied generated revenues that exceeded current operating expenditures (Table 5.9). Generally, the current account surpluses are quite large. This result is surprising for some of the smaller areas in light of the findings above concerning possible scale economies and low employee productivity. Indeed, given current levels of rental rates and stall occupancy fees, most markets would continue to show a current account surplus even if current expenditures were to be as much as 50 to 100 percent more than those reported.

Something might be learned by considering the reasons for operating deficits in Oton and Dumangas. Oton imposes relatively high market fees but has a relatively low stall occupancy rate (Table 5.4). The problem is a deficient volume of market activity, probably caused more by proximity to larger markets in Iloilo City than by high fees. If such is the case, and if the Oton market is not competitive, revisions in the fee structure will not likely bring an operating surplus.

The opposite situation exists in Dumangas—the occupancy rate is high but market fees are low. It would be tempting to take this as an indication that a revision of the fee structure could produce enough new revenues to cover the operating deficit. However, the deficit is so large that fees would have to be more than doubled for the current volume of activities to produce revenues sufficient to cover costs. Here, too, it would appear that volume, or lack of it, is the underlying cause of poor revenue performance.

Two conclusions thus emerge. The first is that markets generally have the potential to cover operating costs and at least a portion of capital costs. General operating subsidies would not seem warranted.[15] The second is that in areas that do not cover operating costs, the problem tends to lie with inadequate volume and probably more with proximity to larger markets than with a fee structure that is out of line.

What portion of capital costs can markets be expected to recover? We might answer this question from the sample of the jurisdictions under study here by comparing the current account surplus with estimated annual capital costs. The results, for a low and high capital cost scenario, are described in columns 3 and 4 of Table 5.9. For example, the current account surplus of ₱133,300 in Barotac Nuevo is larger than either of our estimates of capital costs. Thus, this market generated revenues sufficient to cover its current operating and capital cost with ₱62,500 left over under our low cost scenario. The surplus amounts to a return equivalent of 13.3 percent of the book value of the original investment and a little more than 7 percent of total current revenues of the municipality (Table 5.3). That is to say, it is a profitable undertaking.

More generally, the results of these comparisons are less encouraging. They indicate that even under the better of the terms—20-year loans at 14 percent interest rate—only six of the ten market operations could show an overall surplus. Two of the other four where comparisons are possible, Dumangas and Oton, did not generate revenues sufficient to cover even operating costs and thus required an operating subsidy. Two others, Tigbauan and Sorsogon, did generate a current account surplus, but it was far from adequate to cover amortization payments, even under the low capital cost assumption. These two areas may be exceptional cases as their revenues were below "normal" during this period because they were involved in market renovation and expansion.

Among those markets that appear to be profitable, some have relatively high market fee rates (Barotac Nuevo, Passi, and Gubat) and some have low market rates (Miagao and Tabaco). Some are in large jurisdictions (Iloilo City and Tabaco), and others are in smaller municipalities. Employee productivity is high in some (Miagao, Tabaco, and Gubat) and is low in others (Barotac Nuevo and Passi).

SUCCESS WITH LOCAL GOVERNMENT BUSINESS ENTERPRISES: THE CASE OF BULACAN

There has been much interest in the Philippines in the financial success of four commercial enterprises operated by the provincial government of Bulacan: Hiyas ng Bulakan Convention Center (HBCC), Hiyas Galeria, Hiyas Cafetorium, and Hiyas Agro-Commodities Center (HACC). The first three can be considered nontraditional because they are not usually undertaken by local governments in the Philippines. The fourth, the provincial slaughterhouse (a major component of the Hiyas Agro-Commodities Center), is a traditional local government undertaking but in Bulacan it is managed in a nontraditional way. Indeed, all of these enterprises are characterized by their unusual management and/or operational arrangements.

Considering the very low level of public enterprise activity in the Philippines, the magnitude and variety of Bulacan's undertakings are quite impressive not only in terms of the amount of internal funding that was generated to cover the capital cost of these projects but also in terms of the pace at which the four enterprises were developed. In the aggregate, the construction and equipment costs were approximately ₱10.2 million—₱2.163 million for the Hiyas Agro-Commodities Center, ₱6.919 million for the Convention Center, and ₱1.158 million for the Hiyas Galeria and the Hiyas Cafetorium.

Performance Evaluation

One may legitimately ask how "performance" is to be measured. The answer depends on whether one evaluates economic or financial profitability, whether a short- or long-run view is taken, and on the measurement of costs and benefits.

Financial Versus Economic Profitability

The performance of these enterprises can be evaluated in two ways: financial profitability and economic profitability. Financial profitability is concerned with the present value of the stream of cash flows–revenues less current operating costs–over the lifetime of the project or enterprise, in relation to the initial capital outlay. The enterprise is deemed profitable if, at an appropriate discount rate, the present value of the enterprise's cash flow at market prices exceeds the initial capital outlay.[16] In contrast, economic profitability is concerned with the value of all benefits attributable to the project in relation to the value of all costs (opportunities foregone) as a consequence of undertaking the project. In practice, economic profitability adjusts the cash flows by applying "shadow" or efficiency prices[17] to inputs and outputs and by including indirect benefits and costs, that is, those that are attributable to the project but are not consequences of its primary objective.

The primary concern of this study is financial profitability. The importance of indirect social benefits are acknowledged where appropriate, but these considerations do not enter into our calculations of profitability. In point of fact, there is no strong evidence that these enterprises, with the exception perhaps of the slaughterhouse, are serving any significant social objectives. The one sense in which we do consider economic criteria is in attempting to approximate the annual cost of capital to the local governments.

To evaluate the long-run impact of these enterprises to the province of Bulacan, the net present value (NPV)[18] of the enterprises will be estimated. In addition to the NPV, we will estimate the internal rate of return (IRR).[19] The performance criteria, based on financial profitability, are as follows: (1) NPV–the enterprise is profitable if the discounted cash flow (DCF) exceeds the initial capital outlay or, alternatively, if the NPV is greater than zero. (2) IRR–the enterprise should be undertaken if the IRR exceeds some predetermined rate of interest. It should be noted that if the problem posed is whether or not to proceed with a given project or enterprise, the

NPV and IRR criteria would give the same result if the same rate of discount is used (for instance, the social rate of time preference, that is, the valuation of present consumption relative to future consumption). However, if the problem is how to choose among a set of mutually exclusive projects, given some budgetary constraint, the conventional wisdom is to choose from a set of projects whose IRR exceeds the appropriate discount rate, the one with the highest NPV.[20]

There is one final remark. The IRR and NPV may or may not be the same if these enterprises were undertaken in the private sector. It would be reasonable to argue that private firms would have a higher IRR and NPV because of their profit-maximizing behavior, that is, because the net revenue flow would be greater. Evidence of poor management of public enterprises, due partly to lack of cost minimizing behavior of public enterprise managers is well documented.[21] Moreover, because public enterprises are generally limited in their response to market factors by laws, regulations, and policies on various aspects of public enterprise operation, the observed IRR and NPV may be somewhat understated. This latter point will be carefully examined in the individual case studies.

Method

We consider two major estimation problems: how to compute the annual cost of capital that is required for the short-run analysis and how to estimate the net cash flow of any given enterprise. Implicit in both problems is the need for information on initial capital outlay. For convenience, and in the absence of a good estimate of the replacement costs, we take the historical book value of fixed assets (including structure and facility but excluding land) as the initial investment. Because of inflation, the historical book value will drastically underestimate the true worth of the structure and facilities.

Estimating Capital Costs

In real terms, the cost of capital to be covered should include depreciation and the opportunity cost of financing the project from internal sources. The usual procedure of assuming straight-line depreciation, ignoring the opportunity cost of financing, would grossly underestimate the cost of capital. To make a more appropriate estimate of capital costs, we assume that the investment required to cover the costs of the facilities was financed through a loan. What, then, is the yearly return from the enterprise necessary to repay a loan equivalent to the investment at a given interest rate for a given

TABLE 5.10

Estimated Amortization Required to Replace Book Value of Fixed Assets, Excluding Land, Selected Public Enterprises, 1980 (in thousands of pesos)

Enterprise	Book Value of Fixed Assets Excluding Land	Rate of Interest = 14 Percent			Rate of Interest = 18 Percent		
		$n = 10$	$n = 15$	$n = 25$	$n = 10$	$n = 15$	$n = 25$
Hiyas Agro-Commodities Center	2,163	363	309	276	408	360	335
Hiyas ng Bulakan Convention Center	6,919	1,164	988	883	1,305	1,152	1,073
Hiyas Galeria*	1,158 (Galeria and Cafetorium combined)	117	99	89	131	116	72
Hiyas Cafetorium*		78	66	59	87	77	108

Note: n is the number of annuity periods (years).

*The two enterprises are situated in the same building. No separate figures for the value of fixed assets are available. We assume on the basis of observed space occupied by the two enterprises that Hiyas Galeria accounts for 60 percent of the building, with Hiyas Cafetorium accounting for the remainder. Accordingly, the estimated amortization is assigned on the basis of that assumption.

Source: Book value of fixed assets (excluding land) is based on data supplied by the Office of the Provincial Treasurer, province of Bulacan.

number of years? The answer, simply stated, is the annual amortization required to replace the fixed asset evaluated at its historical book value. We employ alternative assumptions: that the period of the loan or else the life span of the structure and facilities is alternatively 10, 15, and 25 years, and that the interest rate is alternatively 14 or 18 percent. The former is the current interest rate charged by the Land Bank of the Philippines, the latter by the Development Bank of the Philippines.

The estimates of the annual amortization required to reproduce the existing fixed assets based on historical book value are presented in Table 5.10. Hence, for the Convention Center, under the most conservative assumptions (a 14-percent rate of interest and a 25-year loan maturity), an annual capital cost of ₱883,000 results. Under the least favorable terms, the annual capital cost is ₱1.305 million, or 47.8 percent higher. To give some idea of magnitudes, these amounts are 58.0 and 85.8 percent, respectively, of total operating costs.

The local official may well ask how there can be an annual capital cost when the project was financed from surplus. The answer is that there still is a using up of the facility on a year-to-year basis, and this depreciation has to be covered in the pricing structure if the activity is to continue in the long run. Viewed another way, there is a need to replace the original internal funds used in the construction. The fact that cash flow commitments are less because no loan was involved is not relevant to measuring profitability, but it is relevant that the expended funds are not now available for other uses.

The possibilities for measuring net present value and internal rate of return are limited by inadequate data on cash flow. No feasibility studies were prepared before the undertaking of these enterprises, and, in any case, it is doubtful whether such feasibility studies would have adequately dealt with the usual problems of demand estimation and forecasting. It is therefore assumed in this estimation that the cash flow for the last three years will closely approximate the future net benefits of the project. We used alternatively the three-year average cash flow and the "best year" cash flow—the former to minimize the bias from abnormal years, the latter in recognition of the fact that these enterprises are rather new and that they are still essentially operating in the "learning-by-doing" phase. In effect, what we propose to do is re-create the financial appraisal process using observed data on revenues and costs during the last three years.[22]

Hiyas Galeria

Hiyas Galeria was the first of the four enterprises established. It is primarily a business venture whose success may be measured by its profitability, although it also serves some broader purposes in that it is a promotional center for local handicrafts such as brass ornaments, furniture, cabinets, leathercrafts, textiles, and needlecrafts and serves as a broker for local craftsmen.

Sales in the Galeria are made on consignment basis with a 10 percent markup on producer supply price. Total sales for the year ending December 31, 1979, were about ₱1.395 million. Deducting the total payments to consignors, amounting to ₱1.263 million, the commission earned (or total revenue) for 1979 was about ₱132,000.[23] Various efforts have been considered and undertaken to stimulate the volume of sales. First, a liberal credit policy was extended to provincial government employees and employees of the central government working in Bulacan. Promotion of exports has been considered. The Galeria has also considered a working capital lending program. In fact, it has established a ₱100,000 fund in the provincial treasury for this purpose. Because there is a legal prohibition of local government loans to individuals, but not of joint ventures between local government and cooperatives, the Galeria and the provincial government have initiated the organization of a local handicraft producer cooperative.

This enterprise is operated as a regular government department. The Galeria superintendent is not hired on a contractual basis. His salary plus the salaries and wages of some 30 other employees involved in sales, inventory, stock, and accounting are paid out of the provincial budget. The total cost of maintenance and repair and other miscellaneous expenses for the year ending December 31, 1979, was ₱27,836, and the salaries and wages totaled ₱178,680, for a total current operating budget of over ₱200,000.[24] This sum does not include depreciation or any allowance for the replacement of the existing structure. Our estimate of annual capital cost is between ₱89,000 and ₱131,000, depending on the interest rate and asset life assumed (see Table 5.10).

Profitability

With an operating budget in 1979 of over ₱200,000 and net revenues from sales of ₱104,431, the Galeria clearly is not covering even its current expenditures. Put another way, it received an operating subsidy of about ₱95,000 and a total (operating and capital) subsidy of between ₱184,000 and ₱226,000 in 1979. These results are consistent with the overall impression given by local officials that this enterprise has not been financially self-supporting.

Conclusions

On the basis of the above analysis, and the limited data, two general conclusions can be drawn. First, Hiyas Galeria has not been covering its current costs and therefore has been a drain on the provincial treasury of Bulacan. On the other hand, it can be argued—and in fact has been argued by Bulacan local officials—that the objective of this enterprise is not to generate revenue but rather to promote cottage industries in Bulacan. This argument raises two questions. One is whether the province sees this objective as being worth ₱200,000 (a rough estimate of the Galeria deficit) per year in general revenue subsidy. The other is whether the Galeria has made a *net* contribution to stimulating cottage industry in any case. Assuming a competitive environment, it can be reasonably argued that products placed at the Galeria would have been sold elsewhere if it had not been established.

Second, the poor financial performance of this enterprise appears to be influenced considerably by some factors exogenous to internal management: the 10 percent markup pricing rule (assuming that pricing decisions are beyond the Galeria superintendent's discretion), the legal restrictions on extending loans to individual producers, and the wage and employment structure.

Hiyas Cafetorium

The Hiyas Cafetorium caters to tourists, domestic travelers, and employees of the provincial government. Of the four public enterprises operated by the province of Bulacan, it is the most autonomous, being run on a contract management basis.

The primary objective of the Cafetorium is financial profitability, but there are also important nonpecuniary benefits. Hiyas Cafetorium has been, for instance, an informal meeting place of government employees to whom it offers discounted rates. It can be reasonably argued, as some provincial officials do, that the frequent interaction among government officials has improved their knowledge of the operation of the provincial government and, hence, their performance.

TABLE 5.11

Hiyas Cafetorium, Short-Run Performance Indices, 1977–79 (in pesos)

	1977	1978	1979
	Basic Data		
(1) Gross sales	1,169,358	699,906	816,976
(2) Total expenditures[a]	1,084,942	631,597	779,649
(3) Intermediate inputs	722,612	373,763	493,589
(4) Salaries and wages	196,165	134,953	154,893
(5) Maintenance and repairs[b]	166,165	122,881	131,167
(6) Current account surplus[c]	84,416	68,309	37,327
(7) Estimated annual cost of capital[d]	59,000	59,000	59,000
(8) Full accounting surplus (deficit)[e]	25,416	9,309	-21,773
	Percentage Distribution of Total Expenditures		
Intermediate inputs	66.6	59.2	63.3
Salaries and wages	18.1	21.4	19.9
Maintenance and repairs	15.3	19.5	16.8
	Other Measures of Financial Performance		
Total expenditures as a percentage of gross sales	92.8	90.2	95.4
Current accounts surplus as a percentage of gross sales	7.2	9.8	4.6

[a] (3) + (4) + (5).

[b] Includes gas, fuel, and transportation expenses, supplies, cleaning and paper, miscellaneous expenses, representation expenses, employer ECC, Medicare and Social Security System contributions, telephone expenses, and electric expenses.

[c] (1) – (2).

[d] See Table 5.10.

[e] (1) – [(2) – (7)] = (6) – (7).

Source: Computed from income statements submitted by Hiyas Cafetorium to the Commission on Audit.

Over a three-year period, revenues have fluctuated from ₱1.169 million in 1977 to ₱699,900 in 1978 and to ₱816,900 in 1979 (Table 5.11). Because of this short history and the dramatic fluctuations, it is difficult to make any kind of statement about this enterprise's revenue performance. The largest single item of expenditures for the Hiyas Cafetorium is the purchase of intermediate inputs, which has constituted about 63 percent of total expenditures during the three-year period. Salaries and wages accounted for about one-fifth of total expenditures.

Hiyas Cafetorium is under an operating contract arrangement. As the recent Commission on Audit report states: "The operation of the Cafetorium is being undertaken independently and is operating [in a] private business-like manner."[25] This arrangement was created to avoid government wage rate and benefit regulation. As a result, there is no plantilla of personnel to be found anywhere in the provincial budget. By avoiding the wage and employment restrictions that apply to regular agencies of the local governments, workers are employed according to the level of activity of the Cafetorium and are paid at wages approximating the market wage rates. The provincial government is also able to save on labor-related costs such as life insurance, retirement, and medicare contributions.

The Hiyas Cafetorium, by virtue of the operating contract arrangement, is considered a nongovernmental entity. An important outcome of this arrangement is that it does not have to belong to the Government Service Insurance System (GSIS). Rather its social security obligations are to the Social Security System (SSS), whose employee benefits are more restricted and thus less costly. Thus, its social security contribution as a percentage of salaries and wages was 5.3 percent in 1977, 5.5 percent in 1978, and 6.1 percent in 1979—considerably less than what the enterprise would have had to pay if its employees were regular government workers. This type of cost reduction clearly indicates the benefits to local governments of separate, that is, contract enterprise, arrangements.

But still, the current account surplus of the Cafetorium has not been large and it has been declining: ₱84,416 in 1977, ₱68,309 in 1978, and ₱37,327 in 1979 (Table 5.11). As a percentage of gross sales, the current account surplus was 7.2 in 1977, rose to 9.8 in 1978, and then dipped to 4.6 in 1979. As a result, both current and full costs were covered in 1977 and 1978 but a deficit of ₱21,773 was necessary in 1979 (under the most conservative assumptions of capital costs).

TABLE 5.12

Hiyas Cafetorium, Results of Financial Analysis (in 1980 pesos)

Assumptions		Investment Criteria			
		Net Present Value		Internal Rate of Return	
Number of Years of Project	Discount Rate	"Best" Year	Three-Year Average	"Best" Year	Three-Year Average
$n = 15$	$r = .14$	52,940	-76,040	16.25	10.61
	$r = .18$	-35,310	-142,267		
$n = 25$	$r = .14$	114,330	-30,010	17.87	12.98
	$r = .18$	-3,780	-118,580		

Source: Computed from case study data.

Based on an extrapolation of recent data, 1977 to 1979, the long-run financial profitability of Hiyas Cafetorium appears marginal. The results suggest that its viability as a profit-making enterprise depends on its ability to operate at its past "peak" level, 1977, and even then it would appear to be a questionable investment. An enterprise or project becomes viable in the long run when its net present value, given some predetermined rate of interest, is greater than zero. At an 18 percent rate of interest, Hiyas Cafetorium, even on the basis of its best performance during the last three years, fails this test (Table 5.12).

Some important policy lessons can be learned from this enterprise. First, there seem to be no legal restrictions in establishing an independently run local government business venture. Under an operating contract arrangement, enterprise management may enjoy wide discretion in wage and employment decisions. Second, an analysis of profitability may give different results, depending on whether one considers the short run or long run and on whether indirect effects are taken into account. Ostensibly, the Cafetorium is a viable proposition. It generated a positive cash flow by covering full costs in two of the past three years, and we project the internal rate of return on this investment at between 10 and 17 percent. Even this performance, however, does not mean that the Cafetorium is a "good" investment for the provincial government.

In the long run, profitability requires establishing that a return greater than 10 percent is not available elsewhere for the local government. In any case, even this relatively low rate of return may be overstated for two reasons. One is the failure to count indirect effects, that is, the fact that competing restaurants now do less business and employ fewer resources than before (the Cafetorium) and hence pay less property, occupation, and business tax than before. The other is the very conservative way we have estimated depreciation, using historical book value. The much higher actual reproduction cost would raise the annual cost of capital and reduce profitability.

Hiyas Convention Center

The Hiyas ng Bulacan Convention Center (HBCC) was established in July 1975 to provide facilities for conferences, seminars, and training for government and private agencies and organizations in Bulacan and neighboring areas. As a matter of policy, the HBCC leases out its facilities at rates that allow it to cover current operating costs.

TABLE 5.13

Hiyas Convention Center, Short-Run Performance Indices, 1977–79

	Basic Data			
	1977	1978	1979	Growth Rates, 1977–79 (Percent)
(1) Revenues[a]	873.1	1,797.5	1,515.0	73.5
(2) Current Expenditures	865.4	1,518.5	1,520.9	75.7
(3) Salaries and wages	174.6	310.6	352.6	101.9
(4) Maintenance and repair	690.8	1,207.9	1,168.4	69.8
(5) Capital outlays[b]	2,822.6	171.0	245.2	NC
(6) Estimated annual cost of capital[c]	883.0	883.0	883.0	—
	Performance Indices (Excluding Accounts Receivable)			
(7) Current account surplus[d]	7.7	279.0	-5.9	
(8) Full accounting surplus (deficit)[e]	-875.3	-604.0	-888.9	
	Performance Indices (Including Accounts Receivable)			
(9) Revenues including accounts receivable	933.9	1,944.0	2,273.0	
(10) Current account surplus[f]	68.5	415.5	752.1	
(11) Full accounting surplus (deficit)[g]	-814.5	-467.5	-398.7	

NC = Not calculated.

[a]Gross profit from sales.

[b]General Fund and Infrastructure Fund.

[c]See Table 5.10.

[d](1) – (2).

[e](1) – [(2) + (6)].

[f](9) – (2).

[g](9) – [(2) + (6)].

Source: Computed from data furnished by the provincial treasurer's office and income statements submitted by Hiyas Convention Center to the Commission on Audit.

From ₱873,000 in 1977, revenues more than doubled in 1978 (₱1.798 million) and then tapered off to ₱1.515 million in 1979. The drop in revenues in 1979 is more a reflection of collection problems than of the volume of business. If the accounts receivable were added to revenues, the adjusted figures would be ₱933,900 for 1977, ₱1.944 million for 1978, and ₱2.273 million for 1979 (see Table 5.13).

While open to all possible clientele and types of activities, the HBCC has been catering primarily to government-sponsored conventions and training programs. As a result, the rates set prior to April 1979 were based on the amount of per diem given by the government to employees attending seminars and conferences at the convention center. However, recent rate increases have been necessitated by price increases, particularly for food and wages. The new daily rates of ₱39.50 for meals and ₱20.00 for lodging took effect in April 1979. Even at higher levels these rates seem competitive. An HBCC comparative study of hotel facilities in San Fernando, Pampanga (approximately 21 kilometers away), showed that food and accommodation costs were about ₱78 per individual per day.

The volume of convention activity depends largely on factors that are beyond the enterprise management's control—principally, central government policy. For example, while the occupancy rate in 1979 was above 80 percent, it fell to 45 percent during the first quarter of 1980 as a result of LOI 981, which prohibited the expenditure of government funds for attendance at conventions, seminars, workshops, and other similar activities conducted by private groups. While the attendance of government officials and staff may be authorized, the payment of fees, per diem, and transportation expenses may not. In addition, except for the Career Executive Service Course offered by the Development Academy of the Philippines and other programs approved by the chairman of the Civil Service Commission and the Ministry of the Budget, all live-in training programs sponsored by government agencies were suspended. The convention center's vulnerability to such a limitation on government-sponsored training is, of course, exacerbated by its heavy reliance on one type of clientele (government employees). As a postscript, LOI 981 has recently been rescinded.

Current expenditures have grown by 75.7 percent over the three-year period, primarily because of rising nonlabor costs. Maintenance and repair, the single most important expenditure item of this enterprise—representing nearly 80 percent of total expenditures in 1979—has increased by more than two-thirds during the period. The rising cost of food and beverages has been another major contributing factor to the dramatic growth of total expenditures. Salaries and wages increased by 77.9 percent from 1977 to 1978 but by only 13.5 percent from 1978 to 1979. As might be expected, the magnitude of these increases corresponded to the level of enterprise activity.

From 1977 to 1979, revenues, defined here as gross profit from sales, rose by 73.5 percent, while current expenditures grew at a slightly faster rate of 75.7 percent. The financial performance of this enterprise during the last three years has been erratic. Its current account surplus rose from ₱7,000 in 1977 to ₱279,000 in 1978 and then dropped dramatically to a deficit of ₱5,900 in 1979. The overall deficit has been substantial. HBCC has received a subsidy of no less than one-half million pesos during the last three years: ₱875,300 in 1977, ₱604,000 in 1978, and ₱888,900 in 1979.

HBCC's financial performance, however, is not quite so dismal as the above figures would seem to indicate. One of its problems, as mentioned earlier, is an inability to collect unpaid accounts. Among the biggest nonpayers are the Ministry of Human Settlements (₱280,205), Ministry of Agrarian Reform (₱92,194), Human Settlements Regulatory Commission (₱98,059), and the Rural Roads Program (₱53,264). As of December 31, 1979, the accounts receivable of the convention center amounted to ₱965,247. If these amounts were collected, the center would certainly cover its current operating costs. More importantly, at least for the last two years (1978 and 1979), it would have covered all current costs plus about half of the estimated annual amortization for the replacement of its fixed assets. While this would result in a positive cash flow, the enterprise would still not be breaking even.

To minimize nonpayment, a new policy has been instituted. Organizations that want to rent the facilities are now required to pay 30 percent of the estimated costs of the service in advance, with the balance due within seven days after the convention. This policy might go a long way toward reducing delinquent payments, but the problem may not be fully solved unless there is a penalty for late payments. The legal restriction on the imposition of interest and surcharges on the initial fees and charges due should be reconsidered. Yet, can a provincial enterprise reasonably expect to penalize a central government ministry?

The possibilities for cost recovery, which seem real enough by these estimates, are based on a very conservative assumption about depreciation allowance. This important source of underestimation of costs arises from a computation procedure based on the historical or book value of fixed assets rather than on replacement cost. The costs

TABLE 5.14

Hiyas Convention Center, Results of Financial Analysis (in 1980 pesos)

Assumptions		Investment Criteria			
		Net Present Value		Internal Rate of Return	
Number of Years of Project	Discount Rate	"Best" Year	Three-Year Average	"Best" Year	Three-Year Average
		Assumption (a): 100 Percent Collection Efficiency			
$n = 15$	$r = .14$	-2,300,090	-4,388,430	6.84	-0.139
	$r = .18$	-3,090,130	-4,821,270		
$n = 25$	$r = .14$	-1,750,560	-4,087,350	9.84	3.34
	$r = .18$	-2,807,890	-4,666,630		
		Assumption (b): Present Collection Efficiency Will Continue			
$n = 15$	$r = .14$	-5,205,340	-6,320,140	-5.71	-15.15
	$r = .18$	-5,498,450	-6,422,570		
$n = 25$	$r = .14$	-5,001,450	-6,248,890	0.06	-6.81
	$r = .18$	-5,393,730	-6,385,980		

Source: Computed from case study data.

of replacing the HBCC building alone has doubled; one local official estimated it at ₱10.8 million.

The implication of the NPV calculations is that, in the long run, the net effect of the Hiyas Convention Center on the provincial treasury will be negative. Even under the best possible set of assumptions—100 percent collection efficiency, 25-year project life, rate of interest of 14 percent, and a level of activity equivalent to recent "peak" performance—the enterprise stands to lose ₱1.75 million (see Table 5.14). That is, an alternative investment of equal amount, which yielded a 14 percent return, would earn ₱1.75 million more over the same 25-year period. Under the worst possible scenario—the present collection efficiency, discount rate of 18 percent, 15-year project life, and a level of activity equivalent to the average level of operation during the last three years—the loss will amount to ₱6.42 million.

Based on varying assumptions, in four out of eight cases considered the computed IRR is negative. More importantly, even under the best possible set of assumptions, the computed IRR is only 9.84, a rate of return on investment much lower than the prevailing government lending rates of 14 to 18 percent and certainly considerably less than existing commercial loan rates.

The financial loss taken from a broader national viewpoint may be even greater. To the extent that the Hiyas Convention Center is, on balance, substitutive (in the sense that it has drawn away business from similar facilities in the adjoining provinces, including Metropolitan Manila), then there may be some other indirect costs associated with it. First, it can be reasonably argued that the profitability of the hostel and convention centers is less than it would have been if the centers did not compete with the HBCC. The immediate effect is a decrease in tax revenues they pay, either in the form of municipal business tax or income tax. Moreover, the ensuing excess capacity—vacant rooms and unused dining facilities—in such centers reflects a misallocation of resources that could rightfully be counted as indirect costs.

But even with these broader social considerations aside, the long-run profitability of Hiyas Convention Center is not very promising. Past experience suggests that it can be expected to break even at a discount rate of about 10 percent. Under the "best" possible set of conditions, it has an implied rate of return considerably lower than prevailing government lending rates. The implication is that the provincial government has overinvested in this enterprise.

Hiyas Agro-Commodities Center

The Hiyas Agro-Commodities Center (HACC) began operations in 1976. It was established mainly to stabilize prices to livestock producers and facilitate the flow, handling, and processing of livestock and meat producers of Bulacan; that is, it was initially set up as a price support program to serve the municipalities in Bulacan Province. The market prices of livestock and meat producers, however, have risen so much that there is no longer a need for a price support program. Its main activity at present is the slaughtering of livestock.

The existing rate structure, based on Tax Ordinance No. 6, April 16, 1980, is patterned after that of Metro Manila. A comparison of the slaughterhouse fees imposed by HACC with those set by other local units surveyed suggests that Bulacan, along with most local governments, imposes the maximum slaughter fees permitted. Bulacan, however, imposes a wider array of slaughterhouse fees than do most local governments. As a result, revenues from slaughterhouse fees, excluding postmortem fees, rose by 137.5 percent over the 1977–79 period (Table 5.15).

Besides the rate structure, another contributing factor to the profitability of this enterprise is its high level of activity. HACC caters primarily to suppliers in three municipalities in Bulacan: Marilao, Obando, and Malolos. The nearest slaughterhouse is located in Balagtas, approximately 5 to 6 kilometers away; within a 20-kilometer radius, there are seven smaller slaughterhouses. But perhaps because of its location near major transportation routes, HACC undoubtedly dominates within Bulacan Province. Indeed, a great deal of slaughterhouse activity was recently diverted to HACC after the closing of some 17 slaughterhouses in greater Manila.[26] But, still, HACC's slaughterhouse activity goes beyond the confines of Bulacan. Because its facilities are one of the few classed A-1, animals slaughtered at HACC can be transported anywhere in the country.

Operating and Capital Costs

From 1977 to 1979, current expenditures grew by 61.1 percent, considerably less than the growth rate of revenues. Salaries and wages, which constitute about three-fourths of total current expenditures, increased by 30.7 percent, and repair and maintenance costs (including utilities) increased by 171.8 percent (Table 5.15). While there is a separate set of accounts for the enterprise, costs do not include a depreciation or allowance for replacement of the existing building and equipment. Also ignored is the imputed rent for the land on which the slaughterhouse building and facilities were constructed.

A unique feature of the enterprise operation is the way it has shifted part of its costs to the slaughterhouse users—food manufacturers and meat dealers. The usual arrangement is that butchers are paid by the sponsoring local governments. Under the Bulacan setup, however, butchers must register with HACC, but they are paid by the meat dealers and food manufacturers. Although we do not have a firm peso estimate, the amount saved by the provincial government must be considerable.

The arrangement is noteworthy for two reasons. First, it provides a way of circumventing a nationally set wage schedule that may be inappropriate for a given local unit and public enterprise facility. In this case, the effective slaughter fees have been increased over and above the national maximum. Second, by shifting part of the cost of slaughterhouse operation to the private sector, it increases the cash flow and the profitability of the undertaking. From the point of view of ease of administration, level of taxpayer resistance, and other benefit taxation arguments, the strategy of mobilizing public funds by shifting the costs to public enterprise users may be preferable to increased enterprise prices or taxation.

Financial Profitability

The disposition of the postmortem fees is an important issue, as it may affect the profitability measures. Table 5.15, therefore, shows HACC's financial performance using two assumptions on the postmortem fees: (1) the total amount reverts to the central government, and (2) 70 percent of postmortem fees are retained at the local level while 30 percent reverts to the central government.

Over a three-year period, the current account surplus rose enormously. On the assumption that the postmortem fees revert to the central government, the current account surplus increased by 668.2 percent, to ₱390,866 in 1979. At this level of current account surplus, HACC slaughterhouse recovered full costs in 1979 with a surplus of ₱114,866. If we assume that 70 percent of postmortem fees are retained at the local government level, we can estimate that full costs were recovered as early as 1978, two years after the beginning of operations, with a surplus that reached ₱649,425 in 1979. To give some perspective, the surplus, as a percentage of book value of fixed assets, was 3.56 in 1978 and 30.0 in 1979 (Table 5.15).

TABLE 5.15

HACC Slaughterhouse, Short-Run Performance Indices, 1977–79 (in pesos)

	Basic Data			
	1977	1978	1979	Growth Rates, 1977–79 (percent)
(1) Revenues excluding postmortem fee	403,946[a]	511,832	959,545	137.5
(2) Revenue from postmortem fee[b]	247,401	365,133	763,656	208.7
(3) 70 Percent of postmortem fee	173,181	255,593	534,559	208.7
(4) Current expenditures	353,066	414,483	568,679[c]	61.1
(5) Salaries and wages	277,061	308,899	362,124	30.7
(6) Maintenance and repair	76,004	105,584	206,555	171.8
(7) Capital outlays	234,224[a,d]	346,055[d]	–	–
(8) Estimated annual costs of capital[e]	276,000	276,000	276,000	–

(Continued)

TABLE 5.15 (Continued)

	Basic Data			
	1977	1978	1979	Growth Rates, 1977–79 (percent)
	Assumption: Postmortem Fees Revert to the Central Government			
(9) Current account surplus[f]	50,880	97,349	390,866	668.2
(10) Full accounting surplus (deficit)[g]	-225,120	-178,651	114,866	NC
	Assumption: 70 Percent of Postmortem Fees Retained at the Local Level; 30 Percent Reverts to the Central Government			
(11) Current account surplus[h]	224,061	352,942	925,425	313.0
(12) Full accounting surplus (deficit)[i]	-51,939	76,942	649,425	NC

NC = Not calculated.

[a]Source: Ministry of Finance budget operation statement.

[b]Data from provincial treasurer's office, January 14, 1981.

[c]For 1979, the annual budget is ₱675,296 disaggregated as follows: ₱432,296 for salaries and wages and ₱243,000 for repair and maintenance.

[d]Financed from the Infrastructure Fund.

[e]See Table 5.10.

[f](1) – (4).

[g](1) – [(4) + (8)].

[h][(1) + (3)] – (4).

[i][(1) + (3)] – [(4) + (8)].

Source: Computed by authors from data supplied by the provincial treasurer's office and the Ministry of Finance.

TABLE 5.16

HACC Slaughterhouse, Results of Financial Analysis (in 1980 pesos)

Assumptions		Investment Criteria			
		Net Present Value		Internal Rate of Return	
Number of Years of Project	Discount Rate	"Best" Year	Three-Year Average	"Best" Year	Three-Year Average
		Assumption (a): Postmortem Fees Revert to the National Government			
$n = 15$	$r = .14$	₱232,450	₱-1,059,870	16.16	2.88
	$r = .18$	-177,280	-1,248,550		
$n = 25$	$r = .14$	523,630	- 949,240	17.77	6.64
	$r = .18$	-25,990	-1,197,540		
		Assumption (b): 70 Percent of Postmortem Fees is Retained at the Local Level; 30 Percent Reverts to the National Government			
$n = 15$	$r = .14$	₱3,520,960	₱ 913,000	42.6	21.99
	$r = .18$	2,548,750	386,860		
$n = 25$	$r = .14$	4,197,210	1,278,960	42.8	25.38
	$r = .18$	2,896,070	574,830		

Source: Computed from case study data.

The prospective performance of Hiyas Agro-Commodities Center, then, depends on how postmortem fees are handled. Under the "best" possible set of assumptions, the computed net present value of the enterprise is about ₱4.197 million. That is, over its 25-year life, the HACC investment will generate a revenue flow sufficient to cover all costs and provide a return of ₱4.2 million (valued in today's pesos). The set of best assumptions includes retention by local governments of 70 percent of postmortem fees, 25-year project life, rate of interest of 14 percent, and a level of activity that approximates that of 1979, its peak year. If we assume, however, that all postmortem fees revert to the national government, the project life is 15 years, the rate of interest is 18 percent, and that the level of enterprise activity will be the same as the average for the last three years, Hiyas Agro will be a huge drain to the provincial treasury. The financial loss will be ₱1.248 million (Table 5.16).

The computed IRR under each of the eight sets of assumptions shows that in six of eight cases, this enterprise's IRR will exceed the prevailing government lending rates and in some cases the current commercial loan rates as well. On the basis of computed NPVs and IRRs, this enterprise is undoubtedly the most profitable of the Bulacan enterprises.

This enterprise is clearly recovering its current costs and has the potential of recovering its "full" costs, even on the assumption that postmortem fees revert to the central government. This impressive financial performance can be partly attributed to three factors: its cost-reducing arrangement of shifting part of the costs to HACC users, its propitious market position (proximity to Metro Manila where several slaughterhouses were shut down), and its A-1 classification. The second reason strongly suggests the limited replicability of this enterprise. The HACC enterprise has shown, however, that while there are legal and administrative impediments to unconstrained public enterprise operation and pricing, they are not overly restrictive. That is, there exists a possibility for effective local response.

Conclusions

The success of the Bulacan provincial government with business enterprises has been uneven. In three of four cases there has not been a record of financial profitability, partly because of external factors, and it is not clear that the long-term performance will be markedly better. In this connection, it is noteworthy that financial feasibility studies were not carried out prior to establishing any of these enterprises. On a more positive note, there have been management successes, particularly as regards the skill and flexibility of local officials in responding to potentially harmful central government policies.

The Bulacan experience makes a good case for central government involvement in the planning stage for private ventures. Two issues arise here. The first is the need for external review of whether the proposed undertaking has reasonable prospects for financial success. The second relates to whether this type of local government investment ought to be undertaken without review and approval in terms of coordination with the goals of the national development plan.

NOTES

1. Much has been learned about the effectiveness of large national public undertakings. A valuable case study on the topic is Leroy P. Jones, *Public Enterprise and Economic Development: The Korean Case* (Seoul: Korean Development Institute, 1975). For a review of more recent studies, see Malcolm Gillis, "Role of State Enterprises in Economic Development," *Social Research* (January 1981). A discussion of the definition of a public enterprise is provided in Andreja Bohm, "The Concept, Definition and Classification of Public Enterprises," *Public Enterprise* (1981): 72–78. Much less is known about local government enterprises in developing countries.

2. The approach espoused by Jones (op. cit.), involves a mandatory degree of cost recovery as a condition for using the public enterprise form.

3. For a discussion of appropriate pricing policies for decreasing cost industries, see, for example, R. Saunders et al., "Alternative Concepts of Marginal Cost for Public Utility Pricing: Problems of Application in the Water Supply Sector," *World Bank Staff Working Paper No. 259* (May 1977); and for electric power, see M. Munasinghe and J. Warford, "Shadow Pricing and Power Tariff Policy," *World Bank Staff Working Paper No. 286* (June 1978).

4. The imposition of any tax, fee, or charge by a local government requires a legislative act, an ordinance passed by the governing local board or council (Section 39).

5. While such externalities may be either positive or negative, our focus is on positive externalities that justify subsidies.

6. The MOF is presently undertaking such a survey.

7. The enterprise activities of Bulacan Province (discussed below) constitute an exception to this generalization.

8. Two additional areas were included in the original survey. However, the data provided were not sufficient to permit inclusion in this analysis. The areas were Barotac Viejo, Iloilo, and Malinao, Albay.

9. Although some larger markets draw from a much larger area, they may also tap the taxable capacity of smaller, nearby jurisdictions.

10. For a statement of these views, see Ministry of Local Government and Community Development, *Public Markets Manual for Local Units*, Manila, undated.

11. These examples are taken from the market in Passi, which revised its fee rates in 1979 to levels that are relatively high in comparison with the other markets considered here.

12. Orlando R. Garcia, *Market Administration Study, Goa, Camarines Sur,* study undertaken in cooperation with the Department of Local Government and Community Development and the Local Counterpart Committee of the Municipality of Goa, Camarines Sur, February 1975.

13. Ibid.

14. The productivity index is calculated from revenue data reported in Table 5.6 and stall fees reported in Table 5.4.

15. Such subsidies can be a substantial drain on general revenues. We estimate here that the Dumangas deficit is equivalent to about 15 percent of general revenues.

16. The discounted present value of the stream of net cash flows, hereafter referred to as discounted cash flow (DCF), is computed as follows:

$$\text{DCF} = \frac{R_1 - C_1}{(1+r)^1} + \frac{R_2 - C_2}{(1+r)^2} + \ldots + \frac{R_t - C_t}{(1+r)^t}$$

or

$$\sum_{t=1}^{n} \frac{R_t - C_t}{(1+r)^t}$$

where R_t and C_t are revenues and current operating costs of the enterprise at period t, respectively; n is the time horizon of the project in years; and r is the rate of discount.

17. Shadow price, in contrast to market or observed price, is what economists may calculate as the price of the commodity or factor (for example, land, labor and capital) under ideal, competitive conditions. Alternatively, it may be viewed as the true scarcity value of any given resource.

18. Net present value is defined as the difference between the discounted value of the stream of cash flows (revenues minus current operating costs) and the initial capital outlay. Formally it is given by

$$-K_o + \text{DCF}$$

or, using the definition of DCF in note 16:

$$-K_o + \sum_{t=1}^{n} \frac{R_t - C_t}{(1+r)^t}$$

where K_o is the initial capital outlay.

19. Internal rate of return is that rate of discount which makes the net present value (NPV) exactly equal to zero. For an elaboration of this concept, see E. J. Mishan, *Cost Benefit Analysis* (New York: Praeger, 1976), pp. 183–86.

20. For the mathematically inclined worrywarts, one problem with IRR as a decision criterion is its non-uniqueness—that is, if the stream of net benefits (or cash flows) is not "well behaved," there may be several internal rates of return.

21. See, for example, Armeane Choksi, "State Intervention in the Industrialization of Developing Countries: Selected Issues," *World Bank Staff Working Paper No. 341*, July 1979; and Malcolm Gillis, "The Role of Economic Enterprises in Economic Development (A Survey)," *Social Research* (January 1981), and studies cited therein.

22. This approach was ruled out in the case of Hiyas Galeria, as the financial data for this enterprise are for 1979 only. In any case, its performance since 1979 will probably not be a good indication of future performance. Its level of operation has been unsteady and it was closed for most of 1978.

23. The financial data are for 1979 only, as reported in the Commission on Audit report. The data on Galeria financial operations were not provided directly.

24. Information on salaries and wages is for 1980, as provided by the provincial budget officer. The figure for the maintenance and repair is from the income statement submitted by the Galeria accountant to the Commission on Audit for the year ending December 31, 1979.

25. Commission on Audit, *Report of the Financial Audit of the Province of Bulacan for the Calendar Year Ended December 31, 1979,* February 27, 1980.

26. National Tax Research Center, "Study of User Charges in Metropolitan Manila," 1977, p. 100, mimeo.

6

Local Government Credit Financing

by L. KENNETH HUBBELL

In recent years national economic development policy has persistently emphasized regional development planning as a means to achieve economic growth, social justice, and an equitable distribution of income within and among regions of the Philippines. The framework for regional planning and its relationship to the national planning process has been outlined in a series of presidential decress (PD 1 and 1200) and Letters of Instructions (LOI 542 and 542-A). Executive Order (EO) 589 in April 1980 represents another step toward the goal of regional development. It attempts to link the planning and budgeting processes at the regional level by requiring the formation of a Regional Development Investment Program (RDIP) in each of the 14 regions. Responsibility for preparation of the RDIP rests primarily with the Regional Development Council. It is charged with the task of identifying, consolidating, and reconciling programs and projects that are to be undertaken by national line agencies, local governments, government-owned and -controlled corporations and other government development authorities, and, to the extent possible, by the private sector.

EO 589 has important implications for local governments within a region and for their residents. First, the development procedures adopted under the order should foster greater local participation in the identification and selection of national projects. Second, it should provide for a more efficient allocation of financial resources within a region. Third, projects financed by local governments from sources should be integrated more effectively with nationally budgeted projects. Knowing what type of projects the line agencies of a region plan to pursue over the next five or ten years should enable local units in the region to plan their own projects more intelligently, in terms of both compatibility with the national projects and meeting local needs. Last, although locally financed government projects are normally independent of the capital expenditure activities of the line agency and should remain so under the new order, central government ministries exercise considerable control over the capital budgets of local governments.

As detailed in PD 752, the Decree on Credit Financing for Local Governments, provinces, cities, and municipalities may borrow to cover expenditures in advance of revenues and to finance the construction, installation, improvement, expansion, operation, or maintenance of local infrastructure and other socioeconomic development projects. The implementing instructions issued by the Ministry of Finance on August 12, 1975, less than a month after the decree was signed, outline the specific provisions, conditions, and limitations for borrowing and the proper procedures to be followed by local government loan applicants. The Philippine National Bank (PNB), the Development Bank of the Philippines (DBP), and the Government Service Insurance System (GSIS) are authorized to grant loans and credits to local governments. As a matter of policy, however, the PNB makes no long-term loans to local governments, providing only short-term advances against tax receipts.

Section 4(a) of PD 752 lists the types of eligible projects for long-term financing by the three lending institutions. Loans are authorized for construction, improvement, and operation of the following: electric light and power plants, public markets and slaughterhouses, waterworks and irrigation systems, telephone and radio communication systems, government housing projects, purchase of rural and urban estates, and other capital investment projects. Furthermore, in Section 4(b), provincial, city, and municipal governments are granted the authority to obtain medium-term and long-term loans from the Land Bank of the Philippines (LBP). These loans may be secured by real estate and/or other acceptable assets and may be used for the establishment, development, or expansion of agricultural, industrial, home building, and other enterprises.

To secure a loan for one or more of these projects, as well as for such other items as heavy equipment or farm machinery, which are not specifically mentioned, a number of documents and/or approvals are required. The most recent checklist of items to be submitted by local governments to the MOF is dated June 1, 1978. Depending on the type of project to be financed, between nine and twelve different documents and/or approvals must be filed before the MOF will process the application. MOF approval is a necessary condition for the submission of the projects to one of the lending institutions for funding, but is not a sufficient condition for approval by that institution. The sufficient condition is that the project meet the institution's standard for financial viability.

In addition to borrowing from designated government institutions, under PD 752 provinces and cities are also authorized to issue bonds, debentures, securities, collaterals, notes, and other obligations to finance self-liquidating and/or income-producing development projects. The issuance of the bonds and other long-term securities is, however, subject to several conditions: (1) "They shall be in registered form and transferable at the Central Bank of the Philippines." (2) "They shall not be sold at less than face value." (3) "They shall be redeemable ten years or more from the date of issue . . ., but may be redeemable earlier by the local government upon approval by the majority of all the members of the local Council." (4) Before the issuance of the bonds, the secretary of finance determines the annual rate of interest payable, as well as the mode of payment. (5) Finally, and perhaps most importantly, the self-liquidating or income-producing project must be certified by the National Economic and Development Authority (NEDA), and the aggregate amount of outstanding bonds or securities at any one time may not exceed 5 percent of the total assessed value of taxable real property within the territorial jurisdiction of the local government unit.[1] Perhaps because of these restrictions, no local governments have made use of this provision of PD 752. Except for very large infrastructure projects, the cost of issuing bonds and complying with the other conditions of this section is prohibitive.

To enable cities and municipalities to finance capital investment projects within areas larger than the legal boundaries of a single jurisdiction, jointly executed projects are also provided for in PD 752. This provision has great potential because a number of such locally situated projects as slaughterhouses and public markets have areas of influence that extend beyond the geographical boundaries of the unit in which they are located. We know of no local governments making use of this aspect of the decree—perhaps local officials feel that local facilities such as public markets are essential to preserve the community's identity and therefore should not be located outside the jurisdictional boundaries.

LENDING PROGRAMS OF THE AUTHORIZED INSTITUTIONS

Although PD 752 gave explicit instructions about procedures to be followed by local governments seeking loans, much discretion over loan conditions was given to the three designated lending institutions. An analysis of the effectiveness of these lending programs includes their legal authority, current policies concerning eligibility, and conditions and terms for repayment.

Development Bank of the Philippines

Pursuant to Republic Act 2081, approved June 14, 1958, the Development Bank of the Philippines succeeded the Rehabilitation Finance Corporation (RFC), an agency established under Republic Act 85 of October 19, 1946. The DBP is owned wholly by the government. It was established "to provide credit facilities for the rehabilitation and development and expansion of agriculture, industry, and reconstruction of property damaged by war and [for] the broadening and the diversification of the national economy, and to promote the establishment of private development banks in the province and cities."[2] With reference to local governments, the charter provides for the financing of provincial, city, and municipal self-liquidating or income-producing projects. It specifically forbids the financing of non-self-liquidating projects. Local governments are eligible to borrow for the construction, installation, improvement, operation or maintenance of electric plants and systems, public markets and slaughterhouses, waterworks systems, telephone communication, agricultural equipment, heavy equipment and machinery, cadastral surveys, and other income-generating projects.

Under Republic Act 2081, the initial authorized capitalization of the DBP was set at ₱300 million. Over the years the government's capital contribution has been steadily raised in a series of amendments to the original act. The most recent change occurred on June 11, 1978, under PD 1461, when the bank's authorized capitalization was increased to ₱5 billion. As of December 31, 1979, however, the actual level of capitalization was a little over ₱3 billion. In round numbers, the other major sources of investment funds at the end of 1979 were: bonds, notes, and loans—₱7.6 billion; demand, time, and savings deposits—₱1 billion; other sources—₱400 million.

The standard repayment period of DBP loans is ten years, with a two- to three-year grace period. Currently (1981) the interest rate on government loans is 18 percent per year, with a 1 percent rebate if the annual payment is received on time. A nominal application fee is collected from each applicant based on the value of the loan. For loans of a million pesos, for example, the fee is ₱5,000, or one-half of 1 percent of the value of the loan.

Bank policy states that the amount advanced for a project be based on the financial needs of the project and its repayment capacity. Providing that the principal amount does not exceed the borrower's legal borrowing capacity and that the MOF favorably endorses the project, the policy permits 100 percent financing of projects that are totally self-liquidating. In practice, the DBP determines the "financial needs" and the total cost of a project from details furnished by the applicant.

A statement or guarantee is required from the MOF to the effect that should loan default occur it will withhold a portion of the local government's BIR Allotment. According to PD 231 as amended, in the event a jurisdiction is unable to meet its annual amortization payments when they fall due, upon notification by the DBP, the MOF is to withhold a sufficient amount from the monthly BIR Allotment of the local government to repay the amortization, penalties, and any accrued interest charges on the loan.[3] If recipient local governments have BIR Allotments equal to or greater than the annual amortized values of their loans to the DBP, one expects that the bank's risk of total default would be very low. In practice this is not the way it works. According to the DBP, when a local government defaults on its loan, the conditions of the loan guarantee are seldom completely honored. In the bank's experience, the MOF normally remits only between 20 and 30 percent of the annual amortized amount owed. The reported response of the DBP's management to this practice is to discount the importance of the guarantee and in general to follow a more conservative lending program than it would otherwise. In defense of the MOF's actions, however, the scaled-down payments may be called for in many cases because withholding the full amount could jeopardize the local government's financial stability.

Land Bank of the Philippines

Creation of a special banking facility to serve the needs of the rural population can be traced back to Republic Act 3844, or the

Agrarian Reforms Code (ARC), approved on September 10, 1971. The legislation called for the establishment of a land bank to finance owner-cultivated family farms and cooperatives involved in the production, processing, marketing, distribution, and financing of agricultural goods. Due to organizational difficulties and inadequate capitalization, the bank was nevertheless ill-equipped to implement the programs of the original charter or the later policies outlined in PDs 27 and 85 on agrarian reform.

In recognition of these limitations, revisions were made in the charter in May 1973 under PD 251, and the subsequent issuance of PD 717 in 1975 boosted the financial resources of the bank still further. Collectively, these revisions and charter amendments have greatly enhanced the bank's ability to support agrarian reform. They have also increased the institution's scope of operation. At present, it can and does engage in such commercial banking operations as extending commercial loans, accepting deposits, and engaging in import-export financing, international banking, and trust operations. From the 1980 Annual Report, the primary financial resources of the bank are shown to be capital contributions from the national government (₱1.4 billion), demand, time, and savings deposits (₱2.2 billion), bank bonds (₱0.7 billion), and retained earnings (₱1.7 billion).

The applicant follows virtually the same process for loan approval at the Land Bank as at the DBP. Repayment terms vary with the type of project to be financed. The normal length of amortization is ten years for slaughterhouses and markets, seven years for heavy equipment, and four years for hand equipment (small implements such as plows). The current (January 1981) interest rate is 18 percent on longer term loans of ten years or more. Medium-term loans (seven years or less) are 16 to 18 percent. Loans are repaid on an annual basis for markets and slaughterhouses and on a semiannual basis for agricultural and heavy equipment.

Most loans have an equity-debt ratio of 15–85, but for some the ratio has been as high as 50–50. The bank has rather wide discretion in determining what it will accept as equity. Land Bank bonds, real estate, buildings, and plant and equipment are the most common equities. Like DBP, all equipment loans are secured by a chattel mortgage and are subject to the special rules and regulations mentioned above.

Government Service Insurance System

Commonwealth Act 86, passed on November 14, 1936, established a permanent pension plan system for eligible government employees. The original appropriation for the Government Service Insurance System (GSIS) created by this act came from the teachers' pension fund. Although the coverage and operating policies have been amended on several occasions since passage, the basic intent of the act remains unaltered–the development of an actuarially sound life and retirement insurance plan for the benefit of government employees. Like all insurance-based programs, the premium payments of members are invested in interest-bearing financial instruments.

Section 22 of the act details the general conditions for the investment of funds by the board of the GSIS. According to this section, portions of the monies not required to meet the current payments in the form of life annuities, death claims, and expenses incidental to carrying out the purpose of the act are to be invested in interest-bearing deposits, bonds, securities, or in loans to local governments or to the government of the Philippines for the construction of self-liquidating projects.

Standardization of the loan application process by the MOF means that the GSIS documentation requirements and approval process are identical to that of the DBP and of the Land Bank. To the extent that a difference does exist between the GSIS and one or both of the other institutions, it is with respect to the terms and conditions of loans. In contrast to the DBP and the Land Bank, the GSIS is much more flexible on the terms of repayment. The stated policy is to amortize loans over a maximum of ten years, but in practice, the repayment period may be twice the stated length. Ordinarily, however, the loan period does not exceed 15 years.

Since June 1980 the interest rate has been 14 percent. The current (January 1981) rate for local governments is a full four percentage points less than the Land Bank and the DBP interest charge. According to GSIS officials, the more favorable rate stems from the unique source of funding–insurance premiums–and the requirement that all local governments purchase insurance from the GSIS.

With regard to debt-equity ratios, the GSIS generally attempts to keep the ratio at 5 to 1. However, if the project is judged to be totally self-supporting from current operations, 100 percent financing is possible and at least on one occasion has been granted. Finally, the GSIS tends to interpret the debt-carrying capacity rule liberally: It has given loans beyond the paying capacity limit if the outside collateral or self-financing looks very strong. This suggests that the two lending requirements are not legally binding, and the institution feels free to extend loans in excess of a local government's paying capacity if in the lender's judgment the project is an acceptable credit risk.

LEVEL OF CREDIT FINANCING

An overview of the magnitude of local government borrowing or, conversely, of institutional lending leaves little doubt that local project credit financing is not widely practiced in the Philippines (Table 6.1). Over the five-year period from 1976 to 1980, the three authorities combined underwrote only 180 projects totaling ₱573.5 million. During the five-year period approximately one of every ten local jurisdictions had a project loan approved, and the cumulated borrowings in 1980 amounted to slightly more than 14 percent of the gross revenues of local governments in that year. Furthermore, the 1980 figure for total outstanding balances plus partially funded projects of ₱415.1 million is some ₱158.4 million less than the total for the five-year period, which suggests that the rate of loan repayments is outpacing the growth of new loans.

Of the institutions identified, the DBP was the largest lender during the period 1976–80. It accounted for nearly 53 percent of all the funds borrowed and 50 percent of loans made to local governments. The Land Bank was the second most important source of financing, contributing a little over 40 percent of the total funds over the five-year period. With just two loans, representing slightly less than 7 percent of the total, the GSIS was the least active of the three institutions.

Heavy machinery loans dominate the list of projects financed by the DBP both in terms of number of loans and total value (Table 6.2). During the period 1976–80, 46 projects were financed at a value of ₱135.7 million. This represents 44.9 percent of all DBP loans to local governments during the five years. Loans for public markets and slaughterhouses accounted for nearly 40 percent of the total. Loan amounts for projects that one assumes would dominate the institution's portfolio (waterworks, electrical systems, and telephone systems) are, in contrast, presently performed largely by special national authorities. For water projects, the Local Water Utilities Administration (LWUA) has become the dominant institution; in the case of electricity, the National Electrification Administration (NEA) now handles most of the financing.

TABLE 6.1

Consolidated Statement of Approved Loans to Local Governments by the Development Bank of the Philippines, the Land Bank, and the GSIS, 1976–80
(in thousands of pesos)

	1976		1977		1978		1979	
Type of Project	Number	Amount	Number	Amount	Number	Amount	Number	Amount
Markets and slaughterhouses	10	16,313	17	47,968	4	22,081	6	32,540
Commercial buildings					1	3,000	2	33,593
Waterworks	1	12,000	2	200				
Electrical systems								
Heavy equipment	9	20,237	16	57,728	9	45,577	26	107,062
Farm equipment			8	5,927	16	9,088	14	7,529
Fire fighting equipment					1	43,500		
Cadastral surveys					1	1,350		
All other	–	–	1	2,881	–	–	1	7,425
Totals[a]	20	48,550	44	114,764	35	124,596	49	188,149

Type of Project	1980		Total 1976-80		Total Outstanding December 31, 1980	
	Number	Amount	Number	Amount	Number	Amount
Markets and slaughterhouses	9	37,169	49	156,071	167	101,620
Commercial buildings			3	36,593	6	25,498
Waterworks			3	12,260	25	12,309
Electrical systems					12	4,287
Heavy equipment	15	52,723	75	283,327	50	112,132
Farm equipment	7	2,539	45	25,083	36	14,295
Fire fighting equipment			1	43,500	1	27,580
Cadastral surveys			1	1,350	7	1,498
All other	1	5,000	3	15,306	4	6,532
Totals[a]	32	97,431	180	573,490	308	305,751[b]

[a]The annual totals reflect the number and amount of loans approved by the various lending institutions. All the funds were not disbursed during that year.

[b]An amount of ₱109.3 million should be added to the ₱305.7 million figure for partially funded projects.

Source: Unpublished data, Development Bank of the Philippines, the Land Bank, and the GSIS.

TABLE 6.2

Approved Loans to Local Governments by the Development Bank of the Philippines (1976–80), the Land Bank of the Philippines (1977–80), and the Government Service Insurance System (1979)

	DBP (1976–78)				LBP (1977–80)				GSIS (1979)			
	Total 1976–80		Total Outstanding Dec. 31, 1980		Total 1977–80[f]		Total Outstanding Dec. 31, 1980		Total 1979		Total Outstanding Dec. 31, 1979[h]	
Type of Project	Number	Amount	Number	Amount	Number	Amount	Number	Amount	Number	Amount	Number	Amount
Markets and slaughter-houses	38	109,443	146	–	11	46,628	–	15,591	–	–	15	14,290
Heavy equipment	46	135,741	50	–	29	147,586	–	89,519	–	–	–	–
Fire fighting equipment	1	43,500[a]	1	–	–	–	–	–	–	–	–	–
Waterworks[b]	3	12,260	26	–	–	–	–	–	–	–	1	564
Electrical systems	–	–	3	–	–	–	–	–	–	–	7	6,482
Cadastral surveys	1	1,350	4	–	–	–	–	–	–	–	–	–
Farm equipment	–	–	–	–	45	25,083	–	17,564	–	–	–	–

Commercial buildings	–	–	–	–	2	5,493	–	4,252	1	31,100	5	34,332
Road construction	–	–	–	–	2	7,881	–	2,080	–	–	–	–
Cemeteries	–	–	–	–	–	–	–	–	–	–	1	40
Bridges	–	–	–	–	–	–	–	–	–	–	1	73
Beautification project/												
Manila	–	–	–	–	–	–	–	–	1	7,425	1	7,425
Other	–	–	6	–	–	–	–	–	–	–	–	–
Totals[c]	89	302,294[d]	236	176,751[e]	89	232,671	–	129,000[g]	2	38,525	31	63,206

[a]A single loan to Metropolitan Manila for purchase of equipment in 1978.

[b]With the formation of Local Water Utility Administration (LWUA) and National Electrification Administration (NEA), few loans are now being made for utilities.

[c]Annual totals include projects that have been approved but not necessarily totally funded.

[d]Of the 1976–80 total, ₱139,194, or 44 percent, was for local governments in Region IV.

[e]To the outstanding total of ₱176.7 million, an amount of ₱101.5 million should be added for approved but as of yet only partially funded projects. This would bring the aggregate total to ₱278.2 million.

[f]Land Bank's loans to local governments started in 1977.

[g]To the outstanding total of ₱129 million, an amount of ₱7.8 million should be added for four approved but as yet only partially funded projects.

[h]The period covered is from 1956 to March 1979. Excluding the two loans in 1979, the GSIS made no loans to local governments between 1974 and 1979.

Sources: Unpublished data, Development Bank of the Philippines, January 1981; unpublished data, Land Bank of the Philippines, January 1981; Government Service Insurance System, May 1980.

Compared to the Development Bank of the Philippines, lending to local governments is a relatively new activity of the Land Bank, beginning only with the passage of PD 752. The first loan requests were received during 1976, and funds for 15 projects were committed in 1977. In total, over the four-year period ending December 31, 1980, 89 loans were extended to qualified local governments. Approved borrowings during that period amount to nearly ₱233 million, most of which went to finance the purchase of heavy equipment (Table 6.2).

The Land Bank is a more specialized lending institution than the DBP. This difference is clear from the types of loans the Land Bank makes and is primarily a result of its commitment to agricultural reform and development. An examination of the breakdown of projects by type reveals that heavy equipment loans made up 63 percent of the total and that most of this amount went to provinces for the purchase of road construction equipment to extend and upgrade farm to market roads. The other two major categories of loans, public markets and slaughterhouses and farm equipment represent 20 and 11 percent, respectively, of the total. These purposes are justified because markets are seen as a method of improving the agricultural distribution system, and the provision of the farm equipment as a technique for increasing agricultural production through the rental of custom farm machinery to farmers. Although cities can and do borrow from the bank, the bank's agricultural orientation favors financing of the projects of provinces and municipalities.

Of the three lending institutions, the GSIS has been least involved in local government credit financing. With the sole exception of a commercial building loan in 1979, no self-financing loans have been made to local governments since 1972. In the 24-year period (1956–79) that the GSIS has been making loans to local governments, it has underwritten an average of less than one project per year. To the extent that it has financed projects in the past, approximately three-fourths of the funds have gone for markets and slaughterhouses and commercial buildings. In recent years the agency has elected to limit its loan activity to large national projects and national enterprises such as Philippines Airlines.

Delinquencies

There is a relatively high rate of delinquency among borrowers. Data from the three lending institutions show that nearly a third of

TABLE 6.3

Past Due Local Government Loans with the Development Bank of the Philippines, the Land Bank, and GSIS, 1980 (in thousands of pesos)

Lending Institution	Total Accounts	Number of Past Due Accounts	Percent Past Due	Amount Past Due	Total Loans	Percent Past Due	Subject to BIR Allotment
DBP	193	63	33	₱19,440	₱143,172	14	8
Land bank	71	4	6	3,390	129,000	3	4
GSIS	31	27	87	22,000	63,206	35	8
Total	295	94	32	44,830	335,378	13	20

Note: The Central Bank of the Philippines defines the term "past due" as follows: for monthly accounts, a loan that is ten months in arrears; for quarterly accounts, four quarters behind; for semiannual, three payments in arrears; and for annual accounts, two payments behind.

Source: Unpublished data, the DBP, the Land Bank, and the GSIS.

the 295 current loans are past due (Table 6.3). The incidence of delinquencies, however, varies considerably among lenders. Primarily as a result of poor administrative practices in the past, the GSIS has an astonishing 87 percent of its loans classified as past due, accounting for approximately half of the ₱44.8 million in delinquent loans.

In contrast to the GSIS record, the Land Bank lists just 4 out of 71 loans (6 percent) as past due. In part, this very low figure is attributable to the newness of the bank's lending program and the fact that annual loans are not considered in arrears until a local government has missed two annual payments.

The oldest and largest of the lenders, the DBP reports one-third of its loans as past due. Many of the loans go back several years and are for rather small amounts: The 63 delinquent accounts represent less than 14 percent of the bank's total outstanding loans to local governments. Both the DBP and the GSIS have made little use of the BIR Allotment guarantee in collecting past due accounts; only 20 of the 94 delinquent loans are being repaid in this manner.

OBSTACLES TO CREDIT FINANCING

The unmistakable conclusion to be drawn from the discussion thus far is that local governments have borrowed very little to finance capital projects. A first reaction is to think of constraint in terms of availability of funds or availability of suitable projects. The former would not seem to be a binding constraint at present. According to DBP officials, no constraint or limit has been placed on the amount of funds available for financing local government projects by that institution. The current policy is to budget an amount for the local government sector based on projected loan demands. Available loan funds are reported to have exceeded project loan applications by local governments.

Neither would a binding constraint appear to be on the project side. From analysis of local government public enterprises, it appears that viable income-generating projects with some degree of cost recovery are available to local governments. Why, then, is more borrowing not occurring at the present time?

Administrative and Management Issues

Administratively, the credit financing system operates under the rules and regulations established by the Ministry of Finance. Project financing falls outside the sphere of MOF responsibility and is controlled by the lending institutions. This arrangement introduces a number of operational and managerial problems. With at least three and sometimes four or five agencies involved in the approval process, significant delays in the processing of a loan can occur. Of the total 396 loan applications received by the DBP, the Land Bank, and GSIS over the six-year period from 1974 to 1980, nearly 40 percent (155 projects) are still pending further action. The lack of proper endorsements or incomplete documentation are major reasons for such a backlog, according to lending officials. Both the DBP and the Land Bank, however, reported that fully documented applications are processed in 60 to 90 days.

Although it is hazardous to generalize from a small sample and anecdotal evidence, a review of several recently approved loans indicated that it does take an inordinate length of time to approve and fund projects. The municipality of Magsingal in Ilocos Sur received a commitment letter on May 2, 1979, for an agricultural equipment loan—nearly three years after the process was initiated. Similar lengthy waits of two to three years were also noticed for such other projects as public markets and slaughterhouses. In Cadiz City, the local resolution authorizing the mayor to seek financing of a public market was passed in September 1978, but final loan approval for that project was not received until August 1980. In the case of Tagbilaran City, a ₱4 million loan for a market took 22 months for final approval, from October 1977 to August 1979.

A second problem relates to the preparation of a financial feasibility study, an integral part of the application. Local governments lack the professional staff to accomplish this important preliminary step, and the lenders, a logical source for such assistance, find it difficult to justify organizing a professional staff for this purpose because of the low volume of loan activity. The Land Bank, for example, has a very small professional staff with all loan applications currently handled by the division chief and four analysts. In addition to scrutinizing project proposals, the staff is responsible for following up existing loans to ensure that prescribed accounting procedures are observed. By comparison, little staff time is spent assisting local governments in the preparation of proposals.

The GSIS recently reorganized its Business and Investment Department, which administered all loans prior to October 1978. The new Government Investment and Loans Department is headed by a director and supported by fourteen professionals, a technical assistant, three lawyers, four accounts and/or finance analysts, and three engineers. Nevertheless, at the time of our research in May 1980, the department was still grappling with a number of internal management problems and spending the bulk of its time revising existing loans.

The DBP funnels all local government loan inquiries through the Community Development Department. Depending on the type of project, the loan application is routed to one of two divisions—heavy equipment or construction. Each unit has seven professionals—a division chief and an assistant, two technical analysts, and three financial analysts. Similar to the GSIS, the department was reorganized in 1978, but unlike the GSIS, the changes were less apparent. The major focus was improved managerial procedures for evaluating projects.

In general, the Land Bank and the DBP appear to be staffed at a level insufficient to provide specialized assistance to local governments. Furthermore, with the exception of department directors and some of the division chiefs, the professional staffs appear to be inexperienced in local government affairs, both operations and finance.

A third obstacle to local officials applying for loans is the highly centralized nature of the process. Each national government agency (MOF, MLGCD, and COA) and each lending institution require that local jurisdictions deal directly with the Manila office. Field offices may not process loan requests. This centralization may be defensible on important grounds, but such a policy makes the local government official's job much more difficult. Jurisdictions located some distance from the Manila area find communication with the lenders and other agencies to be a major stumbling block. One municipal mayor reported that in order to keep the application process moving, frequent trips to Manila were necessary, at times as often as once each week.

Inadequate Information and Attitudes of Local Officials

In order to understand better why local governments do not borrow more, we interviewed mayors and treasurers of 13 jurisdictions.[4] Of the jurisdictions contacted, approximately half had existing or pending loans. Thus, local governments who had none were also covered in the case studies. When appropriate, the views and attitudes of the two groups have been separated.

Ignorance about borrowing powers is not a major problem. Although local officials varied in their understanding of the details of

PD 752, all those interviewed were aware of the credit financing provisions of the decree. Provincial and city officials were the best informed, most having either been granted or having recently applied for a loan. Municipal officials, by comparison, were less well versed on the provisions of PD 752, but certainly well enough to initiate the loan process.

General agreement existed among the mayors and local treasurers on three basic points. First, for large self-financing projects such as public markets and slaughterhouses, local units often must turn to outside consultants for technical assistance. This problem applies both to the preparation of the feasibility study and to required architectural plans. According to one mayor, the fees charged by consultants for these services range from 3 to 7 percent of the value of the project. In his city's case, preparation of a proposal and preliminary drawings for a new market will cost between ₱500,000 and ₱600,000. As with most projects, this is "up front" money that must be paid by the jurisdiction whether or not the project is funded. The problem is magnified for municipalities, as few possess the technical capability to perform these tasks and must purchase the services from even more limited financial resources.

Without exception, those not borrowing pointed to high interest rates as a major impediment. When pressed on the subject, most of the mayors were of the opinion that the central government should subsidize local projects with below-market interest rates of 6 to 8 percent. Elected officials of jurisdictions with recently approved projects also expressed some concern over the current high level of interest rates, indicating that if rates were to rise above the current level they would in all probability postpone any new projects.

The third view shared by local officials and treasurers was a conservative fiscal attitude. The mayors and treasurers in the survey had a "pay-as-you-go" philosophy of local government: Revenues are accumulated until such time as a project can be fully paid for. To leave office with the municipality in debt is viewed as the mark of an irresponsible public official and as bad management. This cautious attitude is not always irrational. Many mayors feel that the revenue sources of the municipality are so limited that large reserves must be maintained to meet such unforeseen calamities as typhoons and collapses in the market price paid for their agricultural products.

The attitude of public officials in the two cities visited was much less conservative. Both cities had sought loans and were looking forward to their funding. One explanation for this observed difference in attitude is the contrasting nature of the financial resources of the two types of governmental units. Cities have a broader and more diversified revenue base and are more financially secure. Many treasurers have conservative attitudes toward investment projects because they believe Section 10 of PD 752, which deals with remedies, sanctions, and penalties for nonpayment of loans, holds them personally and officially liable for such defaults. While we know of no local government treasurer who has been held personally accountable for a loan default, the language of the decree has created apprehension on the part of treasurers. The important of this cautious attitude is underlined when it is remembered that local government treasurers, particularly the provincial treasurers, have considerable influence when it comes to credit financing matters, as a loan application must have the favorable recommendation of the provincial treasurer in the province and municipalities and the city treasurer in the case of cities.

Unrealistic Loan Standards

Apart from the procedures, endorsements, and policy rules connected with the loan application process, two financial requirements must be satisfied for institutional approval. First, as certified by COA, the loan must be within the legal borrowing capacity of the government—7 percent of assessed value. Currently this particular requirement does not appear to be a major stumbling block for city governments. As shown in Table 6.4, of the 58 cities for which data could be obtained, only two have exceeded the ceiling and another three might be considered close to their limit. For municipalities, a similar situation is believed to exist, but the small number of units surveyed does not permit a definitive statement. None of the 11 municipalities in Table 6.5 exceeded its legal borrowing capacity in 1979. Thus this financial requirement would not seem a constraint on local government credit financing.

A more binding constraint is the paying capacity requirement. This requirement is imposed in order to exclude governments that do not have the financial ability to cover the amortization requirements of a new obligation. The formula used first determines the average yearly excess of gross revenues over total budget charges—excluding sinking fund installments and repayments of loans and capital outlays—for the past three years. A jurisdiction's gross paying capacity is found by dividing the calculated average yearly excess figure by a yearly amortization factor. To illustrate, for a ten-year loan at

TABLE 6.4

Debt Limitation of Cities, 1977

City	Total Population (1975)	Assessed Value of Taxable Property Dec. 31, 1977 (₱ million)	Value per Capita (₱)	Debt Limitation (7% of Value) (₱ million)	Present Debt (Dec. 31, 1977) (₱ million)	Remaining Legal Borrowing Capacity (₱ million)
Manila	1,479,116	5,087.9	3,440	356.2	7.4	348.8
Quezon City	956,864	2,866.8	2,996	200.7	–	200.7
Caloocan City	397,201	654.0	1,647	45.8	–	45.8
Pasay City	254,999	445.2	1,746	31.2	12.1	19.1
Metropolitan Manila	4,970,006	15,891.9	3,198	1,112.4	26.3	1,086.1
Oebu	413,125	1,103.3	2,671	77.2	13.2	64.0
Iloilo	227,027	404.0	1,780	28.3	3.6	24.7
Bacolod	223,392	780.5	3,494	54.6	0.4	54.2
Davao	484,678	844.5	1,742	59.1	15.3	43.8
Angeles	151,164	250.7	1,658	17.5	1.1	16.4
Olongapo	147,109	213.7	1,453	15.0	6.4	8.6
Baguio	97,449	351.4	3,606	24.6	0.02	24.6
Lucena	92,336	143.0	1,549	10.0	0.0	10.0
Dagupan	90,092	83.5	927	5.8	0.0	5.8
Naga	83,337	116.0	1,392	8.1	3.6	4.5
Cavite	82,456	90.6	1,099	6.3	0.1	6.3
Lapu-Lapu	79,484	81.3	1,023	5.7	0.9	4.8

(Continued)

TABLE 6.4 (Continued)

City	Total Population (1975)	Assessed Value of Taxable Property Dec. 31, 1977 (₱ million)	Value per Capita (₱)	Debt Limitation (7% of Value) (₱ million)	Present Debt (Dec. 31, 1977) (₱ million)	Remaining Legal Borrowing Capacity (₱ million)
Mandaue	75,904	129.9	1,711	9.1	3.1	6.0
Tacloban	80,707	105.8	1,311	7.4	0.0	7.4
Marawi	63,332	25.1	396	1.8	0.0	1.8
General Santos	91,154	169.7	1,862	11.9	1.2	10.7
Butuan	132,682	135.1	1,018	9.5	1.6	7.9
Cotabato	67,097	169.7	1,862	11.9	0.0	11.9
Zamboanga	261,978	200.8	766	14.1	1.8	12.4
San Pablo	116,607	126.7	1,087	8.9	0.0	8.9
Legaspi	88,378	83.6	946	5.8	0.0	5.8
Tagbilaran	37,335	47.7	1,278	3.3	0.2	3.1
Cagayan de Oro	165,220	265.8	1,609	18.6	6.8	11.8
Cabanatuan	113,814	109.1	959	7.6	2.0	5.6
Laoag	66,259	113.2	1,708	9.1	2.2	6.9
Silay	104,887	137.5	1,311	9.6	0.9	8.7
Pagadian	67,499	45.4	673	3.2	0.1	3.1
Cadiz	127,653	108.4	849	7.6	0.0	7.6
Surigao	66,027	46.3	701	3.2	0.0	3.2
San Carlos, N.O.	90,982	86.3	949	6.0	0.0	6.0

Dumaguete	52,765	67.1	1,272	4.7	0.2	4.7
Dipolog	48,493	42.9	886	3.0	0.0	3.0
La Carlota	40,984	128.8	3,143	9.0	0.1	8.9
Batangas	125,363	287.8	2,296	20.1	7.4	12.7
Iligan	118,778	484.9	4,108	34.2	0.01	34.2
Lipa	106,094	104.8	988	7.3	0.7	6.6
Calbayog	102,619	46.4	452	3.2	0.2	3.0
San Carlos, Pang.	90,882	53.5	589	3.7	0.0	3.7
Ormoc	89,466	155.6	1,739	1.1	2.6	(1.5)
Bago	89,213	121.9	1,366	8.5	0.1	8.4
Ozamis	71,559	75.1	1,049	5.3	0.2	5.1
Iriga	75,885	45.2	596	3.2	0.0	3.2
Roxas	71,305	66.0	926	4.6	2.2	2.4
Toledo	76,521	176.7	2,309	12.4	0.4	12.0
Gingoog	66,577	65.4	982	4.6	0.0	4.6
Tagaytay	58,274	104.9	1,800	7.6	0.0	7.6
Davao	50,260	91.2	1,815	6.4	15.3	(8.9)
Oroquieta	42,497	30.3	713	2.1	0.03	2.0
Tangub	40,461	15.0	371	1.1	0.02	1.0
Puerto Princesa	45,709	55.0	1,203	3.8	0.0	3.8
Bais	45,672	126.7	2,774	8.9	0.04	8.8
Canlaon	29,152	15.8	542	1.1	0.2	0.9
Dapitan	46,261	22.6	489	1.6	0.0	1.6

Source: Computed from basic data provided in the Commission on Audit, *Report on Local Governments,* 1977.

TABLE 6.5

Legal Borrowing Capacity and Net Paying Capacity Data for 13 Local Jurisdictions, 1979 (in thousands of pesos)

Local Jurisdiction	Type[b]	Assessed Value of Taxable Property	Seven Percent Rule	Out-standing Loans	Legal Borrowing Capacity
Passi	M	82,151	5,750	–	5,750
Sorsogon	M	51,861	3,630	2,628	1,002
Gubat	M	39,224	2,746	731	2,014
Barotac Viejo	M	34,211	2,437	244	2,193
Tigbauan	M	20,060	1,404	169	1,235
Tabaco	M	28,126	1,969	–	1,969
Malinao	M	12,458	872	–	872
Albay	P	313,805	21,966	–	21,966
Miagao	M	21,318[a]	1,492[a]	18	1,474
Legaspi City	C	151,157[a]	10,577[a]	1,760	8,817
Dumangas	M	31,000	2,170	–	2,170
Barotac Nuevo	M	34,500	2,415	–	2,415
Oton	M	44,602	3,122	–	3,122

Local Jurisdiction	Average Yearly Excess 1976-79	Gross Paying Capacity (based on .24)	Adjusted for Slippage (40%)	Less Loans Out-standing	Net Paying Capacity
Passi	204	849	509	–	509
Sorsogon	83	348	209	2,628	(2,419)
Gubat	271	1,130	678	731	(53)
Barotac Viejo	40	166	97	244	(147)
Tigbauan	35	145	87	169	(82)
Tabaco	261	1,089	653	–	653
Malinao	19	80	48	–	48
Albay	–	–	–	–	–
Miagao	103	428	257	18	239
Legaspi City	8,894	3,706	2,224	1,760	464
Dumangas	143	595	357	–	357
Barotac Nuevo	118	492	297	–	297
Oton	19	80	48	–	48

[a]Assessed value as of December 31, 1980.
[b]Legend: P–province; M–municipality; C–city.
Source: Furnished by local treasurers.

14 percent interest per year, an amortization of .269 would be used. To allow for possible slippages or a sudden fall in revenues, the gross paying capacity figure is adjusted downward even further. In the case of revenue-producing projects, 60 percent of the paying capacity figure is allowed, whereas for non-revenue-producing projects, the gross paying capacity figure is cut in half. From the remaining discounted figure, outstanding loan balances are deducted to determine finally the local unit's net loan absorption capacity. The formula outlined essentially assumes that the calculated current surplus will be indefinitely extended into the future and that the present value of that income will be available for debt repayment. Deducting for possible revenue slippage and previous debt repayment commitments, the jurisdiction's paying capacity is determined.

A review of some recently granted loans shows that the lending institutions sometimes ignore the financial viability or paying capacity requirement, believing it to be too restrictive. In essence, lenders seem to believe that the measure is overly conservative because it ignores the self-liquidating aspects of projects. Reducing the revenue slippage adjustment ratio from 60 to 40 percent, they believe, gives far too little weight to the revenue generation aspect of such projects. Therefore, loans that fail to qualify under the narrow net paying capacity standard have not been automatically rejected by the lenders if the project merits consideration from a self-financing standpoint. That many local governments do not meet the specific standard, and lenders often choose to overlook it, raise some question as to the usefulness and appropriateness of the net paying capacity measure.

THE FEASIBILITY AND FORM OF A SPECIALIZED LOCAL GOVERNMENT CREDIT AUTHORITY

Assuming that the above accurately characterizes the major impediments to local government loan financing, substantive changes are called for if local governments are to be encouraged to undertake credit-financed projects. The options are either to modify appropriately the present system by changing current policies, procedures, and practices, or to propose a bolder solution and recommend the creation of a new, specialized entity. Although neither approach is without its problems, we think that the weight of the evidence tips in favor of the establishment of a new credit facility for local governments.

The major reason for favoring a specialized entity is the commonly shared belief of many local government credit experts that project planning, appraisal, and management assistance are so critical to the credit financing process that technical staffs, skilled in the different fields of public sector investments and in local government finance, must be maintained. It is doubtful that this could happen without the establishment of a specialized institution.

Typology of Specialized Credit Authorities

According to information compiled by the International Centre for Local Credit (ICLC), a wide variety of organizations and practices is found throughout the world.[5] Some specialized authorities, for example, have developed as public agencies, completely controlled by the central government; others have been organized by local governments or by associations of local governments. In some cases the credit authority is wholly funded by the national treasury, and in others, the authority is expected to finance projects from its own funding sources. Finally, some are controlled by mixed boards composed of representatives from the private sector. This variety underscores the marked differences in circumstances and conditions of the countries, and in particular, the degree of local government autonomy, the maturity of the country's capital markets, and the emphasis of the central government with respect to social and economic development.

Generally speaking, credit institutions for local governments may be classified into three categories according to their legal status and administrative structure: centrally controlled authorities, locally controlled authorities, and authorities with shared managerial responsibilities, that is, mixed participation. The structure and management of a local government authority is influenced by a number of factors, including the division of supervisory control between the central government and the local governments, the division of managerial responsibility within the institution, and the degree of influence of the other national agencies with which the credit authority is either formally or informally linked. Clearly, considerable latitude exists in defining the division of responsibilities between the board of directors and the management of the authority.

Almost without exception among the credit institutions surveyed by the ICLC, policymaking powers are vested in a group of high-level officials that constitute the board of directors. As the top management body the board must formulate policy, represent the authority in its official business, evaluate the authority's operations, and render the final decision on policy matters. Members of governing boards, according to the study, are usually appointed by higher authorities, selected by local units, or chosen through a combination of the two.

With respect to the Philippines, it is recommended that the credit authority be established by law and governed by a board of directors. It is further recommended that the board be composed of representatives of ministries presently involved in local government development projects and of local government officials. A reasonable composition of this board would include the ministers of finance, local government and community development, economic development (NEDA), the governor of the Central Bank, and representatives of the Budget Ministry and the Ministry of Human Settlements. If it is to be a balanced body, an equal number of local government representatives also should be appointed. Care should be taken, however, to include representation from provincial, municipal, and city governments. One way to ensure this is to have the respective local government national organizations elect members to the board. From among the permanent members of the board, the president would appoint a chairman.

Apart from the practical considerations, there are some fundamental economic reasons for placing the three previously mentioned ministries on the board. First, from a fiscal management standpoint, their presence helps ensure that the credit authority's lending activities conform to the broader economic, fiscal, and monetary policies of the country. This may prove to be an extremely important consideration in the long run if the institution becomes large enough to have an impact upon monetary stability, foreign exchange transactions, and domestic cyclical and countercyclical policies. In addition, the format accommodates the national effort to coordinate all public sector expenditures within the country. Second, to the extent that the credit authority wished to raise investment capital by the issuance of debt, it can do so at a lower cost as a national government entity. The economies of scale associated with large scale capital financing are well known and need not be repeated here.[6]

The chief executive officer (who may carry the title of president, chairman, or managing director) is the most important member of the management team. This is particularly true during the early stages of the institution's organization and development, because he will bear the brunt of the responsibility for the recruitment of staff, formulation and implementation of policy, and representation of the institution in its official business with other governmental agencies. In general, managing directors are either appointed by the central government, or selected directly by the board of directors. While no preferred method of appointment emerges from the ICLC study, an approach similar to that used in the United Kingdom and Norway would seem appropriate for the Philippines: The director should be appointed by the president based on the recommendation of the board.

LOAN REQUIREMENTS, CAPITALIZATION, AND FUNCTIONS OF A NEW CREDIT AUTHORITY

In developing countries, local government credit authorities rely on the following capitalization methods: central government grants in the form of initial capital grants and/or other grants that are either recurrent or nonrecurrent; central government loans; revenues from specified taxes, national or local, earmarked for the credit authority; contributions of local governments, often a fixed percentage of local tax revenues; and required deposits from reserve accounts, cash balance, and pension funds.[7]

It is unreasonable to expect that a new credit authority will be funded solely from a new central government appropriation. Such a recommendation would ignore national economic resource constraints and would not be in keeping with the objective of mobilizing more resources through the local public sector. On the other hand, it would be unrealistic for the central government to believe that any scheme for increasing local government use of credit financing would be costless. Indeed, it is the lure of more central government revenues (including interest subsidies and technical assistance) that will induce local governments to increase their own efforts to finance development outlays.

Before considering specific alternatives for initial and continuing funding, the important relationship between method of capitalization and the functions and operations of the credit institution must be considered. The consequences of ignoring this relationship may be disastrous and quite far-reaching, as it is virtually impossible to divorce the institution's lending policies and practices from its capital structure, and vice versa. At an early stage, decisions must be rendered on the type and duration of loans and the kinds of financial activities other than credit financing in which the institution will engage. An important example is that the credit institution's decision to extend long-term loans (20 to 30 years) must be related to its ability to command funds for the same period. In essence, this means a matching of loan maturities with the maturities held by their own creditors and with the long-term dependability and stability of continuing government subsidies. The need for local government loans with a longer maturity suggests that a central government grant, recurring and dependable, should provide the bulk of the capitalization of the authority.

What will be the demand for loans in the event a specialized authority is established? Past history records no consistent trend. In fact, there was a sharp drop of nearly 50 percent in the amount borrowed between 1979 and 1980. If the establishment of the authority is successful in reversing the sudden decline in government loan demand, a reasonable estimate of first year loan demand might be ₱200 million. For the sake of developing an optimistic target, let us suppose that the increase would be 40 percent in each of the next two years—25 percent because of new borrowing and 15 percent because of inflation. This assumption would place an annual requirement of ₱392 million on the fund by 1983.

The projections are optimistic, but not unrealistic if a specialized authority were properly staffed and managed. The average loan during 1978–80 was ₱3.5 million; allowing for inflation we might assume that it could rise to 4 million by 1983. Hence, our projections would imply an approval of 98 loans by 1983, up from 32, 49, and 35 in 1978, 1979, and 1980, respectively. A specialized authority should be able to generate at least this increase in volume by shortening the application process, assisting in project preparation, and in adjusting loan terms to make the issuance of debt a more viable proposition.

These projections lead to the central question: Where might the government find enough need capital or continuing contributions to support nearly ₱900 million in long-term loans to local governments over this three-year period and commensurate annual amounts beyond? Several promising possibilities exist: annual shares of the BIR, Specific Tax, or National Tax allotments, partial capitalization from local government cash balances, and capitalization from an external donor.

The alternative of a share in the Specific Tax Allotment is particularly appealing for several reasons. Local government revenue entitlements from this source have increased dramatically in the last two years. From 1979 to 1980, the amount due jumped an astonishing 665 percent, rising from ₱115.3 million to ₱766.9 million. In the

1981 budget year the amount is scheduled to rise an additional 15 percent to ₱881.7 million. As little as a 20 percent annual share of the Specific Allotment would provide a substantial proportion of the necessary capital for a credit authority.

Channeling a share of the increased revenue to a local credit authority could also provide an efficient mechanism for converting these additional monies in capital projects. As discussed in Chapter 1, some local governments, in aggregate, have maintained rather large cash balances. Increased revenues from the Specific Tax Allotment could simply be accumulated rather than stimulate additional capital investment, which would certainly occur if the major stumbling block to local capital investment is the inability of local governments to plan and execute relatively large projects.

There are problems with using the Specific Tax Allotment for this purpose. First, the credit authority will require a "certain" revenue source, and actual disbursements from the Specific Tax Allotment have been sporadic (see Chapter 4). Second, the funding of local government capital projects with a share of specific taxes on petroleum products raises enough problems to make one wonder if the practice will continue much longer. This implies that an important revenue source to the authority might be abolished or markedly revised, thereby compromising the flow of funds to the authority. Third, the Specific Tax Allotment is quite income inelastic and grows only because of increases in the tax rate on petroleum products. The demand for loans may be responsive to income, population, and urbanization, which are rising, but natural growth in this funding source would be in proportion to the volume of petroleum consumption, which is flat or declining. Finally, the Specific Tax Allotment is an important revenue source for some local governments, and sharing it with the local credit authority will delete local government's ability to make capital expenditures.

A second possible source of continuing funding is an annual share of the BIR Allotment. In 1980, ₱1.9 billion in annual BIR Allotment was due, but, as in the two previous years, only ₱659 million was distributed. Present practice requires that 20 percent of this amount be earmarked for development expenditures, but there is no good evidence that the BIR stimulates local government economic development expenditures. Hence, one might argue that allocation of this share to the credit authority would be a better course. A 20 percent share would amount to ₱131 million annually at the present level of distribution, and ₱165 million at a possible 1981 BIR Allotment distribution of ₱823.6 million.[8]

There are drawbacks to such a proposal. First, the disbursements, although more certain than those from the Specific Tax Allotment, have been subject to frequent government alterations. Second, some local governments have come to depend quite heavily on the BIR Allotment, and its withdrawal could cause a major hardship.

Two other grant programs that might be legitimately redirected toward the capitalization of a credit authority are the National Tax Allotment and the barangay shares of the Specific Tax and BIR allotments. Both programs have the purpose of supporting community development projects; hence, using the funds for local government loans would not distort the basic program intent. At 1979 levels, the total annual amount due barangays and local governments from this program was ₱703 million. Obviously, only a small share of this amount, as an annual contribution, would go a long way toward meeting the annual lending requirements of a credit authority.

Again, there are important problems with such a proposal. First, these programs exist much more in law than in practice—only 11 percent of the 1979 amount was actually distributed and only 7 percent in 1980. Second, the use of the barangay shares would be conditional on the government's backing away from its commitment to strengthen the financial participation of the barangay unit.

An alternative source of initial funding of a credit authority is use of the cash surpluses or reserves of local governments. Most of these are kept in current accounts and time deposits. As shown in Table 6.6 the aggregate amount of these funds is very large and relatively stable. In the first quarter of 1978, demand deposits were ₱796.6 million. They were steadily drawn down over the year, falling to ₱660.2 million in the fourth quarter. From that low point, fourth-quarter balances have continuously climbed, reaching ₱860.0 million in 1980. Savings and time deposits have shown somewhat more fluctuation, but also have remained large over the period.[9] Combined, the savings and time deposits amounted to ₱626.7 million in the last quarter of 1980.

Clearly, from the recorded data, local government deposits offer an attractive alternative for initial funding. The balances are both large and stable enough to underwrite a significant portion of the institution's initial capital. For example, ₱200 million might be obtained from surplus cash reserves, that is, exchange of local government cash balances for capital stock in the credit authority. Given that local government cash reserves in the aggregate are large and have remained so for several years and are primarily held at the PNB, the Central Bank could require that a portion of these reserves held

TABLE 6.6

Summary Schedule of Local Government Deposits First Quarter, 1978 to Fourth Quarter, 1980 (in thousands of pesos)

Year	Quarter	Demand Deposit	Savings Deposit	Time Deposit	Total Deposits
1978	1st	796,641	9,754	691,774	1,498,169
	2nd	731,821	7,445	733,299	1,472,565
	3rd	710,418	32,653	730,147	1,473,218
	4th	660,252	12,990	683,433	1,356,675
1979	1st	792,478	13,615	693,252	1,499,345
	2nd	843,220	9,238	699,553	1,552,001
	3rd	946,242	9,951	766,128	1,722,321
	4th	840,808	15,340	751,207	1,607,355
1980	1st	1,070,583	17,236	826,509	1,914,328
	2nd	941,177	22,210	553,198	1,516,585
	3rd	877,822	49,000	565,495	1,492,319
	4th	859,955	41,300	585,497	1,484,752

Sources: Data supplied by Development Bank of the Philippines, Land Bank of the Philippines, Philippine National Bank, and Philippine Veterans Bank.

by PNB be earmarked for purchase of capital stock in the new authority. As long as the cash reserves held at the PNB in the aggregate did not fall below the capitalization amount (₱200 million), the financial obligations of the local governments could be met from their own cash reserve balances. In essence, PNB would alter its portfolio by reducing excess reserves or exchanging other assets for the capital stock in the authority.

Capitalizing the credit institution from local government balances, however, is not so straightforward as is suggested by this simple illustration. One issue to be addressed is the impact that the shift in funds will have upon the portfolios of the depository banks—PNB, Land Bank, and Veterans Bank. Unless the depository banks have excess reserves equal to the capitalization amount, they will be unable to adjust without liquidating some of their own assets and/or trimming their lending programs. Thus, from a macroeconomic standpoint, if all public savings are fully invested, capitalization of the credit facility will come at the expense of some other investment opportunities.

In defense of the suggested alternative, it should be pointed out that inasmuch as PNB makes no long-term loans to local governments, these cash balances are currently being used to finance investment projects in other sectors of the economy. Thus, requiring that part of these balances flow into local projects through the purchase of capital stock in the authority simply ensures that part of the savings of the local government sector is invested in that sector.

There are drawbacks to this option. First, we are not certain how much of these balances are restricted and hence whether some expenditure earmarking requirements will have to be relaxed. Second, we do not know how concentrated these holdings are among local governments; for example, is it possible that a relatively few large governments have saved substantial amounts in anticipation of making a major capital outlay? Tying these funds up in the share capital of a lending authority, probably at subsidized rates of return, would initially cause postponement of the capital expenditure and could discourage local government savings. If holdings are more widespread and if the percentage allocated to the credit authority is not large, this problem may not occur. Finally, one needs to be concerned about the consequences of various combinations of these capitalization alternatives. For example, will the allocation of a share of the BIR and Specific Tax allotments substantially dry up the local government cash balances?

The fifth possible source of capital funding is an international donor. In late 1978, after considerable consultation with the Ministry of Finance and other government offices, USAID proposed to make a concessionary loan of $10 million to help capitalize a credit authority for "poor" local governments. Proceeds of the loan, plus counterpart funds from the Philippine government, were to be used to finance projects at low interest rates–6 percent plus a 1 percent DBP service fee. The proposal was shelved, but recently there has been renewed interest in the Ministry of Finance. In its original form, the proposal might be viewed as a method of augmenting the capital base of the new credit authority and as a way of widening the institution's scope of operation. As discussed below, such funding, if obtained, would permit the credit authority to establish two different credit windows–one for bankable projects, the other for projects requiring concessionary terms.

The major danger in such an arrangement is that the government may become committed to a program designed primarily to benefit poorer jurisdictions. Social benefits aside, this would run contrary to the goal of strengthening local government finances, promoting local autonomy, and mobilizing more local government revenues. Some low income jurisdiction assistance is possible under a credit authority, but it must be a secondary rather than a guiding objective.

The proper choice of a financing scheme is a key matter. We would capitalize the new authority from a combination of sources rather than from a single source.[10] This approach provides the authority with a broader financial base, permits greater flexibility in meeting future capital demands, and in all probability would be received more favorably by local and central government officials than would a plan for funding from a single source. The rationale behind this strategy is that there is enough slack in each of the programs considered here to allow for some reductions without great harm, but as the cuts are deeper, unwanted local finance adjustments might be induced.

A major source of continued funding could be from a share of regular allotments. It was recommended in Chapter 4 that the grant system be consolidated, and it was suggested that the allotment share be set at about 30 percent of collections. Since we are unable to determine the exact Specific Tax Allotment entitlement under the present system, we can only roughly estimate the "equal yield" share of BIR collections under the proposed Consolidated Allotment. We would further recommend that a share of this Consolidated Allotment be directed, annually, to the credit authority.

Assume that 10 percent of the Consolidated Allotment flows to the credit authority. Under the more conservative distribution assumed in alternative B (see Table 6.7), funds sufficient to cover loan requirements are generated. Under alternative A, more resources are available to the authority, but no growth in the annual contribution. In the long run, a scheme will have to be developed to guarantee both an adequate amount and a regular flow of resources to the authority.

In addition to the Consolidated Allotment share, we would propose making use of the cash balances that local governments hold in banks. For the three-year period, we recommend a total of ₱218 million. As noted in Chapter 4, the contributed amount is to rise gradually from ₱50 million in the initial year to ₱98 million in the third year.[11] Structuring the paid-in capital in this way should allow the bank(s) to comply without any serious short-term adjustments in their portfolios.

TABLE 6.7

Capitalization of a Credit Authority, 1981–83 (in millions of current pesos)

	1981	1982	1983
Alternative A: Consolidated allotment held constant at ₱1540	150	150	150
Alternative B: Consolidated allotment growth of 25 percent per year	150	210	292
Local government cash balances	50	70	98
Total loan requirements	200	280	390
Shortfall under alternative A	–	60	142

Under either assumption about the distribution and growth of the Consolidated Allotment, this plan generates resources adequate to cover loan requirements for our illustrative three-year period (Table 6.7). Beyond this period, without further recourse to local government cash balances, a shortfall could arise if the allotment distribution is not allowed to increase with BIR collections. This problem will be especially important in the early years of the authority, when the volume of loan repayments will be low and the default rate relatively high.

The Problem of Reallocation

As noted, capitalizing the authority primarily from a share of the Consolidated Allotment reduces the amount that would otherwise have been directly distributed to local governments. More importantly, however, because these funds are presently distributed on a formula basis, some jurisdictions with greater land areas and larger populations, and those that have a better capacity to absorb funding for capital projects will be the biggest losers. Loans to local governments obviously will result in some redistribution, since we cannot believe that the present or proposed allotment formula is a reasonable way to establish eligibility to borrow and since the loan amount will be concentrated on a relatively small number of jurisdictions.

The credit authority, then, will effect some redistribution of resources among local governments, and the redistribution of resources will be larger to the extent that the credit authority's annual share of the Consolidated Allotment is larger. This raises the need for the authority to establish clear rules for the distribution of loans. Two possibilities are to use a formula approach, perhaps based on need, to target loans on lower income jurisdictions, and to allocate on a basis of repayment potential, merit of the project, and local matching shares. We would recommend the second alternative.

To focus on lower income jurisdictions, with such a limited capitalization of the authority, is to invite a greater risk of default and to stimulate less additional local spending and taxing than might otherwise be the case. With respect to the latter, more populous and higher income jurisdictions appear to have more discretionary resources that might be directed to capital projects, a greater potential for tax revenue increase, and a greater potential for project implementation and financial success. One should not enter the process of developing a credit authority with the idea that it may primarily serve the poorest jurisdictions, unless one places the short-run equalization goal above that of strengthening the financial participation of local governments in the development process. At least for the present, the two goals are not fully compatible.

This is not to say that all funds should be allocated to cities, large municipalities, or to the wealthiest jurisdictions, or that constraints should not be placed on the distribution of loans. Since the 10 percent share of the Consolidated Allotment would be taken from provinces, cities, and municipalities in the ratio of 28 percent, 44 percent, and 28 percent, loan ceilings of like percentage could be established. A similar rule might be established for the 12 economic development regions. To address the possible redistribution of funds among regions of the country, the authority might want to establish a simple rule that local governments in each region would have an opportunity to borrow an amount up to that which would have been allocated to the region under the Consolidated Allotment, or according to some other government criteria for the regional distribution of funds. Within the region, however, loans would be allocated on a merit basis.

New Lending Policies

The terms of lending to local governments might be adjusted for two purposes. The first is to lower the "price" of borrowing. The sharp decline in the level of local government borrowing, from ₱189.2 million in 1979 to ₱97.4 million in 1980, suggests that the current terms of repayment (seven to ten years) and interest rates (16 to 18 percent) may be unmanageable for many local governments. The second is to use the availability of loan funds to stimulate increments in local government spending for capital projects. We suggest the following program as a method of achieving both objectives.

The loan rate should be set to vary inversely with the amount of cash equity a local government has in the project. Moreover, we recommend lending rates that, at least in the initial years of the authority, are set below the market rate of interest. The variable interest rate program provides, first, an incentive for local governments to mobilize more resources for an equity contribution. That is, the greater the equity contribution, the lower the interest rate and the lower the loan service fee. Second, if the authority is capitalized by funds originally earmarked for local governments (the allotment, or local government cash balances), offering a below-market interest rate is justified because local governments are in essence borrowing from themselves. Third, inasmuch as the amount of loan coverage rises with the percentage of equity, the risk of default decreases and a lower rate of interest is justified. Fourth, if local governments are permitted to borrow for non-revenue-producing projects (and we would argue that this can be good public policy), loans for this purpose should bear a higher interest rate because of the greater risk of default.

A major weakness in the current credit financing arrangement is the relatively short period of repayment for the number of projects that are normally considered to be long-term investments—that is, projects that have an expected life much greater than the duration of the loan. To remedy this situation, the authority should structure its loan repayment schedules to be more in line with the economically useful life of the projects it finances. This would probably mean extending the period of amortization for projects like public markets and slaughterhouses to 20 years.

A third recommendation is that, apart from the type of self-liquidating projects detailed in PD 752, the government should consider using the credit authority to broaden the list of eligible investments to include certain non-revenue-generating projects, for instance, to permit local governments to assume general obligation debt. Local officials emphasized on numerous occasions the importance of allowing for the financing of such projects. Those most often mentioned were public office buildings, recreational facilities, and road improvement projects. Assuming that the local jurisdiction can meet some objective standards of creditworthiness, there seems little reason to exclude such projects from credit financing.

Standards for Project Analysis

In a capital-scarce country like the Philippines, a major responsibility of the credit institution is to develop its capacity to analyze the technical, economic, and financial viability of proposed projects. Technical assistance provided by the authority should also enhance the ability of local governments to prepare and implement projects. To meet these objectives, the credit authority should develop strict but reasonable rules for approving loan applications; develop a staff with the technical skills to analyze, implement, and monitor the success of investment projects; and develop the capacity to train and assist local government officials in the preparation and development of projects. In developing these capacities the authority will overcome some of the problems that have discouraged more local government borrowing.

In the Philippines, a critical mass of talent does exist, and if the new authority carries the same civil service status as the DBP and the Land Bank it should have no difficulty in attracting qualified personnel. Hence, the authority could have a much better view of local government financial problems than now exists, and because of this expertise should be able to reduce drastically the time necessary to gain loan approval.

Administrative Cost

A credit authority will not run on its capitalization alone. A target of nearly ₱900 million in loans in three years and perhaps as many as 200 new loans implies a staff of substantial size and quality. Moreover, the newness of the effort implies a substantial setup cost, including an important training component.

The operation of the authority might be funded from four sources. First, a 1 or 2 percent add-on to the interest rate could fund a substantial portion of costs to the authority.[12] We propose a lower service charge for a larger equity contribution as another inducement

TABLE 6.8

Illustrative Lending Terms for a Specialized Local Government Credit Authority (in percent)

Cash Equity Required	Annual Interest Rate	Loan Service Fee	Total Annual Interest Charge
	Self-Liquidating Projects		
15	10	2	12
20	9	2	11
25	8	2	10
30	7	2	9
35	6	2	8
40	5	2	7
	Non-Revenue-Producing Projects		
20	16	2	18
25	15	1	16
30	14	1	15
35	13	1	14
40	12	1	13

for larger local government allocations to revenue-producing projects. The service charge does raise the cost of borrowing, but under the present system there is a 1 percent service charge and an additional cost of preparing the feasibility study. In any case, the resulting price of the loan, including the service charge, will be below the market interest rate under this proposal (Table 6.8). Second, a charge could be made for "extra" assistance in project preparation. Third, a central government operating subsidy could be granted. Finally, if external assistance were solicited, it could provide a substantial share of the initial setup and training costs.

Soft Loans for Poor Jurisdictions

The primary purpose of the credit authority is to generate local government spending on capital projects and to encourage the mobilization of additional local resources. There should be no backing away from these primary objectives. Yet, there may be a way to provide some funds for poorer jurisdictions that can neither propose economically viable projects nor satisfy even minimal equity participation or financial soundness criteria.

Suppose an external donor contributed to the capitalization as had earlier been proposed. Some of these funds could be earmarked for a "soft-loan" window where poorer, smaller local units would be eligible for low interest/low equity loans. This program would serve broader social purposes rather than the objectives of the credit authority. Indeed, it is unlikely that increases in tax effort or new income-generating projects would emerge.

There are advantages to a second window approach. It does provide some measure of equalization and channels some resources to very poor jurisdictions. Inevitably it will strengthen the capacity of participating local governments to administer and manage their fiscal affairs. It permits lending for socially desirable projects that cannot meet cost recovery tests. Finally, some portion of the external funding, and probably the majority, could be used to capitalize the bankable loans window of the credit authority and to underwrite some of the initial training effort.

In one sense this discussion of equalization objectives is misleading. Nearly all of the jurisdictions we have been discussing are poor, most have heavy rural components, and few can easily justify heavy debt obligations. Equalization objectives may have much more to do with the kinds of projects being financed by the authority. Certainly for non-revenue-generating projects—those which may be most pro-poor—there may be dim prospects for justification in some communities. It is here that a second window approach may have important distributional effects.

CONCLUSION

It is obvious from this analysis of local government credit finance in the Philippines that the present system poses severe constraints to increased borrowing by local governments. Several courses of action are open to the government of the Philippines that could prompt greater activity. We favor the institution of a new local government credit authority. A review of the structure and functioning of credit institutions in other developing countries would seem to support our view that a new authority would be more effective than piecemeal reform of existing institutions.

NOTES

1. Presidential Decree 1195 (March 20, 1978) amended Section 6(a) of PD 752 and raised the aggregate amount from one-half of 1 percent to 5 percent.

2. Development Bank of Philippines, *1979 Annual Report*, p. 32.

3. Land Bank and Government Service Insurance System are also covered this provision of PD 231.

4. Thirteen jurisdictions were surveyed, one city, one province, and 11 municipalities (see Table 6.4 for a full listing).

5. A comparative study of 34 local credit authorities in 29 countries was carried out by the United Nations with the collaboration of the International Centre for Local Credit in 1970. United Nations, *Credit Institutions for Local Authorities* (New York, 1972).

6. Joseph A Kane, *Development Banking* (Lexington, Mass.: D. C. Heath, 1975).

7. See also United Nations Commission on Human Settlements, *Meetings of the Ad Hoc Group of Experts on Ways and Means of Establishing or Strengthening Financial Institutions for Human Settlements Financing and Investment*, (Nairobi, January 28, 1981).

8. As suggested in an interview at the MOB.

9. As of January 1981, three-year time deposits bear an interest rate of 15 percent and one-year deposits pay 12 percent.

10. This approach differs from the B. M. Villanueva proposal, which recommended that the credit authority be funded from the undistributed portion of the BIR Allotment and other unencumbered balances in the national treasury.

11. Instead of setting aside or designating a specific amount of funds, an alternative is to allocate a fixed percentage of the bank cash balances directly to the authority. For example, the banks could be required to place ₱218 million or no less than 25 percent of local government cash balances with the authority.

12. This is the service charge amount used by the DBP.

7

Strengthening the Fiscal Performance of Philippine Local Governments

by ROY BAHL

One might question the feasibility, if not the wisdom, of strengthening local government fiscal performance in the Philippines. It has been pointed out that even in the face of a national government policy favoring fiscal decentralization, local government fiscal performance did not improve during the 1970s. Despite strong policy declarations, fiscal decentralization is not occurring. In light of this history, does it seem possible that more policy changes will promote a growing local government sector? Another major issue is that, compared to the entire economic structure and development strategies of the Philippines, local government finances appear to be almost negligible. Thus, does it make sense for the government to give a high priority to the improvement of local government financial performance?

Neither of these issues, it seems to us, can defeat the enthusiasm or possibility for strengthening local government fiscal performance in the Philippines. In terms of the feasibility, it should be recognized that changes in the local government financial system can take place in a context of considerable strength. First, the basic system of local government is fundamentally sound. To be sure, there are changes that need to be made, but the administrative procedures, assessment practices, budget format, authorization to borrow, and the like suggest a more workable system than is seen in many other countries of similar income level. The central problem in the Philippines has much less to do with the structure of the system than with the implementation of the system. Second, the quality of public administration seems quite good by comparison with that in many other developing countries. This impression is particularly strong in the case of assessors and treasurers.

Furthermore, the central government's stated objective of strengthening the role of local government in the financing and delivering of public services is a correct priority and should remain at the center of these reforms. The benefits of decentralization are well recognized and consistent with goals of the national plan: to induce local governments to mobilize more revenues, to stimulate infrastructure/economic development expenditures by local governments, to improve the financial management and accountability aspects of local government finances, and to provide local governments with an adequate and dependable source of revenue.

This study of local government finances has led to a suggested program of reform and new initiatives in five areas: financial management and budgeting, local taxation, the allotment programs, the use of public enterprises, and the use of credit financing. Ironically, a major prerequisite to strengthening the financial performance of local governments is a strengthening of the central government's ability to administer and control local government finances.

LOCAL GOVERNMENT BUDGETING, FINANCIAL MANAGEMENT, AND EXPENDITURE MANDATES

It quickly becomes clear to anyone working on local government finance in the Philippines that two important bottlenecks to increased revenue mobilization and to a more efficiently functioning local government sector are inefficiencies in the local government budgeting/ financial management process and the substantial restrictions placed on local government expenditures by the central government.

Budgeting and Financial Management

To the outsider, budgeting by local governments in the Philippines appears to be less an exercise in fiscal planning or control than a response to particular statutory requirements placed on the financial managers of the locality. Supplemental budgets are used as a general rule rather than as an exception. This practice does not stimulate serious fiscal planning for the full fiscal year, as it is widely recognized that the annual budget need be only a crude first approximation. While some degree of flexibility is desirable in any managerial context, the provision for numerous supplemental budgets in the Philippines surely leads to less efficient overall planning of fiscal affairs. The practice of permitting numerous supplemental budgets should be discontinued. The elimination of supplemental budgets and the general improvement of local budgeting practices will call for training of local budget officers, a more rigorous budget approval process at the central government level, and a new set of instructions regarding local government budget preparation and execution.

Attempts have been made to establish longer term capital planning as a part of the financial management responsibilities of local government. Each local government, even the barangay, is supposed to produce a capital improvements program (CIP), which contains five-year revenue projections and lists proposed capital projects. However, in the financial review process there is to be a coordination of the annual budget and the CIP. We could find little evidence that these improvements had been implemented or that they had contributed to improved fiscal planning. Until annual budgeting is improved and made an integral part of the financial management process, there is little likelihood that capital budgeting can be effective. Nevertheless, if additional use of credit financing and an increased focus on capital spending by local governments are part of future plans, well-designed capital budget statements will be essential. Capital budgets, in specified form and including financing plans, should be a general requirement for larger local governments and certainly for all of those borrowing for capital projects. Again, this means that the MOB, MLGCD, MOF, and lending institutions must have the staff necessary to scrutinize the capital budget submissions and certify their acceptability.

Coordination of Central Government Controls

The local fiscal management function is overseen by at least four different arms of the central government. While there may be considerable rationale and even need for this division of labor, it must be recognized that such fragmentation imposes costs. Different ministries have different priorities, which leads to conflicts in the directives and requirements given to local governments. Because of these conflicts and the time cost of complying with these requirements, local government fiscal management is less efficient than it otherwise would be. The central government seems to have decided that local fiscal activities must be highly controlled, yet by not coordinating the control of fiscal affairs, the government is losing one of the significant advantages of centralization. At the very least, techniques and practices of the primary central agencies involved in aspects of local government financial affairs (Ministry of Finance, Ministry of the Budget, Ministry of Local Government and Community Development, and the Commission on Audit) should be reexamined periodically to ensure that their review processes are not at odds with each other or with overall central government objectives.

Expenditure Mandates

The centralized orientation of local financial management is nowhere more evident than in the various restrictions placed upon localities in terms of what they can or must budget for certain functions. This practice enhances the direction the central government can give, but it also markedly reduces the discretion that local governments have in determining the size and makeup of their budgets. We estimate that about 40 percent of the typical local government budget is so constrained. These constraints raise two problems. The first is that if local governments do not control all of their budgets, they can be held that much less accountable for their fiscal performance. For example, because their budgetary discretion is limited, local governments may have to accumulate substantial balances and thus may be less willing to increase their own tax effort. The granting of more local autonomy by easing some of these restrictions is a strategy that may well lead to more resource mobilization and capital spending by local governments.

The second problem relates to the methods by which the expenditure mandates are imposed. One of the simplest, albeit at times misguided, methods to ensure that particular objectives are pursued is to require local governments to spend certain amounts on specific activities. The more or less uniform application of such rules to over 1,600 diverse local government units further complicates the situation and is unlikely to lead to an optimal allocation of resources. If these mandates are to be retained, each should be reviewed in terms of whether the intended objectives are being attained and whether reform is necessary. In particular, the following should be examined:

1. Is an amount as much as 18 percent of general revenues still necessary for recovering INP costs and is a uniform 18 percent

requirement an equitable way of spreading the INP financing burden?

2. The statutory contingency reserve of 2 percent of general revenues should be replaced by a contingency fund. This fund could be specified in size as a percent of total General Fund revenues, but the government needs to establish criteria for determining the size of this fund.

3. The statutory transfer to the Infrastructure Fund may no longer be necessary in light of potential increases in the Specific Tax Allotment and should be reconsidered.

4. The required 20 percent of the BIR Allotment earmarked for development expenditures may be an inefficient practice. The evidence suggests that the 20 percent is as likely to wind up in cash balances as in capital expenditures. Moreover, there is the question of why 20 percent?

We cannot say where a review of these mandates will or even should lead—some of the possibilities depend on changes in the allotment system and others depend on broader objectives of government policy.

Cash Balance Accumulations

Some municipal governments have been accumulating substantial cash balances and unappropriated surpluses. As purely liquid cash, these resources cannot be used for development purposes by either the public or the private sector. This problem is partially addressed by other policy directions suggested in this study, namely, a credit financing scheme and the untying of some local funds from central mandates. Nevertheless, improved cash management techniques need to be implemented to maintain a minimum level of purely idle reserves. The issue should be brought under further study and a manual should be prepared describing standard procedures. A proper consideration of this issue, however, must await a decision on the proposal to create and capitalize a specialized local government credit authority.

THE REAL PROPERTY TAX

The structure of the property tax in the Philippines is sound and the quality of assessors and assessment practices impressive. On the other hand, the revenue performance has suffered from a poor record of enforcement. This trend can be reversed and the property tax made a more effective method of mobilizing domestic resources–but only if the central government takes some important steps.

The first step is to accept the fact that increasing the effectiveness of the local government property tax will mean raising overall tax burdens. The second is to initiate vigorous legal actions against delinquent (and often influential) taxpayers. Third, the central government must coordinate several ministries' activities to improve property tax administration. A fourth step is to recognize that some central government investment in improving the tax will be required. Finally, there is need to create a set of incentives and penalties to induce more active local participation in property tax improvement programs.

To be sure important administrative and management improvements have to be made at the local government level, but in the highly centralized Philippine system, the most important reforms must be initiated by the central government. This research has led to recommendations for change in the following six areas.

Structural Reform

The current practice of assessing certain higher valued improvements at a higher rate than land imposes a penalty on some property investments. This practice is at odds with the government's objective of promoting the mobilization of local resources for capital investments. Moreover, although fractional assessment may be viewed as a method of enhancing the equity of the property tax, it is not an especially effective means of doing so. It would be beneficial to abandon the practice of fractional assessments, that is, to begin assessing all improvements at the same percentage rate, regardless of their value.

Exemption of government-owned properties, religious properties, low valued properties, and "favored industries" tends to erode the real property tax base of local governments. These properties utilize services provided by local governments, and though they may confer employment benefits on the local area, they also confer national benefits. Moreover, the decision to provide the exemptions, and the designation of eligible firms in the case of pioneer firm exemptions, are matters of central government tax policy. In the case of government properties, a system of payments to local governments in lieu of property taxation would well be instituted. In the case of pioneer industry exemptions, there should be a serious reconsideration of eligibility. In many instances the pioneer industry exemption may no longer be called for and may be, in fact, an unnecessary relinquishment of local government resources.

Increased Intensity of Use

In comparison with many other developing countries, and in comparison with other taxes in the Philippines, the property tax is not heavily used. By law, the basic property tax rate is limited to 1 percent of assessed values in municipalities and provinces and 2 percent in cities, with an additional 1 percent designated to the SEF. When fractional assessments on land and improvements are taken into account, the effective rate for the two funds combined is unlikely to exceed 1 percent of market value. If underassessment and collection problems are considered, the actual effective rate is even lower. The ratio of tax collections to assessed value was less than 1 percent in the reassessment years of 1974 and 1979 (0.7 and 0.9, respectively).

While better implementation will contribute to an increased property tax effort, an increase in the legal rate ceiling would also seem appropriate. Limits on the basic rate of 1.5 percent for municipalities and provinces and 3 percent for cities would provide some needed amount of flexibility for local governments. The option to exceed the present rate limit might be restricted to those communities with "acceptable" collection rates and those which are tax mapped. The proposed 50 percent increase in maximum rates, together with the recommended elimination of fractional assessments, would greatly increase the overall revenue potential of the property tax.

Holding land out of productive uses may be rational from the standpoint of an individual landowner but it imposes serious social and economic costs on society. Application of the idle lands tax as it is currently constituted under Philippine law would be a socially beneficial policy. It would increase property tax revenues, but its more important contribution would be to improve the efficiency of land use and penalize speculation. Implementation is the major bottleneck. Local governments will make use of the idle lands tax but only if the central government sees the merit in this tax and mandates its use. If idle lands taxation is part of an increased emphasis on taxing large landowners and delinquents, and if firm directives are sent from MOF, provincial and local officials will be more likely to implement the tax.

Some structural reforms in the existing idle land taxation legislation, however, are called for. The National Tax Research Center has recommended that the idle lands tax rate be increased to 6 percent and also that the tax be broadened to include smaller parcels, especially in urban areas, and that while a grace period before development be given to persons acquiring idle lands, subsequent transfers should not be allowed any grace period. These are sound recommendations.

While a large proportion of local government spending is devoted to services generally available to all residents, many construction-type projects are quite location-specific. In such cases, the use of a special assessment imposed upon the landowners who benefit most directly from the project is justified and desirable. These "special assessments," when used in the place of general tax revenues, free local government revenues for other uses. Very possibly this could be linked to the use of credit financing. For example, lending authorities might provide favorable terms for projects whose cost recovery is partially guaranteed through the use of special assessments. Special assessments are important fiscal instruments in many developing countries and could be important in the Philippines.

Tax Mapping and Records Management

The virtues of tax mapping are generally accepted, and the idea of having complete parcel identification and ownership information has few foes. The problem is that the costs of tax mapping have become too high to overcome the inherent short-time horizon that characterizes most political decisions. The issues, then, are how to mobilize more resources for tax mapping, how to improve the efficiency of tax mapping practices, and how to induce more enthusiastic local participation and some local financing.

More central government funding should be allocated for tax mapping loans via the MOF revolving fund and for staffing to increase the MOF capability to distribute and monitor these loans. Less than 20 percent of local governments have even begun tax mapping, and the process is not going very far on a ₱50 million revolving fund. By combining these programs of the MLGCD and MOF, it may be possible to provide initial seed money on a grant basis and the remainder on a loan basis. Moreover, if loan repayments are deferred, the obstacle of local governments having to make substantial initial contributions might be removed and more local participation might be induced.

Additional incentives should be provided by the central government in order to induce more local government participation in tax mapping. This could be done in two ways: by providing more initial seed money to reflect the higher cost of mapping and to cover a larger share of the initial cost; and by lowering interest costs and deferring repayment on the loan-financed portion. The capitalization of the revolving fund will suffer from the stretched-out repayment, but this could be partly offset by increased central government contributions and the infusion of grant assistance from international agencies. Additionally, it might be beneficial to allow the use of a share of allotments earmarked for infrastructure expenditures for covering the local government portion of tax mapping costs.

The problem of inefficient record keeping and management remains. In the long run, a more satisfactory method must be developed to ensure that as the ownership of parcels is transferrred, the property tax rolls are adjusted. Because total reliance upon the parties to the transaction leaves too much to chance, the central government must take steps to ensure that recorders of deeds, issuers of building permits, and surveyors relay all transactions and other relevant information to the assessor's office. These communications are already required (PD 464), so all that is necessary is the imposition of proper incentives or penalties by the central government to ensure that this information transfer is carried out. Not to do this is to compromise the sustainability of the tax mapping achievements.

Addressing the Land Reform Program

There is no question but that the land reform program in the Philippines has complicated the administration of the real property tax. Because records are inadequate, it is not clear where tax liability lies, whether and how the tax might be collected from former tenants, and what to do about back taxes owed by former owners. The blame for the problem can be rightfully shared by many parties—former tenants and owners, MAR, and local finance officials—but the basic problem seems to be with the system.

The case of long-delinquent tenants requires special consideration. The objective is to integrate these new landowners into the taxpaying population as soon as possible, rather than to penalize them for not having paid property taxes since 1972. This goal could be attained partly through a tax amnesty on a portion of past due taxes, but this amnesty should not be advertised or granted until a method to assess and collect taxes in land reform areas is established.

Obviously, completion of the tax mapping process in reform areas will help, but until mapping is completed, property taxes should be included in the annual payment by tenants to the Land Bank. While this would require a basic change in the relevant statutes, it would greatly improve the likelihood of compliance with the tax, albeit with some increase in administrative costs.

The central government needs to make a concentrated effort to inform new owners of their legal responsibilities to pay property taxes, of the potential benefits to be had from the increased government revenues, and of penalties to be faced for failing to comply. The MAR, MLGCD, the co-ops and the barangays are information-dissemination channels that could be used. Local assessors and treasurers must be encouraged, if not pressured, to gain an understanding of the administrative processes involved in land reform. Interagency dialogues between local representatives of the MAR and the treasurers and assessors, as well as explanatory manuals, would assist both groups in gaining an understanding of their mutual problems.

Assessment and Reassessment

Philippine assessment practices seem reasonable and appropriate, and there does not seem to be the same dire shortage of assessors that plagues local governments in so many developing countries. There are, however, two major problems with the current triennial reassessment cycle. First, it requires complete reassessments of all properties at a single point in time, thus adding to the overall costs of administering the tax. This peak loading of the work means that it is necessary to hire large amounts of casual labor at particular times during the cycle and also increases the likelihood of errors in administrative performance. Second, taxable values experience large incremental jumps once every three years and then are relatively flat during the interim period. The local government must anticipate slow growth in property tax revenues during the interim period while taxpayers experience large single year increases in tax bills. The result is a lowered willingness to comply with the tax and/or pressures for rate reduction.

Two changes in the assessment system might be considered. First, each jurisdiction should be divided into three parts, with each part formally reassessed every third year. This would help avoid the peak workload problem and also would provide a buoyancy to the property tax system since approximately one-third of the tax base would be revalued annually. Second, the increases in tax liability on individual properties should be phased in over the three-year period. In this manner the taxpayer would realize that tax liabilities would be increasing during the next three years but in no single year would the entire increment be felt.

Collection Efficiency

The largest single problem with property tax administration in the Philippines is tax collection. Efforts centered on this problem will have the largest and quickest payoffs and should concentrate on coordinating the collection of various taxes, ensuring that taxpayers do not become delinquent, and collecting previous years' taxes.

One way of ensuring taxpayer compliance is to require that taxes owed on a parcel of property be paid before the owner is allowed to transact other business with the government. The current statute already contains this idea in requiring that the previous owner must show proof of payment of past due taxes before a deed is issued to a new owner. Another opportunity is to require businesses to show proof of property and business license taxes before a mayor's permit is issued.

No one enjoys paying taxes. Yet efforts to lower compliance costs and to show the taxpayer that compliance with the tax is in his self-interest can lower the resistance. These aspects of the tax collection process suggest that efforts be continued to allow the taxpayer to comply with the law at the lowest possible cost and to educate the taxpayer concerning his legal liabilities. Both of these initiatives can be effectively carried out at the barangay level. Sending tax collectors to the barangay can help reduce compliance costs. More use of barangay-level campaigns designed to show residents the direct benefits they might gain from compliance with legal statutes, and more use of the barangay captains in the campaigns and in the collection process would also be effective measures.

Despite their political unpopularity, the legal remedies for collection of delinquent taxes must be aggressively enforced by the central government. All other good efforts notwithstanding, the property tax collection record will not improve dramatically until the central government makes it clear that the consequences of delinquency and evasion will be serious. The central government should initiate a well-publicized attack on delinquents, focusing initially on larger delinquents. The extreme remedies, sale of land or personal property at public auction, should be emphasized.

Local assessors might also be induced to push the use of extreme remedies. The provincial treasurer could provide a monetary inducement to municipalities such that those jurisdictions collecting the greatest proportion of past due taxes would, in effect be allowed to maintain use of around 60 to 70 percent of the delinquent tax received rather than the legal 45 percent. This may provide sufficient incentive to a local political leader to accept the acrimony generated by the auction of delinquent properties. Barangay captains might be given a share (for example, 5 percent) of all delinquent taxes they are able to collect, in the case of smaller taxpayers.

Another necessary change in the treatment of tax delinquencies is to increase the penalty rates. The current maximum of 24 percent after one year is insufficient in the inflationary environment of the Philippines. An increase of 3 percent per month in the penalty rate and its extension for an additional two years would not seem inappropriate. Finally, and especially in smaller rural areas, the use of public knowledge of delinquency, such as posting of delinquent taxpayers' names, could provide a nonmonetary yet effective incentive for compliance.

THE BUSINESS LICENSE TAX

The business license tax (BLT), which yields more than the property tax for many Philippine jurisdictions, has good potential as a local government revenue source. There are two possible routes to reform, altering the current administration and structure of the tax or replacing it with a shared central government general sales tax. There would seem to be more wisdom in the former approach at the present time.

The legal structure of the business license tax suffers from no serious defects with respect to its equity, neutrality, or income elasticity of yield, but the necessary administrative machinery to achieve these goals may be beyond the capabilities of many jurisdictions. The principal administrative difficulty lies with the determination of the tax base—gross receipts. Local governments do not have the staff to assess this base, hence most business taxpayers self-report. This makes the BLT, in effect, a voluntary payment where understatement of gross receipts is more likely the rule than the exception. In the case of larger businesses that do produce financial statements, interpreting and verifying the accuracy of such records are beyond the current capabilities of many local government administrations.

It is feasible that all businesses above a threshold size be required to produce records of their past year's business. To ensure that these records can be interpreted, training programs could be instituted in each province to train designated business tax collectors in the rudiments of business accounting. The central government would do well to underwrite the training cost of these collectors and a share of their annual salaries for the first three years. Business tax collectors might also be charged with the task of reorganizing the BLT roll and monitoring the relationship between payment of the BLT, the property tax, and the mayor's permit.

Rate structure reform is necessary to improve the yield and growth in the BLT. Present rates are quite low on average and are lower for large than for small firms. This regressive structure could be improved with a flat rate set at a level 10 percent higher than the average rate currently levied on larger businesses. The differential rates among types of businesses, however, should be retained. Such a policy should yield a substantial revenue increase.

Inasmuch as record keeping is minimal among small businesses, a flat annual charge would be suitable; however, this charge should be indexed in some manner to the general level of inflation. This reform would permit an easy administration of the tax while still ensuring a certain amount of income elasticity in this component of the BLT.

THE ALLOTMENT SYSTEM

There is a substantial difference between the Philippine grant system that exists in the statutes and the one that is actually practiced. A first positive step would be for the central government to establish and stay with a grant system and avoid ad hoc, year-to-year adjustments. In this context, the structure of the grant system should be rethought and appropriately reformed. Possible reforms fall in four areas: combining the various grant components into a consolidated allotment system; providing incentives to stimulate the mobilization of additional local revenues; providing incentives and financial resources to stimulate development spending; and rethinking the proper role of the barangay in financing and delivering local government services.

Consolidating the Allotment Programs

The present allotment system, which includes the BIR Allotment, the Specific Tax Allotment, and the National Tax Allotment, is unduly fragmented and does not well serve the fiscal decentralization objectives stated at the beginning of this chapter. A consolidated allotment system could be created in place of these components. At 1979 statutory funding levels for each program, such a consolidation would imply an amount equivalent to about 30 percent of BIR collections (with the BIR basis lagged three years). Whatever share of BIR revenues is chosen, however, should be adhered to rigidly.

The consolidated BIR Allotment, in keeping with the percent distribution of the current system, should earmark as much as two-thirds of the grant for the Infrastructure Fund. This policy would protect the more stimulative features of the Specific Tax Allotment and the objective of promoting capital expenditures.

A full distribution of these grant funds may be more than local governments can absorb, at least in the short run. A full distribution in 1979 would have been about twice the actual distribution, and because two-thirds are earmarked for capital projects, one possibility is that local government cash balances could increase. Although more research is necessary on the absorption capacity of local governments, their problems with preparing and implementing projects are well known. If local governments cannot easily absorb this increased flow of grant funds, the objective of mobilizing more local resources might be helped in other ways. In this regard a share of the grant could be held back to capitalize and subsidize a local government credit authority.

A need to tie the Specific Tax Allotment to petroleum tax revenues no longer exists, and there are a number of good reasons to change the basis for this grant program. The funds are presently used for much more than road and bridge construction and maintenance—hence, it is not possible to justify petroleum taxes as a benefit charge to road users. Moreover, because petroleum taxes are specific rather than ad valorem, revenues from the Specific Tax Allotment do not grow in response to GNP or inflation but because of increases in the petroleum tax rate. This raises the most substantial problem with the basis for the Specific Tax Allotment—discretionary petroleum tax actions are guided more by energy policy than by local government financial needs. It makes little sense to tie local grants to energy policy—the potential windfall gains to the local sector from increased specific tax rates in the past two years attest to this.[1]

Mobilizing Additional Local Revenues

The current formula distribution system does not provide a major inducement for increased revenue mobilization. Two changes in the system would help. First, some measure of tax effort could be introduced into the distribution formula. This could provide a substantial reward for increasing tax collections, and it might also increase the accountability of local governments for their fiscal performance. Second, the allotment distribution might be amended to provide other incentives for improving the capacity of local governments to assess and collect property taxes. Allotments earmarked for economic development expenditures should be available for coverage of the local share of tax mapping costs. Likewise, the allotment might be used to cover the partial cost of an additional property tax clerk (for a specified short period) to deal with a backlog of record-keeping problems.

Stimulating Economic Development Expenditures

Many of the suggested reforms lead to increased spending for capital projects by making more resources available. The objective of more capital spending, however, raises the specific question of what incentives might be provided to redirect general revenues to capital projects. One effective incentive seems to be the earmarking of a share of the allotment to the Infrastructure Fund. A second, and potentially much more powerful, technique is to encourage the use of credit financing by eligible local governments.

Barangay Problems

The time is right to assess definitively the role of barangays in the local finance system. Some of the increased barangay involvement is beneficial and clearly should be retained; for example, the 10 percent property tax share for barangays serves many useful purposes. The merit of some other programs and their cost calls for reevaluation. Although it is clear that more input at the barangay level can improve the decision-making process markedly, it is unclear whether the barangay unit is capable of providing the requisite technical or financial planning and management.[2] The barangay unit has not been studied here in any detail. It might be observed, however, that the present practice of earmarking 12.4 percent of the total BIR and

Specific Allotment may be a great deal of financial support for a unit of government whose ability to absorb funds is quite limited. It would be unfortunate for the barangay shares to be dropped, but that eventuality should be studied carefully.

LOCAL GOVERNMENT PUBLIC ENTERPRISES

A more widespread use of local government public enterprises (LGPEs) would be consistent with the fiscal decentralization objectives of the central government and with the goal of increased revenue mobilization. Although the use of LGPEs is provided for in Philippine law, the practice has been largely restricted to markets, and the financial success record has been spotty. The limited use of LGPEs might be traced to a number of factors: limited possibilities for cost recovery, inadequate central government incentives to induce local governments to use the enterprise form, management and administrative problems, and inadequate provision for capital financing. More generally, there seems to be an ambiguity at the central government level about whether LGPEs should be providing a service at subsidized rates or selling a service to recover full costs. The central government could remove some of these ambiguities with a clear policy statement about its goals for the use of local government enterprises and about the operating autonomy that will be given. This statement should distinguish clearly between enterprises that serve social purposes and those that are more purely commercial ventures.

This research suggests that local enterprise activities can be financially viable, that they can be an effective way to mobilize additional resources, and that management and administrative problems can be overcome. What is most needed is for the central government to regulate and monitor firmly the design stage, granting maximum pricing and operational autonomy, reforming the accounting system so that costs and profitability can be more accurately measured, and finding a way to assist in the provision of adequate capital financing.

Public Markets

Most market operations can cover variable costs and some can also cover capital costs, but without capital subsidies, full cost recovery would not appear likely for many. The critical factor seems to be size of the market, with smaller markets that lie in the commuting range of larger markets being particularly disadvantaged. Public policy for market enterprises cannot be formulated only on the basis of the few case studies carried out here; however, four fundamental problems and reform possibilities did emerge in the course of this research: accounting and measurement needs, revenue policy, cost and volume considerations, and credit policy.

Resolving the problems of accurately measuring the cost of enterprise activities is an essential first step in rationalizing the role of public markets in the system of local government finance. The existing accounting system falls short of answering this need in two important respects. The first problem arises because of the special circumstances of small governments. Levels of market activity require heavy work efforts on market days and very little work effort at other times. Thus, either the market plantilla must be supplemented by the efforts of other government employees during peak times or the regular market work force is assigned other tasks on nonmarket days. Moreover, since a full administrative staff cannot be justified, management tasks such as accounting, personnel management and the like are performed by personnel whose plantilla assignment is in other departments. Under either condition, it is unlikely that personnel costs would (or even could) be prorated among market and other accounts in a way that actually reflects the uses of an employee's time. In effect, any monitoring of the financial success of small markets may be ruled out.

What might be done about this problem? The prorating of personnel costs in small areas would be difficult, imprecise, and possibly not worth the effort. Indeed, the very difficulty of separating the enterprise activities may be telling one that the enterprise form is just not a good idea for very small jurisdictions. The public market may be much more a general government function in smaller than larger jurisdictions.

The second accounting problem has to do with the measurement of capital costs. Because capital costs are "lumpy" and capital facilities are long-lived, cash outlays do not give a reasonable estimate of the annual cost of using up the resources embodied in a facility. These costs would be better reflected in annual depreciation reserves that, when accumulated during the lifetime of the facility, would provide for its replacement. An approximation of this amount, which we have used in this analysis, is the annual payments on a loan of amount sufficient to cover the cost of reconstructing the facility. The central government would do well to adopt a standard practice in accounting for the annual capital costs of local government market facilities.

An important barrier to full cost recovery has to do with pricing policy, that is, prices are set too low and revised too infrequently. This practice is partly due to a concern with the cost of foodstuffs and other necessities to low income groups, and partly due to the fear of lowering stall occupancy rates. Our view is that this reasoning is not well founded except, perhaps, in the case of some small markets. First, market stalls are usually all rented. Second, the evidence suggests that market revenues could be increased with little effect on the prices of goods sold in the market. Local governments should be encouraged to increase market fees and to make regular fee revisions in line with rising costs of operation.

The capital-intensive nature of public markets works against smaller markets by keeping their per capita (and presumably per unit) costs high. Our analysis has indicated that these efficiencies become effective when markets service a population of about 40,000. This is not to say that municipalities with larger populations will necessarily realize these efficiencies, for they may not if they fall within the service area of a larger market. Rather, it implies that the technology of market operation is a barrier against the profitability of small markets.

In sum, the key to the profitability of public markets seems to be volume. Our findings suggest two important barriers to market profitability, both of which are related to volume. The first is a lack of access between municipalities and their hinterlands. The policy implication is that road projects that link urban areas with their rural hinterlands should have an important positive effect on public markets, especially larger markets. Second, they suggest that markets of larger municipalities dominate those of smaller nearby municipalities. This competition places smaller markets at a disadvantage and thus constitutes a barrier to their financial success.

In establishing a credit policy for public markets, what might be reasonable expectations? Our sample suggests that recovery of current cost may be expected, but recovery of full capital costs would be less common. Public markets are income generating, but if costs are measured correctly, many will not be completely self-financing. Credit policy might include two features: (1) Capital subsidies could be provided in the form of lower interest costs than the present 14 to 18 percent, and (2) loan maturities could be extended to match better the expected life of market facilities.

Commercial Ventures

The study of four commercial ventures of the Bulacan provincial government suggests that there are good possibilities for local government commercial ventures and that the management constraints may not be so great as one might expect. A number of lessons emerge from the Bulacan experience, particularly in the areas of project design and review, pricing policy, management autonomy, and proper accounting.

Concerning project design and review, the Bulacan experience makes a good case for central government involvement in the planning stage for private ventures. One issue that arises here is the need for external review of whether or not the proposed undertaking has reasonable prospects for financial success. The other relates to whether this type of local government investment ought to be undertaken without review and approval in terms of coordination with the goals of the national economic development plan. If financing is from internal sources, a MOF or MLGCD signoff on the feasibility study should also be required. The establishment of a review procedure and standards for financial feasibility studies would facilitate project planning.

The second issue is more problematic. One could argue effectively that for purely business ventures, the central government should give the local governments maximum discretion in project selection. Only where the project must be justified partly on grounds of providing social benefits should normal central government review and signoff occur.

Pricing decisions should be made by local governments because preferences and economic conditions vary from one community to another. Nationally prescribed price schedules, such as slaughter fees, are changed infrequently and in any case may be unsuitable for some local governments. Furthermore, for some enterprises, pricing autonomy may spell the difference between failure and success. Where the objective of commercial ventures is solely to raise funds for the local government, then the central government should give maximum incentive for local governments to achieve this goal. For purely commercial enterprises, there should be no restrictions on the level of profits that may be earned or on the disposition of these profits.

Regarding management autonomy, many lessons can be learned from Bulacan's management of less traditional public enterprises. A major ingredient for "success" appears to be the ability of the enterprise to function as a private firm. With the exception of the Galeria, the enterprises have been run with some form of private sector participation–management contracting for the slaughterhouse and Convention Center and operating contract for the Cafetorium. In addition, and again with the exception of the Galeria, which operates as a regular government department, the Bulacan enterprises have resorted to various labor-cost saving mechanisms that are largely unconventional by government standards. It appears, therefore, that business enterprises should be given flexibility in terms of hiring and wage determination and in terms of general operating decisions.

Lastly, accounting reforms should be considered. Proper measurement of profitability is a requirement if management is to be held accountable for its efficiency and if subsidies provided to the enterprise are to be detected. To improve overall decision making, to generate a more cost-conscious management behavior, and to facilitate performance monitoring of the enterprise, some structural changes in existing government accounting practices are envisioned. These include adopting a system of enterprise accounting that includes depreciation (or consumption of fixed capital) in the product accounts; requiring the measurement and accounting of all forms of subsidy–either explicit (capital subsidy, statutory transfer, grants) or implicit (tax exemptions, preferential loan subsidy); and the maintenance of a separate set of accounts for the enterprise which records transfers to and from any government funds (General, Infrastructure, Trust, Sinking, Fiduciary, and so on).

INCREASED USE OF CREDIT FINANCING

One important barrier to increased capital formation by local government and to increased participation in "income-generating" projects is the high start-up cost of constructing the capital facility. The government has taken steps to remove this barrier by making loans available to local governments through DBP, the Land Bank, and GSIS, but participation levels are low.

It is apparent that substantive changes must be made in the present system if local governments are to be encouraged to undertake credit-financed projects. Essentially, there are two options: to rectify the problems of the present system by pursuing changes in current policies, procedures, and practices; or to propose a bolder solution–the creation of a new, specialized entity. Although neither approach is without problems, we think the weight of the evidence favors the establishment of a new, specialized credit facility for local governments. The rationale is that project planning, appraisal, and management assistance are so critical to the credit financing process that technical staffs experienced in the different fields of public sector investments must be maintained by the institution.

The organization of such a new authority should pose no great problems. Although the matter requires some careful study, one could envision an authority established by law and governed by a board of directors, comprising both representatives of central ministries involved in local government affairs and local government officials, and with its chairman appointed by the president. Specifically, the board could consist of the ministers of the budget, finance, local government and community development, economic development, and human settlements, and the governor of the Central Bank. An equal number of government representatives might be appointed with equal representation from provincial, municipal, and city governments. The director or internal manager could be appointed by the president, based on the recommendation of the board and with the approval of the Ministry of Finance.

The major drawback to this proposal is the problem of funding. Ultimately the central government is going to have to invest in this activity if it is to be successfully used in inducing local governments to generate more revenues. On the other hand, this funding may not require new allocations of funds to local governments. In fact, with some reallocation of resources already earmarked for the local government, it would be possible initially to capitalize a specialized local government credit authority. It is important to note that the choice of a financing source involves far more than simply finding the pesos. It should be made on a basis of fulfilling the government's ultimate reasons for wanting to increase local government use of credit financing: to stimulate the undertaking of capital projects, to encourage the initiation of income-generating projects, and to stimulate local government tax effort. The objective, in sum, is to design a credit authority financing scheme that promotes these three objectives while diverting funds from other local government activities.

Firm estimates of capital requirements, necessary initial and continuing appropriations, and operating costs of the authority require a detailed financial study, but we can estimate only very roughly the magnitudes of funding involved. Capitalization could come from two sources. The first is an annual share, perhaps 10 to 20 percent, of the proposed Consolidated Allotment. This financing source presumes, of course, that the government begins distributing the full allotment. The second source is approximately ₱200 million of the balances held in banks by local governments, which might be exchanged for share capital in the authority. There are two other potential sources of funding. One is the annual barangay shares of the allotments, and the other is funding from external donors, such as the U.S. Agency for International Development. With external funding it should be possible to allocate some proportion of loanable funds, at subsidized rates, to low income jurisdictions or for "social" projects that might not otherwise qualify.

To stimulate borrowing and tax effort to support capital projects, a change from present lending policies is called for. The strategy is essentially to lower the "price" of borrowing. The interest rate should be set to vary inversely with the amount of cash equity a local government has in the project and to lengthen the maturity of loans to more accurately reflect the economic life of the asset being financed. The authority should consider funding some capital projects that are non-income generating but that may enhance the performance of the local economy. Interest rate subsidies could also be provided for local government loans. The size of these subsidies, however, will be heavily dependent on the method of capitalization chosen.

THE COSTS AND BENEFITS OF REFORM

The costs of any comprehensive program of reform should be weighed against the potential benefits to be received. On the cost side of this program, there is the initial and perhaps continuing outlay required of the central government and the loss of some control by the central government over local government finances. On the benefits side there is the potential for increased revenue mobilization by local governments, more efficient fiscal operations of local governments, increased capital project activity, decentralized government fiscal activity, and a stronger local government sector in the long run. Whether the costs outweigh the benefits depends on the probabilities for success of this program and on the importance placed on local government financial reform by the central government. One thing is sure: A piecemeal reform, such as one that leaves out the incentive elements, is likely to generate costs without benefits. But to try to reform local finances at no cost, by not providing the funding for inducements or for increased ministry staffing, generates little improvements.

Costs

The costs of this reform program are enumerated, insofar as is possible, in Table 7.1. The major cost is associated with the full distribution of the allotment system (exclusive of barangay shares). At 1979 levels (the latest year for which we can make an estimate), this change would amount to about ₱1 billion. In 1982, the level of the undistributed share will depend on the recent growth in the BIR basis, petroleum tax revenues, and discretionary government decisions. In any case, it will be considerably greater than ₱1 billion. Careful study will be required to update the undistributed amounts, but one might guess that a sum roughly equivalent to 30 percent of the lagged BIR basis could fund most of the initiatives suggested here. In one sense this expenditure is a cost only if the outlay needs exceed the undistributed portion, as the present allotment system is already earmarked for the local government sector.

At present there is insufficient information with which to estimate the other costs implied in Table 7.1. The cost of supplementing the MOF revolving fund for tax mapping depends on a number of factors: how much the government wants to push tax mapping, whether an integration between the MOF and USAID/MLGCD program can be worked out, and whether the MOF staff is shored up to accommodate an increased volume of tax mapping activity. Doubling the size of the revolving fund would add measurable support to tax mapping efforts.

If local government finances are to be strengthened within the highly centralized Philippine system, the size and expertise of the central government agencies that monitor and control local finances must be strengthened. It is almost axiomatic in the Philippine case that the center must be strengthened if the local sector is to be strengthened. Additional personnel and training in tax mapping, budget preparation and review, financial analysis, and governmental accounting are essential to the efforts proposed here. A government appropriation of as little as ₱2 million spread over the next five years for capacity building would go a long way toward strengthening the operations of local government. Supplementary funds for this purpose might also be sought from external sources.

Another proposal that would require additional central government funding is the cost sharing for a business tax collector, although the cost should be rather small. For illustration, assume two such collectors per province and assume that the government bears (a) an initial training cost of ₱5,000 per collector, (b) a salary and benefits

TABLE 7.1

Funding Required from Central Government Sources: A Comprehensive Program for Local Government Financial Reform

Reform Action	Funding
1. Consolidated allotment program	There should be a full distribution of the authorized BIR, Specific Tax, and National Tax allotments. At 1979 levels, this would imply distribution of $1 billion, more than was actually the case.
2. Local government credit authority	To be capitalized with a share of the Consolidated Allotment and the cash deposits of local governments in banks. Other potential sources are external funding and the barangay shares of the allotment.
3. Supplementing MOF revolving fund for tax mapping and providing additional staff to review mapping proposals	New central government funding; merger of USAID/MLGCD with MOF revolving fund would provide further support.
4. Supplementing MOF/MOB/MLGCD staff for a. tax mapping b. budget review c. training local officials in (a) and (b) and business tax collection and monitoring d. monitoring design phase for local government public enterprises e. Reforming accounting system for local government public enterprises	New funding from central government; merger of MLGCD program with MOF revolving fund would provide further support for (b)
5. Cost sharing for local business tax collector for three years	New central government funding.
6. Payment in lieu of property tax on government properties	New central government funding.

cost of ₱14,000 per collector per year, and (c) a central level supervisory cost of ₱50,000 per year. The total three-year cost would be about ₱3 million.

Finally, there is a proposal for payment in lieu of property taxes on government property and on some government-granted exemptions. A rough estimate from sample data on Iloilo and Albay suggests that about 10 percent of total assessed values are exempt. If half of these exemptions are covered under this proposal, the annual cost to the government would have been about ₱40 million in 1979.

Obviously, these estimates are rough, but they give some idea that the cost of this program is not unmanageable. In 1979, the cost of this program would have been less than 3 percent of total central government expenditures. By comparative standards, the program may be affordable—the level of tax effort in the Philippines is low. But more to the point is whether the benefits of such a reform program warrant these expenditures.

Benefits

This reform program brings two kinds of potential benefits. The first is improvement of the efficiency of local government operations

TABLE 7.2

Programs to Increase the Efficiency of Local Government Operations

Reform	Effect
1. Form a review office to deal with interministerial conflicts concerning local government finance.	1. Increased revenue generation, improved expenditure and managerial efficiency.
2. Eliminate the practice of supplemental budgets.	2. Increased efficiency in local government expenditures.
3. Require capital budgets of larger local governments.	3. Improved fiscal planning.
4. Eliminate fractional assessments in real property taxation.	4. Will remove property tax disincentive to real property investments.
5. Instigate a program of phased reassessment of property values.	5. Improved taxpayer compliance.
6. Make more use of barangay campaigns.	6. Improved taxpayer compliance.
7. Install accounting reforms for local government public enterprises.	7. Increased efficiency in local government operations.

TABLE 7.3

Incentive Programs to Increase Local Government Revenue Mobilization

Reform	Response from Local Government
1. Earmark 60 percent of Consolidated Allotment for Infrastructure expenditures.	1. Stimulate economic development expenditures; increase revenue generation.
2. Permit use of Infrastructure share of Consolidated Allotment for covering some portion of local share of tax mapping cost and a share of the cost of a property records clerk.	2. Increase revenue generation from real property tax.
3. Introduce a tax effort component into the Consolidated Allotment formula.	3. Increase local government tax effort.
4. Increase the size of the MOF revolving fund for RPTA improvement; provide additional MOF staffing to support these loans; and relax the terms of repayment.	4. Increase real property tax collections and administrative efficiency.
5. Merge or coordinate the MOF and MLGCD tax mapping programs and provide greater incentive grants for tax mapping.	5. Increase tax mapping activity.
6. A cost sharing program for a local business tax collector.	6. Increase business tax collections.
7. Variable interest rate program and lengthened maturities for local government credit financing.	7. Stimulate spending for income-generating projects; increase revenue effects.
8. Increase penalty rate for property tax delinquency; barangay campaigns.	8. Increase property tax collections.
9. Vigorous central government action against property tax delinquents.	9. Increase property tax collections.
10. Reduce earmarking and restrictions of local government budget allocations: a. Eliminate transfer to Infrastructure Fund b. Review 18 percent INP requirements	10. Increase local government revenue effort.
11. Encourage idle lands taxation and special assessments.	11. Increase local government revenue effort and stimulate capital spending.
12. More flexibility in pricing and disposition of surplus for local government public enterprises.	12. Increase local government revenues.

(Table 7.2). In effect, these improvements can be had without the major reforms described above and with little cost, although an increase in the budget review capabilities of the MOF/MOB would be essential. This part of the reform program can result in an improved ability of local governments to deliver services and manage their affairs, but it falls short of achieving government objectives in other areas. It does not provide incentives for the local governments to mobilize additional revenues, to spend more for capital purposes, or to improve their capacity to accommodate future expansions in their fiscal activities. These objectives are served by the second component of this reform program.

The potential benefits described in Table 7.3 are more in the areas of increased revenue generation and capital spending. Twelve areas are listed where the incentives provided should induce local governments to increase tax effort and capital expenditures, although it is not possible to estimate the extent of the increase. Moreover, in some cases the benefits are long run.

FUTURE RESEARCH

With respect to needed reform, the research reported in this book has perhaps raised as many questions as have been answered. On the other hand, much has been learned about local government financing in the Philippines and much of the experience may be transferable. Furthermore, the general direction of the reforms proposed is consistent with government policy and all are administratively and financially feasible. This momentum could be built on with a further research effort in three areas: analysis of the financial performance of local governments from a nationwide sample; working out the implications of specific reforms, particularly in the case of the proposed Consolidated Allotment and credit authority; and determining data needs for tracking and monitoring local government finances.

This analysis of fiscal performance and behavior has been carried out largely on a sample of four provinces and needs to be extended to a nationwide sample. For some questions, such as measuring the stimulative effects of the allotment system and measuring tax effort, an analytic framework has been developed but requires further testing before it can serve as a firm basis for policy changes. In other cases, such as our discovery of surpluses and cash balances, the question arises as to how widespread the phenomenon is. Finally, in some areas of inquiry, such as the fiscal structure and performance of market enterprises, the sample was too small to expose regularities that may exist.

The second important research task is to work out the specific details of some of these reform suggestions. For example, the case for a local government credit authority seems persuasive to us, but there is much to be done in working out the details of organizing and operating such an authority. Similarly, we know that a different kind of allotment system based on local matching requirements would stimulate greater local tax effort and we believe that a Consolidated Allotment system would have great merit. To design such a system would entail a significant amount of effort.

Finally, there is an important research need in the area of improved local government fiscal data. If the local government sector is to grow in importance in the Philippines, its performance will have to be understood and monitored. The producing of annual, timely data on local government finances is a requirement. The monthly reports to the MOF and the annual COA data could serve as the basis of an annual "census of local government finances." However, given the state of municipal accounting practices, detailed design work would be a first step. Our opinion, based on working with these data, is that such an undertaking is feasible. The analysis of the four provinces is evidence, we hope, of the valuable uses to which such data might be put.

NOTES

1. There is a similar problem with the BIR basis, but the parallel is really not so close. Both BIR collections and local finance needs bear some relationship to income growth and inflation.

2. Field research that found substantial local government potential at the barangay level is reported in Buenaventura M. Villanueva, "A Study of the Competence of the Barrio People to Conduct Barrio Government," Ph.D. dissertation, University of Southern California, 1959.

Appendix: Research Areas and Sample

This study focuses on two levels of local government in the Philippines: cities and municipalities. Certain kinds of data were gathered for all cities within each region in the Philippines. More detailed studies concentrated on four provinces: Albay, Bulacan, Iloilo, and Sorsogon. The provinces were chosen to represent a broad range of economic variation in different regions of the country and to exhibit diversity in income level and degree of urbanization and other indicators of development. Within the four provinces, certain kinds of data were gathered for all municipalities and cities.

Lengthy fieldwork was also carried out in selected municipalities in the four provinces. In 15 municipalities and two cities in Iloilo, Albay and Bulacan, detailed data were gathered on budgetary matters, in addition to data on the growth of particular revenue sources for the 1977–79 period. For in-depth information on market enterprises, 11 local government operations were studied: one city and one municipality in Albay, one city and six municipalities in Iloilo, and two municipalities in Sorsogon. In studying local government commercial enterprises, four cases in Bulacan were selected: a convention center, a handicrafts emporium, a cafeteria, and a slaughterhouse. For the survey of credit use by local governments, localized information was gathered in 13 jurisdictions: two cities, Albay and Legaspi City, and 11 municipalities of which two were in Sorgoson Province, two in Albay Province, and seven in Iloilo Province.

A listing of the cities (by region) and the municipalities (by province) included in the sample is given in Table A.1.

TABLE A.1

List of Jurisdictions Included in the Sample

Cities by Region			
Region	Cities	Region	Cities
Region I	Baguio	Region VII	Bais
	Dagupan		Canlaon
	Laoag		Cebu
	San Carlos		Danao
			Dumaguete
Region III	Angeles		Lapu-Lapu
	Cabanatuan		Mandaue
	Olongapo		Tagbilaran
	Palayan		Toledo
	San Jose		
		Region VIII	Calbayog
Region IV	Batangas		
	Cavite	Region IX	Dapitan
	Lipa		Dipolog
	Puerto Princesa		Pagadian
	Tagaytay		Zamboanga
	Trece Martires		
		Region X	Butuan
Region V	Iriga		Cagayan de Oro
	Legaspi		Gingoog
	Naga		Oroquieta
			Ozamis
Region VI	Iloilo		Tangub
	Roxas		
		Region XII	Iligan
			Marawi

(Continued)

TABLE A.1 (Continued)

Municipalities by Province

Province	Municipalities	Province	Municipalities
Albay	Bacacay		San Rafael
	Camalig		Santa Maria
	Daraga		
	Guinobatan	Iloilo	Ajuy
	Jovellar		Alimodian
	Libon		Anilao
	Ligao		Badiangan
	Malilipot		Balasan
	Malinao		Banate
	Manito		Barotac Nuevo
	Oas		Barotac Viejo
	Pio Duran		Batad
	Polangui		Bingawan
	Rapu-Rapu		Cabatuan
	Santo Domingo		Calinog
	Tabaco		Carles
	Tiwi		Concepcion
			Dingle
Bulacan	Angat		Duenas
	Balagtas (Bigaa)		Dumangas
	Baliwag		Estancia
	Bucaue		Guimbal
	Bulacan		Igbaras
	Bustos		Janiuay
	Calumpit		Lambunao
	Guiguinto		Leganes
	Hagonoy		Lemery
	Malolos		Leon
	Marilao		Maasin
	Meycauayan		Miagao
	Norzagaray		Mina
	Obando		New Lucena
	Pandi		Oton
	Paombong		Passi
	Plaridel		Pavia
	Pulilan		Pototan
	San Ildefonso		San Dionisio
	San Jose del Monte		San Enrique
	San Miguel		San Joaquin

(Continued)

TABLE A.1 (Continued)

Municipalities by Province

Province	Municipalities	Province	Municipalities
	San Miguel		Castilla
	San Rafael		Dansol
	Santa Barbara		Gubat
	Sara		Irosin
	Tigbauan		Juban
	Tubungan		Magallanes
	Zarrago		Matnog
			Pilar
Sorsogon	Bacon		Prieto Diaz
	Barcelona		Santa Magdalena
	Bulan		Sorsogon
	Bulusan		

INDEX

Aguinaldo, Eduardo, 80n
Allotment system, 100-139
evaluation of, 130-133
steps for reform, 240-243
See also BIR Allotment; National Tax Allotment; Specific Tax Allotment

Baas, Hessel, 45n, 81n
Bahl, Roy, 43n, 45n, 79n, 80n, 81n, 139n
Barangay, 1-3
barangay brigades, 2-3
shares in BIR Allotment, 102, 242-243
shares in Specific Tax Allotment, 123, 242-243
Barrio. *See* Barangay
BIR Allotment, 22, 100-122, 136
accountability of local governments, 116-119
and barangay shares, 127-129, 242-243
elasticity and certainty, 119-122
equalization impacts, 103-105
fiscal stimulation of, 106-107
and per capita income, 104-105
possible reform, 241-252
and a specialized local government credit authority, 215-217, 219-221
Bird, Richard M., 139n
Bohm, Andreja, 185n
Budgeting and financial management, 5-28, 229, 233
cash balance accumulations, 37-42, 232
coordination of central government controls, 230-231
expenditure mandates, 231-232
Business enterprises (of local governments), 163-185
Hiyas Agro-Commodities Center, 179-184
[Business enterprises]
Hiyas Cafetorium, 169-173
Hiyas Convention Center, 173-178
Hiyas Galeria, 168-169
performance evaluation, 163-167
possible reform, 246-247
See also Public enterprises (of local governments); Market enterprises (of local governments)
Business license tax, 22, 26, 82-99
base, 82-84, 239
collection, 85-86, 240
possible reform, 239-240
rate structure, 84-85, 240
revenue performance, 86-98

Cash balance accumulations, 37-42, 232
and a specialized local government credit authority, 221
Census data for the Philippines, 12, 44
Chelliah, Raja, 45n, 81n
Choksi, Armeane, 187n
Commercial ventures. *See* Business enterprises
Compliance
with business license tax, 85, 90
with real property tax, 60-61, 65
Credit financing (of local governments), 188-227
borrowing capacity, 206-211
level of borrowing, 195-202
obstacles to, 202-211
See also Development Bank of the Philippines; Government Service Insurance System; Land Bank of the Philippines; Specialized local government credit authority

Delinquency
and land reform, 236-237
on local government loans, 200-202
on real property tax, 61-65, 232
Development Bank of the Philippines, 189-190, 195-202, 219, 224-227, 247
Doebele, William A., 81n

Eichengreen, Barry, 45n
Expenditures
of central government, 3-5
of local government, 15-26

Financial management. *See* Budgeting and financial management
Fiscal decentralization
benefits of, 229
program of reform for, 228-255
Fiscal surpluses, 41-42
Fossett, James W., 43n
Fractional assessments on real property, 49-50

Garcia, Orlando R., 186n
General Fund, 6-7, 15-26, 37, 107-116
Gillis, Malcolm, 185n, 187n
Government Service Insurance System, 189, 194-195, 247
Gramlich, Edward, 138n
Grant system. *See* Allotment system
Gratz, Wilfred, 45n
Grimes, Orville F., Jr., 81n

Hicks, Ursula K., 79n, 139n
Hinrichs, Harley, 44n
Holland, Daniel, 79n

Idle lands tax, 59, 234
Incentive programs, 252-254
Income levels, 12-15
and the BIR Allotment, 104-105
and the business license tax, 89-94
[Income levels]
and the Specific Tax Allotment, 104-105
Income tax, 83-84
Infrastructure Fund, 6, 26, 28, 107-116, 123
Intergovernmental fiscal relations. *See* Allotment system; BIR Allotment; National Tax Allotment; Specific Tax Allotment
International Union of Local Authorities, 227

Jones, Leroy P., 185n

Kane, Joseph A., 227n
Kelly, Margaret, 45n, 68n, 81n

Land Bank of the Philippines, 189, 192-193, 247
Land reform, 50, 236
Land valuation, 48-50
Linn, Johannes F., 81n, 139n
Local government structure, 1-3
Lotz, Joergen, 44n

Marcos, Ferdinand, 3
Market enterprises (of local governments), 143-146
expenditure levels, 152-161
fiscal importance, 147
possible reform, 243-245
revenue determinants, 147-152
stall fees, 149-151
Ministry of Finance Revolving Fund, 235-237, 253
Mishan, E. J., 186n
Morss, Elliott R., 44n
Munasinghe, M., 185n

Nathan, Richard P., 43n
National Tax Allotment, 127-129, 137
barangay shares of, 127-129
possible reform, 241, 251

[National Tax Allotment]
and a specialized local government credit authority, 216-217
National Tax Research Center, 81n, 99n, 187n, 235

Omohundro, John T., 99n

Petroleum tax, 122, 241
Philippine National Bank, 189, 217-218
Population growth and fiscal performance, 12-15
Property Identification Number, 51
Property taxation
in ASEAN countries, 66
in developing countries, 67-68
in the Philippines. *See* Real property tax
Public enterprises (of local governments), 140-187
actual use of, 145-146
criteria for appropriate use of, 140-142
possible reform, 243-245
potential enterprise forms, 142-146
See also Business enterprises; Market enterprises

Quintos, Vicente G., 44n, 66, 79n, 81n

Real property tax, 22, 26, 46-81, 232-239
assessment, 49-57, 237-238
base, 47-58
collection, 60-65, 238-239
equity implications, 55
growth in yield, 69-78
possible reform, 233-239
rate elasticity, 78-79
rates, 58-59, 234
revenue performance, 66-81
Real Property Tax Code, 47
Records management for real property tax, 52-53, 235-236
Revenue structure (of local governments), 22-26

Sales tax, 84
Sample jurisdictions, 11, 257-260
Saunders, Robert J., 185n
Schroeder, Larry, 43n
Smith, Roger, 80n
Socioeconomic structure and fiscal performance, 12-15
Special assessments on property, 59-60, 234-235
Special Education Fund, 6-7, 58-59
Specialized local government credit authority, 211-227
administrative costs, 224-225
capitalization of, 214-222, 248-249
lending policies, 223-226
soft loans, 225-226
standards for project analysis, 224
typology of forms, 212-214
Specific Tax Allotment, 122-125, 136, 241-242
barangay shares of, 127-129, 242
elasticity, 124-125
equalization impacts, 123
fiscal stimulation of, 123-124
possible reform, 241
and a specialized local government credit authority, 215-216, 219-220
Tait, Alan, 45n, 81n
Taxable capacity, 35-37
Tax campaigns, 65
Tax effort, 28-37
and per capita income, 32-33
and population, 34
and urbanization, 33-34
Tax effort index, 30-32

Tax mapping (of real property), 51, 234-235

United Nations, 227n
Urbanization and fiscal performance, 12-15

Veloso Abueva, Jose, 43n
Villanueva, Buenaventura M., 227n, 255n
Virata Cesar, 21, 43n

Warford, Jerry, 185n
Wasylenko, Michael, 79n

Yoingco, Angel, 44n, 66, 79n, 81n

ABOUT THE EDITORS

ROY BAHL is professor of economics and director of the Metropolitan Studies Program, The Maxwell School, Syracuse University. He has worked on problems of local finance in many developing countries, under the auspices of the World Bank, the International Monetary Fund, the United Nations, and the Agency for International Development.

BARBARA D. MILLER is senior research associate with the Local Revenue Administration Project of the Metropolitan Studies Program, The Maxwell School, Syracuse University. She has done research in India and Bangladesh and is primarily concerned with the social aspects of local public finance.

ABOUT THE CONTRIBUTORS

BENJAMIN E. DIOKNO is assistant professor of economics and concurrently director for public affairs in the School of Economics at the University of the Philippines. His primary research and teaching interests are in the area of fiscal policy and theory. His current research is focused on the public economy of local governments and the economics of state-operated enterprises in the Philippines.

DAVID GREYTAK is professor of economics and associate director of the Metropolitan Studies Program, The Maxwell School, Syracuse University. His publications include papers on local government revenue performance, property taxation, and regional economics. He has done fieldwork in Bolivia, Costa Rica, Honduras, Peru, and the Philippines. His research interests include local government taxation, development banking, and public enterprise activities in developing countries.

KENNETH HUBBELL is professor of economics at the University of Missouri at Kansas City. He has written extensively in the area of local finance in developing countries and has undertaken fieldwork in Egypt, Thailand, and the Philippines for the World Bank and the Agency for International Development.

LARRY SCHROEDER is professor of public administration and economics and senior research associate in the Metropolitan Studies Program, The Maxwell School, Syracuse University. He has published articles and reports on local government finance in developing countries based on fieldwork in the Philippines, India, Tanzania, and Bangladesh. His primary research interests include property taxation, revenue forecasting, and financial management.